Girls and Women in STEM
A Never Ending Story

A volume in
Research on Women and Education
Janice Koch and Beverly Irby, *Series Editors*

Girls and Women in STEM

A Never Ending Story

edited by

Janice Koch
Emerita Hofstra University

Barbara Polnick
Sam Houston State University

Beverly Irby
Texas A & M University

INFORMATION AGE PUBLISHING, INC.
Charlotte, NC • www.infoagepub.com

Library of Congress Cataloging-in-Publication Data

A CIP record for this book is available from the Library of Congress
http://www.loc.gov

ISBN: 978-1-62396-556-3 (Paperback)
       978-1-62396-557-0 (Hardcover)
       978-1-62396-558-7 (ebook)

Printed in the United States of America

CONTENTS

PART TWO

INTERVENTIONS ON BEHALF OF GIRLS AND WOMEN
PURSUING STEM FIELDS

INTRODUCTION

Janice Koch
Beverly Irby

It might seem unfair to reward a person for having so much pleasure over the years, asking the maize plant to solve specific problems and then watching its responses.

—Barbara McClintock, upon receiving the Nobel Prize for Science
or Medicine in Stockholm, Sweden, 1983

This quote from Dr. McClintock is a poignant reminder of how compelling and personally gratifying a life's pursuit in the natural sciences can be. It also illustrates how one woman exhibited extraordinary generosity of spirit upon receiving the most prestigious international honor in the field of science or medicine in 1983.

When the RWE series editors examined the topic of girls and women and STEM learning and careers, we were reminded, once more, that encouraging their participation remains as vital today as when many of us chartered this territory in the 1970s, hence, the subtitle *A Never Ending Story*. This volume, however, is not about hand-wringing. It is about ongoing advocacy on behalf of the future workforce in fields that lie on the cutting edge of society's future. We anticipate that this volume will give the reader insight into what works and what does not work for providing the message to girls and women that, indeed, STEM fields are for them in this second decade of the 21st century. Nancy Hopkins (2011), the renowned biologist from MIT who turned higher education on its head when she forged a review of opportunities and facilities afforded to women faculty in the sciences and engineering as compared with their male peers, reminds us that deeply embedded beliefs about social and academic entitlement take generations to overcome and hence, we forge forward in the knowledge that contributions to this volume will resonate with readers and that those in positions of access will learn more about how to provide opportunities for girls and women that propel them into science, technology, engineering, and mathematics. Further, we anticipate that students and scholars in STEM fields will identify with the success stories related in some of these chapters and find inspiration in the ways their own journeys are reflected by the authors in this volume.

The first part of this volume is devoted to stories of girls and young women who pursued studies in STEM despite cultural challenges and because of supports found in family, school, peers, and mentors. Catherine Martin-Dunlop and Whitney Johnson explore the stories of three African American women's journeys toward engagement in STEM fields. This chapter highlights the importance of family and school mentors, peers and teachers, and examines the role of negative stereotyping and the very real differences that individual contexts bring to bear upon future success for minority women in STEM. Ezella McPherson's study reinforces the dire need for institutions of higher learning to design and construct a "welcome mat" for African American women who have expressed interest in and a desire to pursue studies in STEM fields. Hence, they have "made it" to higher education in nontraditional majors, but their stories do not end with entry. Institutional support is necessary to counter the culture of scientific participation, which remains predominantly White. In Carolyn Parker's chapter, the stories of challenges faced by Latina middle school girls in science class are examined. Teachers who are unused to engaging Latina girls in the language of science benefit from instructional strategies to encourage these girls to become engaged with science. Overcoming language difficulties and the stereotypical image of the scientist is only part of the full story for these seventh and eighth graders. Louise Ann Lyon's work, which focuses on mothers' influences on their daughters' potential careers in computer science, highlights that, while all mothers encouraged their daughters to pursue their interests in computer science, their own social class dictated how impacting their encouragement became. This is significant when we view the importance of closing the opportunity gap for economically disadvantaged women pursuing STEM. Finally, Roxanne Hughes' chapter examines the stories of three academic women in science who confronted barriers and biases that were remarkably similar despite spanning three generations. While Part One examines stories of girls and women's pursuits of what remains a nontraditional study and career choice, it becomes clear that equity for girls and women in STEM fields is a pursuit requiring attention to the educational, personal, and cultural messages of the school, college, graduate programs, and academic environments that can foster or discourage the quest.

In Part Two of this volume, the chapters address a wide range of interventions on behalf of supporting the efforts of girls and women in STEM subjects. We begin with grade school students' experiences in and out of school and then explore interventions for the women who work and aspire to work in STEM fields throughout the K–16 continuum. For example, in a South African middle school, Nicole N. Wallace and Annemarie Hattingh explored 8th-grade girls' engagement with alternative assessments in their Natural Science classes and how it became a positive factor in their attitudes toward science in that school year. Informal science learning experiences described in the chapter by Merle Froschl and Babara Sprung as Out of School Time (OST) programs have important implications for encouraging girls in STEM. This is due to their hands-on, inquiry-based curricula as well as the absence of classroom testing constraints. They have implications for expanded day programs, and reading this chapter encourages educators and leaders to consider mimicking these programs. The intervention described by Crystal T. Chukwurah and Stacy S. Klein-Gardner examine the constructs of engineering design with which many girls and young women are not familiar. Specifically, they examine the role of optimization in design and foster an increase in the 9th- and 10th-grade underrepresented girls' self-efficacy. The girls' new understanding of engineering design has important implications for their imagining themselves as participants in STEM fields. Related to this is Cecilia D. Craig's chapter, which provides an overview of the ways in which precollege robotics programs engage students and are important interventional tools for encouraging girls and young women in STEM. Craig found that early experimentation with robotics can inspire girls to venture into the field of engineering, where there is the least female representation. In Sylvia Taube and Barbara Polnick's chapter, 19 female mathematics teachers participate in an intervention designed to improve the teaching of mathematics to culturally diverse students. We see the way in which their entitlement to the study of mathematics can be a tool to empower others through their own self-reflection. From high school teachers to college-level instructors and professors, advocacy takes many forms. The intervention described by Catherine Mavripilis and colleagues—the FORWARD program—addresses the professional trajectory for women in academe who have already entered STEM fields. The FORWARD program, designed to enhance women's opportunities for tenure and promotion in the science and engineering disciplines, provides workshops in writing and publishing, teaching strategies, grant submission, negotiation skills, and work-life balance. These mentoring workshops have an impressive track record for sustaining female science and engineering faculty success. They also encourage doctoral students to persist in science and engineering and pursue academic careers. While this program has roots in the mentoring of undergraduates, it has expanded to enhance the career paths of academic women in science and engineering.

The Research on Women and Education (RWE) book series provides readers with a lens into the experiences of girls and women in many contexts. At no time in our history has the particpation of women been more essential to the fields of science, technology, engineering, and mathematics. An adaptation of a Talmudic expression states, "We do not see things as they are; we see things as we are." The more women in STEM, the more informed the observations of scientists and engineers can become.

REFERENCE

Hopkins, N. (2011). *The changing status of women in science at MIT: 1999–2011. The inaugural colloquium on how to advance women in science and engineering.* University of Chicago. Retrieved March 12, 2011, from http://www.youtube.com/watch?v=IQUB3LeJEJE

PART ONE

STORIES OF GIRLS AND WOMEN PURSUING STEM

CHAPTER 1

INTERSECTIONS OF AFRICAN AMERICAN WOMEN IN STEM AND LINGERING RACIAL AND GENDER BIAS

Catherine Martin-Dunlop
Whitney Johnson

A dearth of knowledge exists regarding the experiences of African American women during their science, technology, engineering, and mathematics (STEM) education. During the mid-1990s, gender research rarely considered the effects of race (Scantlebury, 2012), and any "assumptions about the mismatch between women's interests and STEM often are based on the experiences of white women" (Hill, Corbett, & St. Rose, 2010, p. 23). Despite the progress that women have made, the culture of science and mathematics continues to be a White male culture, with research giving "little attention to subgroups of women" (Hanson, 2009, p. 1). The study described in this chapter attempts to understand the successes and struggles of three African American women with undergraduate degrees in science and engi-

Girls and Women in STEM, pages 3–19

neering who persisted for decades in the face of lingering racial and gender bias in order to reach their goals. The STEM acronym refers to four disciplines, but our chapter focuses on the women's experiences in only two of these areas. Only through deep understanding of the experiences of underrepresented groups such as African American women will educators be able to make significant headway at improving STEM education for the growing diverse workforce of the future.

BACKGROUND

In a recent American Association for University Women (AAUW) report by Hill et al. (2010), the authors state that gender achievement gaps in mathematics and science have decreased and, in some specific subjects, no longer exist. However, our study, which looks specifically at three African American women currently enrolled in a graduate science and mathematics education program at a historically Black college and university (HBCU) in the mid-Atlantic region, reveals that sexism and racism still exist in our schools' classrooms, college lecture halls, and laboratories, and undoubtedly contribute to the underrepresentation of African American women in STEM majors and careers. African American women are less likely to select a STEM major initially and less likely to persist during college compared to males and nonminority students (Chen & Weko, 2009; National Science Board, 2008). In 2006, of all African American freshmen, 27.6% of males and 16.4% of females *intended* to major in a STEM field, with the majority (11%) of females choosing biological or agricultural sciences as their major. Only 1.6%, 0.4%, 1.1%, and 2.3% of African American females initially choose physical science, mathematics/statistics, computer sciences, or engineering, respectively, as a major (Hill et al., 2010). The point here is that these figures illustrate the extremely low numbers of African American females who even *begin* the journey down the STEM pipeline in areas other than biological or agricultural sciences.

Whatever their intended major, many academically capable women drop their STEM major early in their college career. And those who persist represent a tiny fraction of the overall workforce in STEM and those who continue on and earn a graduate degree in STEM. For example, in 2007, only 599 African American women in the United States earned bachelor's degrees in the physical sciences (although this represents 57% of all physical science degrees awarded to African Americans). In the same year, African American women earned only 2.2% of doctoral degrees in biology and less than 2% of doctorates in engineering, computer sciences, physical sciences, and mathematics/statistics combined (Hill et al., 2010).

Negative stereotyping is still prevalent as well. Brotman and Moore (2008) reviewed 10 years of published science education articles on gender issues between 1996 and 2006 and found that, "Students have strong stereotypes that view the physical sciences as masculine and the biological sciences as more feminine" (as cited in Scantlebury, 2012, p. 502). STEM professors sometimes inadvertently discourage women of color—professors who should be going out of their way to recruit and encourage underrepresented students. Johnson (2007) interviewed 16 Black, Latina, and Native American women enrolled in a large, research traditionally White institution (TWI) and reported disturbing results. She found that women were discouraged by the large size of the lecture classes and by asking and answering questions in class. Additionally, they felt negatively impacted by the portrayal "of science as a gender-, ethnicity- and race-neutral meritocracy" (Johnson, 2007, p. 805). Although our study involves women in a *graduate* program, most of the focus was on their *undergraduate* experiences in science and engineering, as we felt experiences in this time period would likely tell a more compelling story and would also provide an explanatory "bridge" to their current career goals.

The science and engineering workforce of the 21st century needs to become more diverse in order to capture lost talent and to more accurately represent the changing demographics of the United States. Underrepresented minorities—the fastest growing segment of the U.S. population—remain hugely underrepresented in STEM fields. But knowing *how* to tap into the minds and talents of these marginalized groups continues to be a challenge for educators. Despite lingering barriers, the women in our study represent examples of those who have persisted and successfully earned a STEM degree. The remainder of this chapter will discuss the design of the study, its results, and then conclude with a discussion and recommendations section.

DESIGN OF STUDY

Our portraiture of three African American women,

> is a method of qualitative research that blurs the boundaries of aesthetics and empiricism in an effort to capture the complexity, dynamics, and subtlety of human experience ... [and] seek[s] to record and interpret the perspectives and experience of the people they are studying, documenting their voices and their visions. (Lawrence-Lightfoot & Davis as cited in Patton, 2002, p. 404)

Our study's objective was to answer the question, "What in-school and out-of-school experiences most influenced African American women as they progressed along their STEM career path?" We mainly focused on memorable experiences, both positive and negative, that our participants reported during their precollege and undergraduate education. Participants were three successful African American women with an average age of 30.7 years. We consider all three women as successful because they already possess a STEM undergraduate degree (in science or engineering) and have worked in STEM-related careers for several years.

The women were purposefully selected for this study because they are currently graduate students in a STEM-education program at an HBCU located in the mid-Atlantic region of the United States where the authors are professors. The women are pursuing either a master's or a doctoral degree in mathematics or science education. The graduate science and mathematics education program has been a successful program within the university's School of Education and Urban Studies for over 15 years. Both authors/professors have been at the university for 2 years. The first author (a White professor) has had all three students in at least one of her courses, and one student—Shomara—has taken four courses with the first author. The second author (a Black professor) has had Danielle in two of her classes. Table 1.1 provides an overview of the women's background.

Data were collected through a preliminary set of questions emailed to the three women, followed by a 1-hour, individual semistructured interview that was audiotaped (after a signed informed consent form was obtained). Table 1.2 lists the interview questions. As can be seen, the open-ended questions allowed the women to explain their experiences in their own words. Additional follow-up emails to the women were used to gather factual information to help produce Table 1.2.

The audiotaped interview responses were transcribed. Reliability was sought by member checking. Transcribed interviews were sent to the women to verify accuracy and to see if they wanted to clarify or elaborate on any details in their responses. Analysis of data followed an inductive process in which transcripts were repeatedly read and reflected upon by the two authors. The goal was to identity salient and recurring themes or patterns (Creswell, 2013) related to our overarching research question. We identified eight themes that served as an organizing framework for this chapter's Results section.

RESULTS

Positive Experiences With Teachers and Professors

All three women had *positive* experiences with professors at college, but only Danielle conveyed positive experiences with teachers at elementary

TABLE 1.1 Overview of the Three African American Women in Study

Pseudonym	Age	Marital Status	Childhood School Background	Parents' Professional & Educational Level	Undergrad STEM Degree(s)	Graduate STEM-Education Degree	STEM Positions
Danielle	28	Single, no children	Mid-SES, urban, 99% Black	Father: engineer, bachelor's degree in Engineering Mother: businesswoman, bachelor's degree in business	Bachelor of Science–Civil Engineering	Completed master's degree in mathematics education, May 2013	5 years as a civil engineer 6 months at an urban middle school teaching mathematics
Shomara	30	Married, no children	Low-SES, rural, majority White	Father: janitor Mother: secretary Both high school graduates	Bachelor of science–molecular biology, biochemistry, and bioinformatics Bachelor of science-biology	Completed master's degree in science education, May 2013	Certified pharmacy technician since 2002 Taught certification course for 2 years Volunteer researcher at herpes virus university lab Taught fifth-/seventh-grade science 2 years Biological sciences technician for federal gov't. for 3 years
Regina	34	Married, two children	High-SES, suburban, 50% White/ 50% Black	Father: rehabilitation counselor, community college certificate Mother: nurse, community college	Bachelor of science-biology Bachelor of science-medical technology	Master's of education with science concentration Currently finishing coursework for an EdD in science education	12 years teaching science (integrated science, physical science, biology, oceanography) in secondary schools Laboratory instruction coordinator at an HBCU Biology adjunct instructor at 2-year community college

TABLE 1.2   Semi-Structured Interview Questions

1. Describe some memorable, *positive* school experiences that you would say are unique to being an African American woman.
2. Describe some memorable, *negative* school experiences that you would say are unique to being an African American woman.
3. What kind of support groups did you have as an undergraduate/graduate STEM student?
4. What were your interactions like with your STEM professors? With other STEM students in your major?
5. Do you believe people were responding or reacting to you during your undergraduate STEM education in a particular way because of your race? Your gender? Please explain.
6. Why do you think there is still underrepresentation of women in the STEM fields? Particularly African American women?
7. What recommendations do you have for increasing the number of African American women in STEM majors and careers?

and middle school. Danielle's teachers recognized that she was intelligent and wanted to use her as a positive role model for the other students. Danielle volunteered to show her work on the board (particularly in mathematics), which teachers appreciated. By being a positive role model, Danielle naturally became a leader. Shomara was pulled out of regular classes in elementary school to attend the Talented and Gifted (TAG) program, but she did not attribute this positive event to a particular teacher.

While pursuing their undergraduate STEM degrees, all three women provided details regarding a professor who made a significant positive impact on their college experience. While attending an HBCU in another state, Danielle talked warmly about Dr. Tames, a middle-aged Black female environmental engineering professor, who advised her during the last 2 years of her degree. Dr. Tames shared with Danielle how things would be in the "real world"—the ups and downs, how engineering would not make her rich, how she would not automatically get to the top, and that engineering was hard work. Danielle explained,

> She took a lot of the females under her belt…she said it's going to be difficult…you're going to have to knock down some barriers. So don't think it's going to be a walk in the park. I mean she gave it to us raw.

In addition to Dr. Tames, Danielle also mentioned the Dean of Engineering (an African male), who took the engineering women to meetings such as those sponsored by the American Society of Civil Engineers (ASCE), which also had a positive impact on her undergraduate STEM experience.

Both Regina and Shomara attended TWIs in their home states for their undergraduate STEM degrees. Regina had no African American professors during her 4 years, while Shomara mentioned that she had one African

American female biology professor. Regina described a special relationship with a White female biology professor who was also her advisor, and gave Regina a laboratory assistant's position in the department. Regina said they became friends and she even babysat the professor's daughter on occasion. Regina's second bachelor's degree from another university in her home state was in medical technology. The Department Chair of Medical Technology (a White female professor) said that she saw Regina "doing great things and advised me to pursue a higher level degree." Shomara was offered a job as a research assistant by a White male professor running a laboratory at the university. She said,

> We developed a really good relationship. And to this day, if I ever need something—help with a class, even graduate classes—he says okay, what do you need? I can ask him anything. He even provided me with a recommendation letter for my PhD program [in epidemiology]. So that's a really positive experience that I have had with a professor.

Negative Experiences With Teachers and Professors

Together with the *positive* experiences with teachers and professors mentioned in the proceeding paragraphs, all three women also had *negative* experiences. In middle school, Danielle said that the principal (a Black female) hated her because she had the perception that Danielle was overly confident, had her nose in the air, and held her head too high. The principal did not sign off on administrative papers and allow Danielle to go to the high school where all her classmates were going "because she said she didn't want me with my class, so they sent me to [the other, "rival," high school across the city]." We interpreted this action as the principal using her power to punish Danielle.

Apart from Regina's biology professor/advisor, she felt no other professors at her TWI really supported her. She said, "I always felt like the sore thumb sticking out." For example, Regina's White chemistry professor said that she should not be getting A's on his exams (after she did in fact receive an A on the first exam). On a subsequent examination, Regina received only a grade of C, but when she looked at a White male's paper, she found her answers did not differ greatly from her classmate's. When she confronted her professor about this, he reluctantly made the change to her paper but said, "You are treading on thin ice." As a result of this experience, Regina felt she always needed to work harder than her White peers, and she never did ask her professor for clarification again on any subsequent work.

Shomara conveyed to us that she felt that, generally, most Black (her term) children do not have many positive experiences in school. Her explanation for this was that teachers expect Black children *not* to have emotions (especially strong ones), and to *not* ask questions. Shomara said she always had lots of questions, but they were not always answered or interpreted positively.

Making the transition from high school to college is a challenge for most students. During her first year as a STEM biology major, Shomara earned C's in chemistry, and this resulted in the premedicine and dentistry advisor telling her that she should change majors. Shomara said,

> Why? And I had to wonder, if I were a White girl, would he have told me the same thing? I had to wonder that. Like why, who has the audacity to say that? It wasn't like I was failing, although a C when you want to go to medical school is not necessarily the grade you want to get, but I wasn't failing. But yeah, that's the game.

Positive Influence From Peers

The extent to which peers had a positive influence during their STEM education varied among the three women. For Danielle, who attended an HBCU in another state, her girlfriends in business inspired and motivated her. In fact, Danielle partnered with a high school girlfriend during graduate school in order to form a mentoring business. Among her STEM peers in college, a support group of eight women was formed for the "cool nerds" as she referred to herself, and they called the group "McNair Maids." Regina mentioned a White male student advisor who helped her and seemed to go beyond the call of duty to support her. Shomara said the few Black students (her term) at her TWI helped each other but only to a limited degree. They wanted to study with her when it served their needs (e.g., when they discovered Shomara was doing well in a challenging class), but if they felt that she did not have anything to offer, they would not include her in activities.

Negative Influence From Peers

In general, the women did not have what we describe as harmful negative experiences with peers (although Danielle definitely came close if we examine her language carefully). A harmful experience would have been one that altered their perception of themselves or their career path. If a negative experience occurred, they were able to learn from it and turn it into a positive experience. For example, Regina's suburban high school friends (who she described as half Black, half White) did not support her decision to go to college, and she received negative comments from them. When she went to college anyway, she was puzzled at first when her White peers distanced themselves and gave her the "silent treatment." She often felt isolated, but with the help of Dr. Tames, she was able to relax and be herself. She expressed that slowly her peers came to see who she really was, and they began to accept her into their networks.

Danielle's experiences with peers in her inner-city school were often challenging, particularly with other girls. Sometimes the other African American girls didn't like Danielle because she was popular and the boys liked her. This made the girls jealous and hateful, she said. As early as elementary school, Danielle felt there was "something wrong with women" because they seemed to have an issue with someone who was smart and confident. She reflected, "I don't know if that had something to do with me becoming an engineer." Later, in middle school, Danielle was in an advanced math and science program in the summertime. "I was tormented in middle school . . . they hated me." We asked specifically which classmates hated her—girls, boys, Black or White—and she said it was *all* kids. She said,

> They hated me most because I was the role model, the leader. I had to have tough skin. The girls absolutely hated me . . . because the boys wanted to like me . . . but they couldn't because all the girls hated me. And it was really, really bad.

Danielle admitted to having a couple of fights with the girls, but she said she was never the instigator. Surprisingly, even when Danielle attended an HBCU in another state for her engineering degree, she still occasionally faced dismissal from her peers. She connected this to being a strong minded, confident, and outgoing person from an urban environment. She believed that her classmates had a stereotyped image of her as a hard, thuggish city girl, and they treated her as such. She said, "A lot of African American women are known as dramatic. We have a lot of negative connotations around us. And to break that stereotype along the way is what matters the most."

Shomara was the only woman who felt that she had no significant peer support in high school or as an undergraduate STEM student. When she was accepted into the TWI in her home state, friends did not encourage her to go. Her peers were all going to a nearby university or community college, but she said she had bigger goals for herself, as we can tell by the following quote:

> Well, I'm not getting stuck here [in her county]. I don't want to say you get stuck but you do get stuck; you get the same people doing the same stuff and half of them are not doing the right stuff, and I just . . . it was time for me to go, and that is what I did.

As soon as she received her acceptance letter for college, Shomara began working to save money for the tuition. However, once on campus, she again felt the other students did not accept her.

Role of Parents and Other Family Members

Two of the three women had a lot of support from family members. Again, Shomara was the only one who felt that pursuing an undergraduate education was solely up to her. She felt she did not receive any encouragement from her parents. (However, she does acknowledge that her husband, whom she married after graduating, was and still is very supportive of her going to graduate school.) Fighting back tears, she elaborated,

> And I say that because my parents didn't have any money. We didn't have a lot when I was a kid and neither of my parents went to college. As a matter of fact, when I got into college, parts of my family told me I should go to a community college instead [starts to cry] because my parents couldn't afford to send me . . . it's not my parents' fault . . . no one told them to go to college.

So without the financial or emotional support of her family, Shomara at times worked three jobs to pay her tuition and room and board.

In contrast, Danielle had the full support of her family. Danielle's father was an engineer and her mother was a business woman, so both had attended college. An example of this support occurred when Danielle's middle school principal told her she was "snooty" and that she held her head too high, as described in an earlier section. Both her parents marched to the school to defend her and told the principal that Danielle *should* be confident and hold her head up high. Danielle reported, "So they pretty much supported me, and I think that's when I learned that my parents are on my team and that they're my safety net." Another example of the support she received from her father occurred when she was forced to go to the high school on the other side of the city. Her father did some research on the Internet and provided Danielle with some statistics to show her that the school was actually a better school to go to if she wanted to be an engineer.

Danielle had known she wanted to be an engineer since she was a little girl, and her parents supported her goal, even when she wanted to get her degree in a neighboring state. Fortunately, Danielle's grandmother lived near the university, and she also provided support. Danielle would often visit her grandmother on the weekends, and her grandmother cooked and washed her clothes while at the same time encouraging Danielle to do well in school. Obviously, higher education was highly valued by everyone in Danielle's family.

Regina mentioned that her family supported her throughout her education, especially her mother. Regina said she was a little apprehensive at first when she began her STEM degree in biology, but Regina's mother convinced her that she could do it.

Other Support Groups

In addition to support from teachers, professors, family members, and peers, two out of the three women had positive experiences with other support groups or individuals during their STEM education. Danielle described how the engineering department secretary played a positive role as the "mother." The secretary would make sure they all went to classes on time and even looked out for them when they were ill. As mentioned earlier, the American Society of Civil Engineers, along with the National Society for Black Engineers (NSBE), and the Institute of Technology and Engineering (ITE) are professional organizations that provide social activities for its members such as Danielle so that she could network and feel connected to her future career.

Regina discussed two events and an older family friend who impacted her in a positive way. In high school, she participated in a 1-week mini–medical school experience that instilled a love of biology in her, and then as an undergrad STEM student, Regina received a Barnes and Noble scholarship for free books. The family friend happened to be an academic advisor, and she met with Regina weekly to help her write a good résumé and to apply to colleges.

Both Danielle and Regina mentioned that their church played a major positive role in their life as well. Danielle says that she relies on God during tough times, and she feels God has a plan for her and that He wants her to be "confident and to ignore all the crazy things that people said."

Perspectives on Race and Gender Contributing to Self-Perceptions

For two of the women, race was a *very* salient part of their experiences and development of their self-perceptions. However, when asked, "Do you feel people were responding or reacting to you during your undergraduate STEM education in a particular way because of your race and/or gender?" all three women said "Yes." Danielle explained,

Yes, I would say yes. So I was stereotyped and labeled... labeled as ghetto... labeled as having an attitude... labeled as I think I'm tough... I think

I'm hard . . . I think I'm cute. I don't know how someone could think that . . . if it's not true. But that didn't keep me from doing anything that I needed to do . . . which is amazing.

Danielle always felt proud to be a successful Black student. Being proud and using her support system has allowed her to fight the challenges to her identity.

Shomara felt that being Black was more significant than being female as a factor for how others responded to her. In addition to the story she told us about being advised to drop her major because she was getting C's in chemistry, Shomara also told us about a troubling experience in organic chemistry. Both Shomara and a White classmate were failing the class by midterm. Shomara decided to drop the class because she knew that an F in a five-credit class would lower her GPA significantly, and it would be nearly impossible to raise it high enough to get into medical school. At the end of the semester, she ran into her classmate, who asked her why she dropped the class. Shomara explained her reasoning and then was shocked to learn that her classmate received an A in the class. When we asked if she thought she too would have received an A in the class if she had not withdrawn, Shomara responded,

All I can say is, I don't know the answer to that. Deep in my heart I don't believe that I would have, but to be fair, I really don't know. I don't know; but inside no. I would have gotten that F on my transcript.

Although she had no proof, Shomara fully believed that this was an incident of racial discrimination or preferential treatment for the White student.

Shomara also recounted a more overt incident of racial discrimination while working as a biological sciences technician for 3 years for the federal government. (She had graduated and obtained her STEM degree with double majors in molecular biology, biochemistry, and bioinformatics.) She applied for a position as a scientist with the federal government and made the eligibility list but was denied an interview by her boss because, she was told, she did not have a doctoral degree. Shomara was shocked that she didn't even get an interview, because she knew White colleagues who had similar positions who did not have doctorates. In Shomara's opinion, she "was getting too ambitious and he didn't like it."

Regina had difficulties separating race from gender. Her earlier description of the "silent treatment" could not be attributed to being a Black student or being female. Nevertheless, she found that her questions during her undergraduate education were sometimes ignored and devalued, whereas questions posed by males were always given priority and answered.

Interestingly, of the three women, Regina seemed to have the *least* negative experiences overall, yet was the *least* confident.

Perspectives on Underrepresentation of African American Women in STEM

When asked, "Why do you think there is still underrepresentation of African American women in the STEM fields," each woman highlighted a different aspect of the problem. Danielle said girls do not see enough role models in school (teachers are mostly White), college, or in STEM-related careers such as engineering. She said girls think engineering is a man's job. Regina felt girls in school lacked interest in STEM education, and both Regina and Danielle thought this is mainly because they're not aware of the scope of various STEM-related careers and only know about premedicine. Both Regina and Danielle said girls think that they're not good at math and that it is too difficult, and therefore girls do not consider a STEM career. Regina pointed out that the media and society in general contribute to a negative image of STEM.

Shomara said the underrepresentation of Black women in STEM is basically because of "people." When we asked for clarification on who she meant by "people," she said, "admissions people, grant writers, and White men still think African Americans can't do it [STEM]." Shomara felt it is the very people who are empowered to admit Black female students into STEM programs and provide funding who don't because they believe that Black women are incapable of succeeding.

SUMMARY

The following is a summary of our findings:

1. All three women had positive experiences with one or more STEM professors. This highlights the power of close interpersonal relationships between student and professor.
2. All three women had negative experiences with a teacher or a STEM professor.
3. All three women experienced negative stereotyping that seemed tied more to their race than their gender.
4. Two out of three women had support and encouragement from family members, who contributed to their success.
5. Others who provided support included professional organizations, church, an older family friend, and a STEM department secretary.

DISCUSSION AND RECOMMENDATIONS

Through this study, we discovered that all three women saw the interplay of *both* race and gender as substantial components of their identity as strong, resilient, and successful women in STEM. We discovered that there were key people in their lives who enabled them to persist as they progressed along their chosen STEM career path. Often, it seemed they persisted in defiance of others (even of their own gender and race) who doubted them or placed roadblocks in their path. In seeking to understand their struggles, we came to admire these three women even more than when we first met them 2 years ago.

Our study revealed that *what* is taught during STEM is not the problem associated with underrepresentation of African American women. Rather, *how* STEM is taught, interactions with STEM teachers and professors, and support networks and learning opportunities outside of the classroom are the crucial factors that must be further examined if we want to reduce racial and gender bias. Current researchers reiterate the fact that negative stereotyping is still prevalent in our society (Brotman & Moore, 2008; Jovanovic & Bhanot, 2008; Scantlebury, 2012). Such a view limits girls' opportunities to learn and succeed in science. However, Danielle was able to use her prior successes and her support systems to change negative experiences related to her race and/or gender into an opportunity to show others that their assumptions about her were incorrect. What is still disconcerting in Danielle's stories of success is that she feels a lot of African Americans do not view African American women as role models. This needs to change so that African American girls can see women such as themselves engaged in interesting and challenging opportunities in science, technology, engineering, and mathematics. Eventually, African American girls will begin to see themselves differently and will continue to study STEM subjects as they progress through school and college.

As mentioned above, teacher–student interactions can have lasting positive or negative effects. Johnson's (2007) study, in which she found STEM professors discouraged minority women majoring in science at a TWI, resonated with our participants' stories. Johnson revealed that she "never saw a woman of color either ask or answer a question" (p. 812) during a lecture class. "It is through answering, not asking, questions that status [in the eyes of the male classmates] is built" (p. 813). Both Shomara and Regina, who went to TWIs for their undergraduate degrees, also experienced subtle undertones of racism when they attempted to ask questions. Regina quickly learned that it was not her place to question her professor's grading on examinations. Even as far back as elementary school, Shomara believed she did not have a voice. She was likely considered a nuisance when she asked too many questions.

A supportive network and learning environment outside of the classroom can often counteract negative influences inside the classroom. Danielle reported that her parents and grandmother served as a safety net during school and college, and Regina said her mother gave her that gentle push of encouragement when she was feeling apprehensive about first starting a STEM degree.

Family support may be complemented by other groups outside of the classroom, which one can seek out or establish themselves. Danielle and Regina mentioned how their religion helps them on a daily basis. In our initial email communication with Regina asking about the people who were most influential, she said, "Most of all, my spiritual guidance gave me faith and empowered me to believe that I could do it and that I can make it, and that it [my goals, dreams, and aspirations] shall come to pass." A recent study by Ceglie (2013) also found that religion may positively influence outcomes for African American women majoring in science and may contribute to their persistence during challenging circumstances. Because our study included only three women and Ceglie's had only six, we recommend further study on the role that religion may play in the lives and experiences of minority women pursuing a STEM degree or career.

Lastly, a self-established group like Danielle's "McNair Maids" or a professional organization such as the National Society for Black Engineers or summer enrichment programs for high school students such as Regina's mini–medical school camp can play a significant role outside of the STEM classroom in combating negative stereotypes.

RECOMMENDATIONS

Some of the recommendations made by the women for tackling problems of underrepresentation of minority women in STEM are closely aligned with the National Research Council's (NRC, 2011) broad recommendations for action. Both the women and the NRC stress the importance of preschool and early education programs in mathematics and science, and the need for more information, counseling, and outreach so that minorities are aware of STEM-related opportunities and careers. Both Shomara and Regina believe young Black children need to do more hands-on science. This seems to echo the findings of Patrick, Mantzicopoulos, and Samarapungayan (2009), who saw low SES kindergarten children experience success during a 5- and 10-week inquiry-based science program; and Hammrich (2002), who developed the Sisters in Sport Science afterschool and summer program for minority girls. Rahm (2008) also recommends afterschool science programs that involve school–museum–scientist partnerships. Similar to this, Regina said communities need more basic information on STEM education, and she suggested creating a STEM community center. Finally, we recommend the establishment of structured mentoring programs and small, collaborative learning communities (Alston, 2008) for women who pursue STEM degrees. We feel mentoring programs and collaborative learning communities have the potential to create a profound positive impact on outcomes in STEM for African American women.

THE FUTURE FOR OUR STEM-EDUCATION GRADUATE STUDENTS

Our participants/students are at a transitional stage in their STEM career—a stage that has been shaped by a mix of negative and positive experiences in school, college, and outside of the classroom, with teachers, professors, friends, and parents, and various support groups. Danielle has temporally left the engineering field in order to teach mathematics in an urban middle school very near to where she went to school. She had always planned for careers in *both* engineering and mathematics education. She said, "I really want students to 'get math'...just simply get it, just as I did in K–12." Shomara is again juggling three jobs (teaching college science courses and tutoring) as she submits applications to PhD programs in epidemiology. She wants to combine her knowledge and skills in education with microbiology so that she can tackle public health problems in the African American community. Despite coming from a low-SES background and having few support groups in place during her education, Shomara also wants to give back to her community. Regina discovered her passion for teaching and plans to use her doctoral degree in science education to teach at a higher education institution.

In the not-too-distant future, American society and the economy will need to rely more and more on a diverse workforce who possess the highly specialized knowledge, skills, and abilities associated with the STEM fields. Our study has shown that three African American women in particular also needed inner strength and perseverance in order to overcome the challenges presented by lingering racial and gender bias. We believe STEM education must be improved at all levels from prekindergarten to graduate school so that other women like Danielle, Shomara, and Regina may be inspired to pursue STEM careers.

REFERENCES

Alston, S. (2008). The effect of learning communities on achievement in STEM fields for African Americans across four campuses. *Journal of Negro Education, 77,* 190–202.

Brotman, J., & Moore, F. (2008). Girls and science: A review of four themes in the science education literature. *Journal of Research in Science Teaching, 45,* 971–1002.

Ceglie, R. (2013). Religion as a support factor for women of color pursuing science degrees: Implications for science teacher educators. *Journal of Science Teacher Education, 24,* 37–65.

Chen, X., & Weko, T. (2009). Students who study science, technology, engineering, and mathematics (STEM) in postsecondary education. U.S. Department of Education NCES 2009-161: Institute of Education Sciences.

Creswell, J. (2013). *Research design: Qualitative, quantitative, and mixed methods approaches.* Washington, DC: Sage.

Hammrich, P. (2002). Gender equity in science and mathematics education. In J. Koch & B. Irby (Eds.), *Defining and redefining gender equity in education* (pp. 81–98). Greenwich, CT: Information Age.

Hanson, S. (2009). *Swimming against the tide: African American girls and science education.* Philadelphia, PA: Temple University Press.

Hill, C., Corbett, C., & St. Rose, A. (2010). *Why so few? Women in science, technology, engineering, and mathematics.* Washington, DC: American Association for University Women.

Johnson, A. (2007). Unintended consequences: How science professors discourage women of color. *Science Education, 91,* 805–821.

Jovanovic, J., & Bhanot, R. (2008). Gender differences in science. In W.-M. Roth & K. Tobin (Eds.), *World of science education: North America* (pp. 427–450). Rotterdam, The Netherlands: Sense.

National Research Council (NRC). (2011). *Expanding underrepresented minority participation: America's science and technology talent at the crossroads.* Washington, DC: National Academies Press.

National Science Board. (2008). *Science and engineering indicators 2008.* Arlington, VA: National Science Foundation.

Patrick, H., Mantzicopoulos, P., & Samarapungayan, A. (2009). Motivation for learning science in kindergarten: Is there a gender gap and does integrated inquiry and literacy instruction make a difference? *Journal of Research in Science Teaching, 46,* 166–191.

Patton, M. (2002). *Qualitative research & evaluation methods.* Thousand Oaks, CA: Sage.

Rahm, I. (2008). Urban youths' hybrid positioning in science practices at the margin: A look inside a school–museum–scientist partnership project and an after-school science program. *Cultural Studies in Science Education, 3,* 97–121.

Scantlebury, K. (2012). Still part of the conversation: Gender issues in science education. In B. J. Fraser, K. Tobin, & R. McRobbie (Eds.), *Second international handbook of science education* (pp. 499–512). Rotterdam, The Netherlands: Springer.

CHAPTER 2

AFRICAN AMERICAN WOMEN'S RESILIENCE IN HARD SCIENCE MAJORS

Ezella McPherson

Historically, few African American women have earned degrees in science, technology, engineering, and math (STEM) fields (Jordan, 2006; L. Malcom & S. Malcom, 2011; S. Malcom, 1993; Warren, 2000). Historical scholarship showed that some African American women rarely had mentors, role models, and parental support while pursuing hard science[1] majors in college or graduate school. In contrast, other African American women who remained in STEM fields displayed early interests in science or mathematics through participation in school or home projects. Teacher and parental support was also found to be present for these women pursuing STEM majors during the 20th century.

African American women are currently one of the largest growing populations in college, but continue to be underrepresented in STEM fields at predominantly White institutions (PWIs) (Bowen, Chingos, & McPherson, 2009; Jordan, 2006; NSF, 2009, 2011; Warren, 2000). Scholars have also found that African American women remain in these fields due to individual and school factors, the home environment, the culture of science, and

Girls and Women in STEM, pages 21–37

career aspirations (Hanson & Johnson, 2000; Henrion, 1997; Jordan, 2006; Justin-Johnson, 2004; Warren, 2000). However, little research has examined how school, home, and the culture of science[2] and multiple identities influence the hardships that African American women experience in STEM majors and how being resilient contributes to their success in these majors (McPherson, 2012).

There is still a gap in the research literature. The purpose of this chapter is to examine African American women's experiences in hard science majors throughout K–16 schooling. It employs the multiple-case research methodology to demonstrate how eight African American women faced obstacles due to their multiple identities while acting in a resilient manner while pursuing STEM majors. The chapter starts by discussing the frameworks of Black Feminist Thought and resilience. It then describes the research methods, findings, conclusions, and implications.

LITERATURE REVIEW

Historical Explanations for Underrepresentation

The modern-day underrepresentation of African American women in hard science majors can be attributed to their historically low enrollment and graduation rates. Consider that in the early 20th century, few Black women were engaged in chemical sciences curriculum in college (Brown, 2011). These included Ohio State University's natural science scholar Dr. Ruth Ella Moore (class of 1933), University of Pennsylvania's biologist Dr. Roger Arlinger Young (class of 1940), Columbia University's chemist Marie Maynard Daly (class of 1948), and physicist Shirley Ann Jackson (MIT, class of 1973) (Jordan, 2006; Rayner-Canham & Rayner-Canham,1998; Warren, 2000).

In addition, few Black women earned doctoral degrees in engineering and mathematics from PWIs (Jordan, 2006; Kenshaft, 2005; Warren, 2000). Black female engineers with doctorates included University of California-Davis' electrical engineer Giovonnae Anderson Dennis (class of 1978), MIT's engineer Jennie R. Patrick (class of 1979), and George Washington University's mechanical engineer Geraldine Claudette Darden (class of 1983). Moreover, mathematicians who received doctorates were Catholic University's Euphemia Lofton Haynes (class of 1943), University of Michigan's Marjorie Lee Brown (class of 1949), and Yale's Evelyn Boyd Collins Granville (class of 1950).

Furthermore, a small number of PWIs produced the first African American medical doctors in American society during the 20th century (Warren, 2000). These included Cornell University graduates such as physician

May Edward Chin (class of 1926), psychiatrist Margaret Morgan Lawrence (class of 1940), physician F. Pearl McBroom (class of 1954), and NASA astronaut and physician Mae Jemison (class of 1984). Others were New York Medical College's Dr. Jane Cook (class of 1945), Columbia's Dr. Barbara Wright Pierce (class of 1947/1948), and the University of Michigan's Dr. Margaret E. Grigsby (class of 1948). One exception to the rule was Dr. Dorothy Lavinia Brown. In 1948, she became the first Black woman to earn a medical degree from Meharry Medical College, a predominantly Black institution (PBI).

These scholars became role models and mentors for the next generation. However, the existing research on this group fails to examine these women's challenges based on their multiple identities while they were pursuing STEM or medical degrees from PWIs and/or PBIs. Additionally, the current scholarship offers little insight into how these women remained resilient despite the barriers they encountered while pursuing these degrees.

Current Explanations for Underrepresentation

Contemporary scholars have observed that African American women are underrepresented in STEM fields in comparison with White and male counterparts (Bowen et al., 2009; NSF, 2011). Researchers have attributed their underrepresentation to individual factors, including sense of belonging in STEM classes and majors (Gilmartin, Li, & Aschbacher, 2006; Hanson, 2006), isolation (Sands, 2009), and academic preparation (Bradley, 1997; Hanson & Johnson, 2000; McGee, 2009). Other barriers include lack of parental support and role models (Jordan, 2006; Warren, 2000). The "chilly" culture of science explained the underrepresentation of African American female instructors and the omission of culturally relevant science curriculum (Bradley, 1997; Justin-Johnson, 2004; Lee & Luykx, 2006). Finally, they had limited access to careers.

In contrast, a growing body of literature discusses African American women's experiences in STEM fields in different contexts, including the home, school, and the culture of science. Evidence also confirms that African American women utilized support systems (e.g., family, friends, and community members) as resources when they faced obstacles in the STEM curriculum in K–16 settings (Edwards, 2002; Jordan, 2006; Justin-Johnson, 2004). For instance, mathematician Vivienne Malone-Mayes received parental support and was motivated to study mathematics (Henrion, 1997). Support from family and friends in graduate school gave some African American women the motivation to persist despite adversity that they encountered in science programs when they were undergraduates (Justin-Johnson, 2004).

Second, in the school environment, support from instructors explains African American women's success in the face of adversity in STEM fields. Consider that historically, African American female scientists, mathematicians, and engineers had supportive teachers to encourage them to pursue STEM degrees and careers in spite of their low enrollment in STEM programs (Henrion, 1997; Jordan, 2006; Warren, 2000). For example, former NASA aerospace engineer Christine Voncile Mann Darden was encouraged by teachers to pursue science and engineering interests (Warren, 2000).

Third, the culture of science environment impacted African American females' experiences in STEM fields. Two Black women revealed that having some supportive secondary school and college math teachers accounted for their success despite challenges in math (Moody, 2003). These teachers encouraged students and made sure they understood mathematics problems. Additionally, being able to engage in real-life applications of mathematical concepts and cooperative learning were important for helping them to fully understand the math course materials. Mathematics is important because it is an integral part of many of the sciences and engineering curricular programs.

The above research provided some insight into the experiences of African American women in STEM majors. However, less is known about how, in the past and present, African American women experienced STEM majors due to their multiple identities. We also know little about how African American women were resilient to the extent that they were able to bounce back from adversity while pursuing undergraduate STEM degrees. The next section closer analyzes the shortcomings of this research.

LIMITATIONS OF EXISTING RESEARCH: RATIONALE FOR THE CURRENT STUDY

The majority of STEM research on African American women lacked an intersectional focus that centered on how race, class, gender, and nation influenced their experiences in STEM majors. Thus, there is a limited understanding of African American women's experiences in these fields based on their multiple identities. Equally important is how different contexts influence their experiences and resilience in hard-science majors. However, few studies have attempted to document African American women's successful experiences navigating through STEM majors (Jordan, 2006; McPherson, 2012; Warren, 2000) using an intersectional perspective and resilience framework. Hence, this study will attempt to fill these gaps by employing both frameworks to better understand African American women's experiences in hard-science majors.

THEORETICAL FRAMEWORK

This study combines Black Feminist Thought and resilience into a unified framework for understanding African American women's experiences in hard-science majors. Black Feminist Thought sheds light on the interlocking forms of oppression (e.g., racism, sexism, and classism) experienced by Black women in their everyday lived experiences (Collins, 2000; Crenshaw, 1995; hooks, 2000). It also privileges Black women's knowledge through everyday life experiences with multiple identities (e.g., race, class, gender, sexuality, nation), which can account for their experiences with discrimination (Collins, 2000; Feagin & Yanick, 1998). These experiences include "being the only one" in employment or educational settings, sexual harassment, rape, domestic violence, and reproductive rights (Collins, 2000; Guy-Sheftall, 2005; hooks, 2000; Ladner, 1995; McPherson, 2012; Reid-Merritt, 1996).

In addition, few studies have connected this framework to better understand how African American women with multiple identities have used strategies to overcome obstacles in STEM majors (McPherson, 2012). Being resilient was one way these women mitigated barriers in hard-science majors. Resilience is "the capacity to rebound from adversity strengthened and more resourceful" (Walsh, 1998, p. 4). Martin and Mitchell-Martin (1978) applied the resilience framework to Black families and discussed how extended families pulled together and pooled their resources to survive in the face of obstacles. Moreover, Black female-headed households thrive and survive through support from extended family members (R. B. Hill, 1997). Black single-parent families also instilled the value of education, especially higher education for their children.

African American women in both single-parent and dual-parent households received support from their home environments while pursuing STEM majors (McPherson, 2012). However, few studies have combined Black Feminist Thought and resilience to better understand African American women's experiences of trials and triumphs in hard-science majors due to their multiple identities. Hence, combining these frameworks will shed synergistic light on the everyday lived experiences of these women. Below is a discussion of the research methods.

METHODOLOGY

The purpose of this chapter is to examine African American women's experiences in hard-science majors throughout K–16 schooling. It answers the following questions: How do multiple identities influence the experiences of African American women in hard-science majors? and How do undergraduate African American women become resilient in hard-science majors? To answer these questions, multiple-case research methodology is employed.

Multiple-Case Study Design

The multiple-case study design differs from a single-case study because it involves replication of the experiment to determine whether similar results occur when there are multiple cases (Yin, 2009). In a multiple-case study, researchers conduct the same experiment using purposefully[3] chosen populations and locations to determine whether similar or dissimilar results are produced in the same context (Yin, 2003), which might be a school or hospital (Miles & Huberman, 1994). The multiple-case study methodology is appropriate when researchers want to compare and contrast findings of experiments using replication (Yin, 2009). The multiple-case research study methodological approach is thus appropriate for comparing and contrasting African American women's experiences in hard-science majors at Town University (pseudonym).

Data Collection

The data for this study was pulled from a larger study on the persistence of undergraduate African American women in hard-science majors at a PWI. The data for this study was collected from March 2011 to December 2011.

Sample

In this study, the multiple cases were eight purposefully chosen African American women who persisted[4] in hard-science majors at Town University. The criterion for participation was (a) women who self-identified as African American or Black with upperclassman status based on credit hours, (b) were hard-science majors, and (3) between the ages of 19 and 23. Each participant provided written consent for the study. The study was approved by the University of Illinois Institutional Review Board.

Interviews

Data collection consisted of four interviews. The interviews lasted from 8 minutes to 3 hours. The researcher asked questions that focused on African American women's experiences in math and science in K–16 settings. What was the questioning protocol?

Research Setting

This multiple-case study was completed at a PWI, Town University, which was chosen because of the undergraduate student population. Consider for example that Town University is a research-intensive institution that serves over 30,000 undergraduate students (U.S. Department of Education & National Center for Education Statistics, 2010). In 2010, there were slightly more men (over 55%) enrolled at the institution than women (about 45%). The population consisted of about 60% White students, 28% minority students, 9% immigrants, and 3% unidentified students. Fewer undergraduate minority students and women were enrolled in STEM majors when compared to their White male and international counterparts.

Data Analysis

The electronically recorded interviews were transcribed verbatim. The data was analyzed by question using data displays to derive meaning and themes. The qualitative data analysis program, Maxqda, was used to code the data and develop patterns consistent with qualitative data analysis (Lofland & Lofland, 1995). The qualitative data results are reported below

FINDINGS

African American Women's Adversity in Hard-Science Majors

African American women who pursue hard-science majors face multiple barriers. The unification of Black Feminist Thought and resilience frameworks revealed that these obstacles occur in home, school, and the culture of science. These obstacles are explored in-depth through the lens of women science majors.

Home Environment
The home environment accounted for some of the adversities that African American women face in hard-science majors. These challenges can include death and homesickness when seen through the lens of Black Feminist Thought. When she wanted to leave the university, Briana stated,

> A couple weeks ago when my [foster] mom died. I didn't feel like it was worth it... She was my sole motivation for coming to college... [I wanted] to find out what's wrong with [her]. [I was] going to take care of [her] one

day... This degree [was] going to allow me to figure out neurological reasons
as to why this disease [was] happening [and]... progressing.

This quote exemplifies how difficult home situations can deter participants
such as Briana, an adopted woman from a working-class family, from even
completing college. Similarly, Jennifer, a woman with a middle-class family
background, departed from another PWI to attend Town University due to
homesickness.

The Black Feminist Thought perspective also noted that some of these
women experience financial hardships due to social class. Finances pro-
hibited some women from purchasing course books or paying tuition.
These women typically came from working-class or lower-middle-class backgrounds. Math major Lara, from a lower-middle-class family, provides an
example. She responded, "First chemistry. I didn't have a book, because
it was a lot of money and they had [a] chemistry tutoring program where
you could use it and do homework in there." This excerpt demonstrates
the role of social class in determining whether or not these women have
textbooks and other materials needed for classes.

Other African American women from middle-class families, like engineering major Simone, lacked financial issues and resisted purchasing
books. She shared books with peers who previously took her classes or
bought books when they were relevant for class sessions. In fact, some middle-class females fell behind in STEM classes at the beginning of the term.
However, they eventually caught up in the class or dropped classes.

School Environment

Using a Black Feminist Thought perspective, the school environment
difficulties faced by African American women in hard-science majors included adjustment to college, communicating with peers and instructors,
and racism. Adjustment to the college culture of studying regularly for the
STEM curriculum was the first hurdle that many African American women
endured at Town University. This is displayed in the narratives of Rachelle
and Patricia below.

Adjustment was a lot, just because I had to get used to studying. (Rachelle,
biology major)

They have all these different people reaching out to you, freshman year
[with] different resources. They guide you. Then sophomore year, you have
to... seek out those resources on your own. At the same time, I'm still new to
the university. I'm still trying to transition, [because]... this is the time when
I have to determine my major. So somebody should be able to help me out.
(Patricia, business major)

In addition, communicating with peers and instructors were obstacles that some African American women faced in classes in hard-science majors. These women described how their instructors and peers looked different than their neighborhood peers. When asked about these experiences, Lara responded, "I had some experiences with not understanding some of my teachers, because English isn't their first language. So accents and trying to understand them . . . [and] the material being taught to me." This narrative addresses the language barriers that these women endured in learning math and science. Of equal importance is the racism outside of classrooms that these women encountered on Town University's campus. When asked about racism as a college student, a biology major, Shannon, responded,

> Last year on a holiday, my friend and I were walking down main street and we were about to go into EXPRESS and I guess that this guy was really drunk, but that is no excuse. He yelled back, "What are you doing going into EXPRESS. That store is "for White people." We were both Black.

Culture of Science

Peers and instructors accounted for some of the difficulties that these women endured at Town University. The Black Feminist Thought perspective of the burden of representation, namely, "being one of the few" emerged, as Rachelle described her math classroom experiences. She stated,

> In math class, I was the "only Black girl" in my discussion, "only African American," "only person of color" . . . I liked working with the Asians with mathematics . . . It feels a little weird. My T.A. knew my name from day one. I wanted to ask him, "Do you know my name, because you're really good with names?" Or "Am I the 'only one' that looks like me?"

Other African American women reported hardships working with peers inside and outside of science and mathematics classrooms. When asked about relationships with White female peers, Simone responded,

> My first couple semesters of engineering classes, I don't think a lot of my peers noticed I was there, or really talked to me . . . They wouldn't say "hi" in the hallway or anything . . . It annoyed me . . . There were definitely a few girls that I remember, we had all our classes together, and it would just be me and them in the hallway sometimes . . . You try to make the eye contact and get ready to say "hi," and they would turn the other way . . . "I'm right here."

The previous quotes are a sample of the racial and gendered experiences that African American women faced in the classroom. Learning to work with and maintain relationships with peers who differed by race and gender was essential for African American women to be able to persist and graduate with degrees in hard-science majors from Town University.

African American women pursuing hard-science majors also had to deal with stereotypes about their academic abilities, due to their racial and gendered identities. Ashley, a biology major, provided a narrative about peers' stereotypes that focused on her academic abilities. She said, "I do work hard all of the time. You don't want to be seen as the 'dumb Black girl' that does not know anything, 'cause I am not that." In this section, the peers might have perceived African American women as being less smart. Hence, some African American women's experiences within the culture of science were different than those of their peers, because they had to prove their intellectual capabilities. This finding is similar to research that has shown that minorities and women were deemed to be less smart in comparison with their White and/or male peers (Fleshman, 2012; Heppner, Wao, & Lee, 2010; Hill, Corbett, & St. Rose, 2010; Litzler, Mody-Pan, & Brainard, 2011; Reid, 2009).

In addition to problems with their peers, many African American women jumped over hurdles when working with science and math professors. Research on the underrepresentation of faculty and women in STEM fields (Griffin, Pérez, Holmes, & Mayo, 2010; Hurtado et al., 2011) has shown that the majority of science and math professors were White males, with a few female and minority instructors being the exceptions. For instance, Jennifer experienced anxiety when meeting with professors for the first time during office hours due to stereotypes about African Americans. She explained that these feelings stemmed from White and male professors' prejudgments about her academic abilities as "one of the few" African American female mathematics majors. In sum, African American women encountered hardships, which were due in part to race, gender, and class experiences inside and outside of classrooms. Some female African American students developed coping strategies for dealing with these problems.

AFRICAN AMERICAN WOMEN'S RESILIENT SUCCESS STRATEGIES IN STEM MAJORS

African American women need to mitigate the barriers that exist in hard-science majors. Some resilient strategies that African American women have used to promote perseverance include individual faith, peer and family support, school resources, and peers. This section examines the methods used by African American women to deal with hardships in STEM majors at Town University.

Individual Faith

Individual faith was cited as one resilient strategy that African American women used within the home environment to navigate hard-science majors and curriculum. An example of spirituality can be found in the narrative of Briana, who lost her foster mother during her third year of college. During this time period, she contemplated dropping out of college. When asked what kept her at Town University, she replied, "Self-motivation. I prayed a lot. I really didn't know. That was one of the questions that I was asking God...Am I supposed to not do this? Or is this a perseverance test?"

Home Environment

In the home environment, family and friends served as important resources who helped these women become resilient and continue in the science curriculum despite obstacles. When asked about the support system that helped her remain, Rachelle responded,

> My dad. He really wants to see me succeed. [If I] say, "I cannot do it. It is too hard, daddy," [then he responds] "Try harder." He has never been the one to pity me. Now that I am older... "Daddy, my stomach hurts." [He says] "Well, get over it; you are fine." I think not having the tender part of it. Just having that hardcore male's point of view just pushed me to go through it.

Similarly, when Shannon endured hardships as a biology major, she consulted her female best friend. She stated, "We had the same ideas at the same time. So we were egging each other on. We can do this, we can just change [our majors]...Neither one of us changed [majors]." These narratives support research (Hanson, 2007, 2009) on the crucial role that support systems play in helping African American women persist in hard-science majors, coping with stress, and dealing with hardships in STEM majors.

Additionally, despite financial barriers, some African American women remained resilient by holding multiple jobs or receiving financial support from parents. For example, Patricia, Briana, and Ashley worked 15 to 25 hours per week as full-time students. They were from working-class or lower-middle-class backgrounds, based on their parents' education and occupations.

The financial challenges that working-class women like Briana and Ashley, who remained in hard-science majors, could have induced them to leave college. Their reasons for remaining in college were twofold. First, they wanted to obtain bachelors' degrees, unlike their parents. Second, they wanted to move out of impoverished neighborhoods with gang violence and teenage mothers. Both women exhibited personal characteristics of self-determination and motivation, which might have explained their resilience in hard-science majors despite financial hardships.

School Environment

Some African American women in hard-science majors relied on resources available in their school environment to address their academic difficulties. For instance, when Shannon experienced challenges with the science curriculum at Town University, she used tutoring at the TU Resource Center. She pointed out, "The tutors would help me break stuff down." Simone also relied on tutoring for mathematics through an additional class. She described this class: "You talk to the teacher, asking questions to the TA working the group that we're in, helping people or asking [questions] if we don't understand something." These quotes point to resources such as tutoring and teaching assistants who can help students understand course materials.

Scholars noted the importance of resources in promoting the persistence of underrepresented students in STEM majors (Hurtado et al., 2011; Seymour & Hewitt, 1997). Other strategies utilized by African American women to tackle the rigorous science or mathematics curriculum at Town University included taking classes at community colleges, visiting instructors during office hours, and retaking classes to improve substandard grades.

Culture of Science

The buddy system served as another resilient strategy that these women used to survive in the culture of science, which was dominated by White and/or male peers and professors at Town University. The peers that these women relied upon were not homogenous in terms of race or gender. These peers were male or female, African American, White, Asian, and Indian, who had successfully passed upper-level math and science courses. Jennifer explained the buddy system used in her mathematics classes. She said,

> The first day, I found a buddy, and me and this person [checked] the homework together, studied for the test together. [In] almost every mathematics class because I have so many [phone] numbers and emails of people that are my mathematics best friends and then I met a few more this semester...I can't name a class where that didn't happen.

This section demonstrated the vital role peers play in facilitating success in math and science in college classrooms, which supports previous studies (Seymour & Hewitt, 1997; Tyson, Smith, & Ndong, 2010).

Furthermore, by being resilient, they fought negative stereotypes about intellectual inferiority through intrinsic motivation and proved their academic abilities to their peers. This is reflected in Ashley's narrative below.

> Sometimes, I feel as though I have to work harder and I have got to prove more. Other people might not "see" that. I wouldn't want to say that the science department did anything specific to make me feel like that. I just think

that is a general feeling that you get when you are "one of few" or "the only one" in a group.

This finding is consistent with research (McGee & Martin, 2011) that showed that African American students can dispel stereotypes about their academic abilities through stereotype management. According to McGee and Martin (2011), stereotype management "explain[s] academic resilience (traditionally valued high achievement in spite of negative intellectual and societal based stereotypes and other forms of racial bias) among Black mathematics and engineering students" (p. 1354). This quote points to the fact that students aspired to disprove stereotypes about their academic abilities. In conclusion, African American females in hard-science majors became resilient by making use of individual faith and parental support within the home environment as well as peer support in the school environment and culture of science.

DISCUSSION OF FINDINGS

Multiple identities contributed to the adversity that African American women faced in home, school, and science culture environments. This finding is similar to previous research on Black Feminist Thought (Collins, 2000; Ladner, 1995) that described how African American women encountered difficulties at home or work. This scholarship complicates STEM education research by providing a better understanding of the lived experiences of undergraduate African American female hard-science majors at a PWI. Additionally, scholars now understand that their home and school environment influence their persistence in STEM majors. We can also visualize how their multiple identities of race, class, and gender could have contributed to their departure from STEM majors and college.

In the context of the school environment, adjustment to the college STEM curriculum, peers, instructors, and racism outside of the classroom created hardships for African American women in hard-science majors. In addition, the culture of science, which was dominated by White and male peers or professors created real barriers for these women. Similar to other research on the underrepresentation of minority faculty members (Griffin et al., 2010; Hurtado et al., 2011), they had few instructors who looked like them and were thus forced to interact with peers and instructors of different races and/or genders. They also had to manage stereotypes that peers and professors had about their intellectual abilities in hard-science majors.

These hardships may have contributed to the departure of some African American women from hard-science majors. However, these women remained in these majors by using resilient strategies, including individual faith, peer and parental support, and obtaining financial support. In the school environment, they used resources, such as tutoring, instructors; and retaking classes. Furthermore, in the science culture environment, they learned to work with peers from different racial and gender backgrounds and reduced stereotypes by working on group projects.

CONCLUSIONS AND IMPLICATIONS FOR PRACTICE

Multiple identities impacted African American women's everyday lived experiences in hard-science majors. This research adds to the ongoing debates about girls' and women's entry and success in STEM fields by facilitating our understanding of how multiple identities influenced African American women's experiences in hard-science majors. This research helps us understand that campus resources as well as parental, peer, and instructor support promoted the persistence of this population. Retaining African American female undergraduate students may require that institutions consider creating more welcoming environments to facilitate the inclusion of this population in the science culture. This environment might include their engagement in research projects, tutoring, group studying, together with warm instructors and peers. Finally, hiring faculty and staff members who can serve as role models and mentors will contribute to the persistence and eventual graduation of African American women and hopefully change their experiences inside and outside of classrooms.

NOTES

1. The National Science Foundation (2009) defines the hard sciences as including biology, computer science, earth science, atmospheric science, oceanography, physical science (e.g., chemistry, astronomy, physics). This study included business as a hard science major, because it requires a thorough understanding and application of mathematical concepts (McPherson, 2012).
2. The culture of science revolves around teaching and learning within the field using a Western mode of thought from the perspective of White males (Harding, 2006; Seiler & Gonsalves, 2010). In the teaching of science, students learn about the contributions of Western scientists but less about the ideas and thoughts of non-Western scientists.
3. Purposive sampling is a method researchers use to "identify the purposefully selected sites or individuals for the proposed study" (Creswell, 2003, p. 185).
4. College persistence is defined as students making progress toward a degree (Pascarella & Terenzini, 2005). In this study, persistence is determined by engagement in upper-level coursework.

REFERENCES

Bowen, W. G., Chingos, M. M., & McPherson, M. S. (2009). *Crossing the finish line: Completing college at America's public universities.* Princeton, NJ: Princeton University Press.

Bradley, R. M. (1997). Science education for a minority within a minority. *American Biology Teacher, 59*(2), 73–80. Retrieved from http://www.jstor.org/action/show Publication?journalCode=amerbiolteac

Brown, J. (2011). *African American women chemists.* New York, NY: Oxford University Press.

Collins, P. H. (2000). *Black feminist thought: Knowledge, consciousness, and the politics of empowerment.* New York, NY: Routledge.

Crenshaw, K. W. (1995). Mapping the margins: Intersectionality, identity politics, and violence against women of color. In K. Crenshaw, N. Gotanda, G. Peller, & K. Thomas (Eds.), *Critical race theory: The key writings that informed the movement* (pp. 357–383). New York, NY: New Press.

Creswell, J. W. (2003). *Research design: Qualitative, quantitative, and mixed methods approaches.* Thousand Oaks, CA: Sage.

Edwards, L. D. (2002). *Creating a virtual community of practice to investigate legitimate peripheral participation by African American middle school girls in science activities* (Unpublished doctoral dissertation). Retrieved from http://proquest.umi.com

Feagin, J., & Yanick, S. J. (1998). *Double burden: Black women and everyday racism.* Armonk, NY: M.E. Sharpe.

Fleshman, P. J. (2012). *Beyond the scores: Mathematics identities of African American and Hispanic fifth graders in an urban elementary community school* (Unpublished dissertation). City University of New York

Gilmartin, S. K., Li, E., & Aschbacher, P. (2006). The relationship between interest in physical science/engineering, science class experiences, and family contexts: Variations by gender and race/ethnicity among secondary students. *Journal of Women and Minorities in Science and Engineering, 12*(2/3), 179–207.

Griffin, K. A., Pérez II, D., Holmes, A. P., & Mayo, C. (2010). Investing in the future: The importance of faculty mentoring in the development of students of color in STEM. *New Directions for Institutional Research, 148,* 95–103. doi:10.1002/ir.365

Guy-Sheftall, B. (2005). The body politic: Black female sexuality and the nineteenthcentury Euro-American imagination. In K. Wallace-Sanders (Ed.), *Skin deep, spirit strong: The Black female body in American culture* (pp. 13–36). Ann Arbor: University of Michigan Press.

Hanson, S. L. (2006). Insights from vignettes: African American women's perceptions of discrimination in the science classroom. *Journal of Women and Minorities in Science and Engineering, 12,* 11–34.

Hanson, S. L. (2007). Success in science among young African American women: The role of minority families. *Journal of Family Issues,* (28), 3–33. doi:10.1177/0192513X06292694

Hanson, S. L. (2009) *Swimming against the tide: Minority women in science.* Philadelphia, PA: Temple University Press.

Hanson, S. L., & Johnson, E. P. (2000). Expecting the unexpected: A comparative study of African-American women's experiences in science during the high school years. *Journal of Women and Minorities in Science and Engineering, 6,* 265–294.

Harding, S. (2006). *Science and social inequality: Feminist and poststructural issues.* Urbana: University of Illinois Press.

Henrion, C. (1997). *Women in mathematics: The addition of difference.* Bloomington: Indiana University Press.

Heppner, R. S., Wao, H. O., & Lee, R. S. (2010). Pedagogy and preparation: Learning to be an engineer. In K. M. Borman, W. Tyson, & R. H. Halperin (Eds.), *Becoming an engineer in public universities: Pathways for women and minorities* (pp. 81–104). New York, NY: Palgrave MacMillan.

Hill, C., Corbett, C., & St. Rose, A. (2010). *Why so few?: Women in science, technology, engineering, and mathematics.* Washington, DC: American Association of University Women.

Hill, R. B. (1997). *The strengths of African American families: Twenty-five years later.* Washington DC: R & B.

hooks, b. (2000). *Feminist theory: From margin to center.* Cambridge, MA: South End.

Hurtado, S., Eagan, M. K., Tran, M. C., Newman, C. B., Chang, M. J., & Velasco, P. (2011). "We do science here": Underrepresented students' interactions with faculty in different college contexts. *Journal of Social Issues, 67*(3), 553–579.

Jordan, D. (2006). *Sisters in science: Conversations with Black women scientists on race, gender, and their passion for science.* West Lafayette, IN: Purdue University Press.

Justin-Johnson, C. (2004). *Good fit or chilly climate: An exploration of the persistence experiences of African American women at predominantly White college science programs* (Unpublished doctoral dissertation). Retrieved from http://proquest.umi.com

Kenshaft, P. C. (2005). *Change is possible: Stories of women and minorities in mathematics.* Providence, RI: American Mathematical Society.

Ladner, J. (1995). *Tomorrow's tomorrow: The Black woman.* Lincoln: University of Nebraska Press.

Lee, O., & Luykx, A. (2006). *Science education and student diversity.* New York, NY: Cambridge University Press.

Litzler, E., Mody-Pan, P. N., & Brainard, S. G. (2011, June). *Intersections of gender and race in engineering education.* Paper presented at the American Society for Engineering Education.

Lofland, L., & Lofland, L. H. (1995). *Analyzing social settings: A guide to qualitative observation and analysis.* Belmont, CA: Wadsworth.

Malcom, L., & Malcom, S. (2011). The double bind: The next generation. *Harvard Educational Review, 81*(2), 162–172.

Malcom, S. (1993). Increasing the participation of Black women in science and technology. In S. Harding (Ed.), *The "racial" economy of science: Toward a democratic future* (pp. 249–253). Bloomington: Indiana University Press.

Martin, E. P., & Mitchell-Martin, J. (1978). *The Black extended family.* Chicago, IL: University of Chicago Press.

McGee, E. O. (2009). *Race, identity, and resilience: Black college students negotiating success in mathematics and engineering* (Unpublished doctoral dissertation). Retrieved from http://proquest.umi.com

McGee, E. O., & Martin, D. B. (2011). "You would not believe what I have to go through to prove my intellectual value!": Stereotype management among academically successful Black mathematics and engineering students. *American Educational Research Journal, 48*(6), 1347–1389. doi:10.3102/0002831211423972

McPherson, E. (2012). *Undergraduate African American women's narratives on persistence in science majors at a PWI.* (Unpublished doctoral dissertation). University of Illinois, Urbana.

Miles, M. B., & Huberman, A. M. (1994). *An expanded sourcebook: Qualitative data analysis.* Thousand Oaks, CA: Sage.

Moody, V. (2003). The ins and outs of succeeding in mathematics: African American students' notions and perceptions. *Multicultural Perspectives, 5*(1), 33–37.

National Science Foundation (NSF). (2009). *Minorities, women, and persons with disabilities in science and engineering* (Report No. 09-305). Retrieved from http://www.nsf.gov/statistics/wmpd/archives.cfm

National Science Foundation (NSF). (2011). *Minorities, women, and persons with disabilities in science and engineering: 2011* (Report No. 11-309). Retrieved from www.nsf.gov/statistics/wmpd/pdf/nsf11309.pdf

Pascarella, E. T., & Terenzini, P. T. (2005). *How college affects students: A third decade of research.* San Francisco, CA: Jossey-Bass.

Rayner-Canham, M., & Rayner-Canham, G. (1998). *Women in chemistry: Their changing roles from alchemical times to the mid-twentieth century.* Philadelphia, PA: American Chemical Society and the Chemical Heritage Foundation.

Reid, E. L. (2009). *Exploring the experiences of African American women in an undergraduate research program designed to address the underrepresentation of women and minorities in neuroscience: A qualitative analysis* (Unpublished doctoral dissertation). Atlanta: Georgia State University. Retrieved from http://proquest.umi.com

Reid-Merritt, P. (1996). *Sister power: How phenomenal Black women are rising to the top.* New York, NY: John Wiley & Sons.

Sands, A. (2009). *Never meant to survive: A Black woman's journey: An interview with Evelyn Hammonds.* In M. Wyer, M. Barbercheck, D. Giesman, H. O. Ozturk, & M. Wayne (Eds.), *Women, science, and technology: A reader in feminist science studies* (pp. 31– 39). New York, NY: Routledge.

Seiler, G., & Gonsalves, A. (2010). Student-powered science: Science education for and by African American students. *Equity & Excellence in Education, 43,* 88–105. doi:10.1080/10665680903489361

Seymour, E., & Hewitt, N. M. (1997). *Talking about leaving: Why undergraduates leave the sciences.* Boulder, CO: Westview.

Tyson, W., Smith, C. A., & Ndong, A. N. (2010). To stay or to switch? Why students leave engineering programs. In K. M. Borman, W. Tyson, & R. H. Halperin (Eds.), *Becoming an engineer in public universities: Pathways for women and minorities* (pp. 53–80). New York, NY: Palgrave MacMillan.

U.S. Department of Education & National Center for Education Statistics. (2010). *2010 college enrollment statistics 2010.* Retrieved from http://nces.ed.gov/

Walsh, F. (1998). *Strengthening family resilience.* New York, NY: Guilford.

Warren, W. (2000). *Black women scientists in the United States.* Bloomington: Indiana University Press.

Yin, R. K. (2003). *Case study research: Design and methods.* Thousand Oaks, CA: Sage.

Yin, R. K. (2009). How to do better case studies (with illustrations from 20 exemplary case studies). In L. Bickman & D. J. Rog (Eds.), *The Sage handbook of applied social research methods* (pp. 254–282). Los Angeles, CA: Sage.

CHAPTER 3

REFLECTIONS OF EIGHT LATINAS AND THE ROLE OF LANGUAGE IN THE MIDDLE SCHOOL SCIENCE CLASSROOM

Carolyn Parker

Some teachers, like you're a Spanish person and you don't know English, like you just can't do anything. There are some teachers, they ignore you, like, if you want to do something, they don't explain it to you. You don't know nothing.

—Individual Interview, Coni, 8th-Grade Student
at Rockland Middle School, March 29, 2000

So, if you want to really hurt me, talk badly about my language.
Ethnic diversity is twin skin to linguistic identity—I am language.
Until I can take pride in my language, I cannot take pride in myself.

—Gloria Anzaldúa, Chicana Feminist, 1987, p. 81

Language use in the science classroom is often thought of as a rather complex series of vocabulary words that describe scientific entities or phenomena. There are numerous studies that examine the student use of language

Girls and Women in STEM, pages 39–52
Copyright © 2014 by Information Age Publishing

to express scientific ideas or to better understand students' thinking about science (Banquet, 1994; Brown & Ryoo, 2008; Lee & Fradd, 1998), however, what we often fail to recognize is the affective role that nonscientific language use, in this case in both Spanish and English, plays in students' interaction with school science.

This chapter is situated within a 9-month study that shares the science stories of eight Latinas of Central American descent. Ivette, Maricela, Belinda, Claudine, Teresa, Erica, Coni, and Sophie were 7th- and 8th-grade Latina students attending Rockland Middle School, an urbanized middle school in the Mid-Atlantic region. Each Latina consented to work with me over an academic year so that I could better understand their experiences with middle school science. My study was informed by the understanding that for decades, scientific literacy for all students has been an educational goal in the United States, but despite our educational community's verbiage reaching every student, we continue to leave behind large groups of students, particularly Latino/as and English language learners.

CENTRAL AMERICA

Seven countries form the region of Central America: Belize, Guatemala, El Salvador, Honduras, Nicaragua, Costa Rica, and Panama. Six of the seven countries (except Belize) share a common political heritage. Each was governed by Spain during the colonial period and from 1823 to 1838; the six countries formed a single state called the United Provinces of Central America. The area has a combined landmass of 524,000 square kilometers or 202,000 square miles, which is about the size of California. As of 2009, the region's population was estimated at about 42 million people (Booth, Wade, & Walker, 2009).

Costa Rica and Panama have had a longer history of stable governments than the rest of region. Economically, Costa Rica and Panama have also been better off (Economist, 2011). Nicaragua is the poorest country in the region (Economist, 2011).

In the 1970s and 1980s, the economic status of large segments of Central America's poor and middle classes began to worsen. Coupled with a post–World War II population growth (Central America's population nearly doubled between 1960 and 1980) and an improved system of communication through television and telephone, many people became aware of the enormous inequities embedded within their nations' social, political, and economic systems. Large-scale political turmoil in the form of public protests erupted, calling for economic and political reform (Barry, 1991). As a result, the region was ravaged by civil wars in the 1970s and 1980s. This period of intense political unrest created millions of refugees, many immigrating to the United States (Booth et al., 2009). Some of these refugees, especially from El Salvador and to a lesser degree from Nicaragua, Guatemala, and Honduras, settled in the Mid-Atlantic region.

The exodus from Central America has contributed to the fast-growing Hispanic or Latino/a population in the United States. According to the 2010 United States Census, a Hispanic or Latino/a person is defined as a person of Cuban, Mexican, Puerto Rican, South or Central American, or other Spanish culture, regardless of race (Humes, Jones, and Ramirez, 2011). From 2000 to 2010, the U.S Hispanic or Latino/a population rose from 13% to 16% of the total population. In the state of Maryland, where this work is situated, the population of people of Central American descent doubled between the years 2000 and 2009 (Brick, Challinor, & Rosenblum, 2011). The U.S. Census Bureau projects that by 2050, people of Hispanic or Latino descent will comprise 102.6 million people or 24.4% of the U.S. population (Humes et al., 2011). The Latino/a population will comprise larger and larger percentages of the U.S. preschool, K–12 school age, and college age populations.

However, Latino/a representation in the U.S. educational system does not mirror the country's population trends, particularly at the college level. "In 2000 Latino/a individuals accounted for 17.5% of the U.S. college-age population. However, only 9.9% of associate degrees, 6.6% of all bachelor's degrees and 3.8% of all doctorates were awarded to Latino/a students (Chapa & De La Rosa, 2006, p. 203–204).

SETTING

This work took place at Rockland Middle School (a pseudonym), an urbanized middle school in the Mid-Atlantic region. At the time of the study, the school enrolled just over 1,000 students. The school's racial composition was 31.2% African American, 12.0% Asian, 28.6% Hispanic, and 28.3% White. Some 42% of the students received free or reduced-price meals, an indicator of poverty by the U.S. Department of Education. And 9% of the students received English language learning (ELL) instruction.

Rockland was and still is the site of a humanities and communication magnet school. In order to attend the magnet part of Rockland, students must submit an application. The application consists of written statements from candidates and their parents, historical coursework and grades, standardized test scores, school-based achievements, and teacher recommendations. If a student is accepted into the magnet program at Rockland, they are driven or bussed to the school from various locations around the county. Rockland Middle School is not typically a magnet student's neighborhood home school.

The faculty and administration at Rockland Middle School assign students one of three academic tracks: magnet, gifted, or "regular." Students who have been accepted into the Humanities and Communication Magnet Program are identified as magnet students. Students in this program take their English and social studies classes with only their magnet peers. Magnet students take their science and mathematics classes with a blend of magnet students and gifted and talented students. Students gain admission to the gifted and talented program with a recommendation from a teacher. Gifted students take their English and social studies classes with only their gifted and talented peers. Gifted and talented students take their science and mathematics with magnet and gifted and talented students. Students identified as "regular" never take classes with magnet or gifted and talented students.

Particpants

Ivette, Maricela, Belinda, Claudine, Teresa, Erica, Coni, and Sophie were 7th- and 8th-grade Latina students who attended Rockland Middle School. Each Latina consented to work with me over an academic school year so that I could better understand their experiences with middle school science and language. In order to connect with Ivette, Maricela, Belinda, Claudine, Teresa, Erica, Coni, and Sophie, I contacted Ms. Mulligan, an 8th-grade science teacher at Rockland, who had completed her teaching certification at the university where I was attending graduate school. Ms. Mulligan introduced me to Ms. Corlin, a 7th-grade teacher. Ms. Corlin and Ms. Mulligan agreed to introduce me to their students and let me observe their classes.

From class lists and demographic information, Ms. Mulligan, Ms. Corlin, and I identified 27 seventh- and eighth-grade Latino/a girls who attended Rockland. So that I could get to know all of the students at Rockland better, I chaperoned two field trips and helped out in Ms. Corlin and Ms. Mulligan's science classes. When I sensed that I had developed sufficient rapport with the 7th- and 8th-grade teachers and students, I asked all of the 27 Latino/a girls to complete a demographic questionnaire that had been used in a previous study with Mexican American girls (Hazelwood, 1996). The questionnaire included demographic information about each student's place of birth, their parents' educational level, language used at home, and such. I also spent 3 days observing science classes at Rockland. As I observed, I took field notes that documented each student's peer group and participation in science class. In order to help me better characterize each girl's background, from my questionnaire and my classroom observations, I developed a characteristic matrix of each of the 27 Latinas, which included relevant information about each student's background such as which language they used at home, which students they socialized with in class, and such.

My intent was to invite four 7th-grade students that I felt would best provide a diversity of emigration, home life, and school experience to work with me. However, at Rockland Middle School, there were no Latina girls whom the school had identified as gifted and talented in the 7th-grade life science classes. As a result, I invited Teresa and Claudine, two 8th-grade girls who had been identified as gifted and talented. Nancy Brickhouse, a science educator, suggested inviting girls who were friends with one another (N. Brickhouse, personal communication, April 1999). Dr. Brickhouse had attempted a similar study at the University of Delaware, and all the Latina girls had dropped out. In retrospect, she said that she wished that she had the foresight to invite girls who were at least acquainted with one another, as she felt that they might have stayed in the study longer if they could be with their friends. Teresa and Claudine appeared to be friends. They always sat and worked with one another in science, and they ate together in the cafeteria. On paper, their biographies were similar: Both girls' parents had been born in El Salvador, both girls were born in the Mid-Atlantic states, and both were the youngest of all their siblings.

The 7th-grade life science classes did not have any Latinas who were also enrolled in English language learning classes, so I decided to invite two 8th-grade English language learner students: Sophie and Coni. I had met Coni the day that I chaperoned an 8th-grade field trip, and she seemed open to working with me. Sophie, who was Guatemalan, ate lunch with Coni. Most Latinos/as at Rockland were from El Salvador. Inviting a student from Guatemala would diversify the ethnic makeup of the group. Sophie had also written that science was her favorite class, the only Latino/a to do so.

I also met Erica the day I chaperoned the 8th-grade field trip. Erica had been born in El Salvador. She had emigrated to the United States as a toddler. Her biography was in contrast to the four girls who had already agreed to work with me. Teresa and Claudine had been born in the United States, while Sophie and Coni were very recent immigrants.

From the 7th grade, Ms. Corlin described Ivette, out of all of the students enrolled in her five classes, as the Latina "closest" to being identified as gifted and talented (Fieldnotes, November 12, 1999). Ivette was Honduran, and she was the only Honduran girl of all 27 Latina girls who attended Rockland. And I decided to invite two girls, Belinda and Maricela, from Ms. Corlin's eighth-period class. My thought was that two girls from the same science class might be at least acquaintances who would continue to work with me through the year. Marciela was Guatemalan and came to the United States 3 years prior to the study. She was living with her dad and American stepmother. Belinda was born in the United States and lived with her father. Her mother lived in Florida. Ivette, Belinda, and Maricela agreed to work with me. Table 3.1 summarizes each participant's biographical characteristics.

TABLE 3.1   Summary of the Participants' Biographical Characteristics

	Place of Birth	Parents' Place of Birth	Length of Time in the U.S.	Language Used With Parents	Language Used With Friends
Seventh Graders					
Ivette	Honduras	Honduras	8 Years	Spanish	Spanish and English
Maricela	Guatemala	Guatemala	3 Years	Spanish	Spanish and English
Belinda	United States	El Salvador	13 Years	Spanish	Spanish and English
Eighth Graders					
Claudine (Labeled G/T)	United States	El Salvador	14 Years	Spanish	English
Teresa (Labeled G/T)	United States	El Salvador	14 Years	Spanish	English
Erica	El Salvador	El Salvador	12 Years	Spanish	Spanish and English, but best in English
Coni (Enrolled in ESOL)	El Salvador	El Salvador	3 Years	Spanish	Spanish
Sophie (Enrolled in ESOL)	Guatemala	Guatemala	2 Years	Spanish	Writes English, but speaks best in Spanish

Once the eight girls were invited and each accepted, I gained parental permission to work with the girls using a Spanish-language permission form. Once permission was granted, I scheduled some initial lunch meetings so that I could begin to better know each girl.

As I got to know the girls a bit better, and not wishing to impose dominant-derived labels on Ivette, Maricela, Belinda, Claudine, Teresa, Erica, Coni, and Sophie, I asked the group how they would like to collectively be referred to as I wrote about our work together. I wanted to dignify the girls' rich cultural, language, and religious experiences by resisting "broad-brushed terms such as Latino or Hispanic when I read education research that is classroom-based" (Gallard, 2009). Therefore, over lunch, I carefully explained to the group how all gender and ethnic labels carry meanings, and I asked whether they collectively preferred to be called girls, young women, adolescents, or something else. I also asked how they wanted their ethnicity described. Should we use their country of origin, or would Hispanic and/or Latina be acceptable as I wrote up their collective voices? The girls were insightful and as a group, chose the terms girl(s), Latino/a girl, or Latina as acceptable. The girls did not feel that they were old enough to be referred to as young women or women.

The girls did not believe that specifying each girl's individual country was necessary, but they believed that the term Hispanic was a term that the U.S. government imposed. They felt Latino/a girl or Latina would best represent their ethnic identity and gender. Also, each Latina chose a unique pseudonym, which was used throughout this manuscript to protect each girl's identity.

Over the academic year that I spent at Rockland, I immersed myself in the school. I asked each girl to meet with me individually, I held monthly focus group meetings, and regular classroom observations. To better understand what their school day was like outside of the science classroom, I shadowed each girl for 3 entire school days, and I interviewed an important adult in their lives. One challenge that I encountered throughout the study was the emergence of collective themes while maintaining the individual voice of each of the informants. Therefore, on a monthly basis, I formally examined all of my individual and group interview transcripts and field notes in order to reflect and refine subsequent interviews and observations. This helped ensure that I was cognizant of emerging group themes while ensuring that each individual girl was heard.

SCHOOL SCIENCE AT ROCKLAND MIDDLE SCHOOL

At the time of the study, Ms. Mulligan had been teaching at Rockland Middle School for 4 years and was fully certified to teach biology, grades 7–12. Ms. Corlin was also fully certified to teach biology and had been teaching at Rockland for 13 years. According to numerous curriculum documents that Ms. Corlin and Ms. Mulligan shared with me, science at Rockland Middle School was supposed to be hands-on and inquiry-based, with the intent of enhancing the scientific literacy of all students. When I observed Ms. Mulligan, who taught in a fully equipped science room, I observed a teacher who relied heavily on students working silently at their desks reading from and answering questions from the textbook or completing a worksheet. Some days Ms. Mulligan allowed students to work with others on worksheets or textbook-based questions copied from the chalkboard. On these days, Ms. Mulligan allowed students to talk with one another while looking for answers. My impression when I observed her classroom was often of a sense of order.

Ms. Corlin filled most of her life science classes' instructional time with teacher-directed lessons. Each day the students started with a question or two directly from their textbooks. As students completed the warm-up, Ms. Corlin walked around the room checking answers. If a student answered the questions correctly, Ms. Corlin gave them a coupon printed on a small piece of paper. The class then began the day's lesson, typically some type of direct-instruction question and answer recitation organized by notes outlined on the blackboard or the overhead projector. Ms. Corlin would read the outline and ask students to elaborate on the information citing facts from the day's warm-up or from previous homework assignments. For each correct answer, a student would earn another coupon. By Friday, the coupons could be exchanged for a piece of candy or extra credit points. Each Friday, well-behaved, eager-to-answer students exited Ms. Corlin's classroom with pockets full of candy.

The girls recognized that their present science experiences were devoid of experiments and primarily consisted of textbook- and worksheet-centered instruction. Seventh grader Belinda reflected on the differences she observed between her 6th-grade science experience and Ms. Corlin's class:

> **Carolyn:** And what do you do in Ms. Corlin's class, how is that different?
> **Belinda:** Well, we don't experiment too much.
> **Carolyn:** Have you done, what experiments have you done this year?
> **Belinda:** Microscope. We looked through a microscope. That is basically it. We haven't done anything else (Individual interview, May 18, 2000).

Maricela described observing the letter "E" in a microscope, the only hands-on science experience she could remember completing in Ms. Corlin's class:

> **Maricela:** Well, in science we have not got a chance to do that—well, yes. But not like using those, you know, like instruments.
> **Carolyn:** Microscopes, or...?
> **Maricela:** Well, we only used it once, but like we didn't get to finish it exactly. We haven't really used, do projects like, you know, like really. We have just talked about science, and we have done like one or two projects, I think (Individual interview, February 1, 2000).

In one of our last interviews, Maricela reflected on her 7th-grade science experience:

> **Maricela:** Uh huh. And Ms. Corlin has never done that. I thought that at the beginning of the year she was like, she was explaining to us all the materials and the microscope and all that, and

I thought we were going to use them, but we haven't used them at all (Individual interview, May 19, 2000).

Teresa described the differences she perceived between her 7th-grade science experience and Ms. Mulligan's class:

> **Carolyn:** So, you did more hands-on?
> **Teresa:** Yeah, like at least once a month we did something about it. I mean, in this class, all we did was once. Then the rest is just written work. I don't like that. It's boring. And then she makes you be quiet all the time. I don't like it (Individual interview, February 1, 2000).

When I discussed this assertion with all of the girls in the spring following the data collection portion of the study, all agreed that their last year's science classes were devoid of experiments. Maricela remembered one instance: "It wasn't an experiment, just to look in the microscope for a letter" (Interview with Maricela and Ivette, March 7, 2001).

Maricela, Claudine, and Teresa used their present science experiences to describe last year's classes. Former eighth grader Claudine commented on her 9th-grade experience: "We have a lab like every other day. And we interact and stuff. I like my science class." Claudine's former classmate Teresa commented on the difference between 8th-grade science and high school science: "We have a lab every day" (Interview with Teresa and Claudine, March 12, 2001).

LANGUAGE USE IN THE SCIENCE CLASSROOM

The girls' use of language, both Spanish and English, seemed to influence with whom the girls socialized and interacted in their classes. Through my day-to-day observations, it was obvious that Coni and Sophie, both of whom spoke limited English, often struggled to function in the English-only worksheet-based environment of Ms. Mulligan's classroom. In response, both girls (if Ms. Mulligan allowed) always chose to work with the three other English language learning enrolled Latinos/as in their eighth-period science class. When the English language learners worked together, they spoke quietly in Spanish to one another as they worked through the day's worksheet or assignment. Sophie, who was the most limited in English, never spoke publicly in science class because, as she stated, I "cannot talk very well in English, so I am afraid to talk, or I am embarr . . . Because when I gave opinion, I think that people are going to laugh at me because I don't speak English very well" (Individual interview, January 18, 2000). Sophie agreed that potentially being embarrassed inhibited her participation.

When I asked her if she was concerned that people may also laugh at the content of her opinions (as opposed to her ability to speak English), she replied, "No, that she '*tengo confianza*' in her science" (Individual interview, January 18, 2000).

Coni shared that she also never spoke publicly in science class because it was scary to speak English in front of people. She stated, "Sometimes there are some people, because I don't know how to speak real English, better English they make fun of me." However, Coni would speak freely in her English language learning class because "There are some people they don't know how to speak English. I show them how to speak English" (Individual interview, January 20, 2000). When I discussed their use of English and Spanish with Coni and Sophie, they agreed and reiterated that their biggest concern was speaking English in public, a concern they continued to hold a year after our initial conversations (Interview with Coni and Sophie, March 14, 2001). Sophie and Coni truly desired to speak English well, but until they felt comfortable in their new second language, they did not want to speak in front of their fluent English-speaking peers.

What was subtler and took much longer for me to understand was how the girls who spoke fluent conversational English—students who were not enrolled in English language learning coursework—were influenced by their classmates and their own perceived English language ability. Maricela, Claudine, and Belinda commented on the use of classmates "big" words:

Maricela: There is this boy, when the teachers asks him something and tries to be all that, use big vocabulary, and he was . . .
Claudine: I have a rule, no more than six letters.
Maricela: I know.
Belinda: We don't really understand, the English language please.
Carolyn: In what class?
Maricela: In health, and the kid is like, use big vocabulary and I'm just like, what did he say (Focus Group Meeting, March, 16, 2000)?

Teresa and Claudine, who had both been born in the United States and who took classes with other gifted and talented and magnet students, reflected on the differences they perceived in the use of English language.

Teresa: She [Claudine] talks ghetto, OK. The magnet people, they talk correctly. Like we talk with some sort of accent and they sound perfect and use the biggest words I ever heard. And most of the time they talk about schoolwork, school work . . . schoolwork. Did you do your homework (Interview with Teresa and Claudine, March 12, 2001)?

The girls' reflections about speaking differently extended to what they expressed as differences in lifestyles. Claudine shared that she did not think that she could get close with anybody in her magnet/gifted and talented science class because they

> lead different lives and they are more, you know, they were raised you know, not in the ghetto. I mean you know because we really can't talk about stuff. I mean I get along with them it's just that we can't just after classes go hang out with them. (Individual interview, February 29, 2000)

In a later interview, Claudine reflected on her gifted and talented/magnet science classmates:

> In here, it is like, they are not my type and I feel kind of dumb when I know, when I want to raise my hand for a question, but I am not confident because I am not comfortable being wrong in front of them. You know, it is like, I don't know, maybe I personally don't care what they think about me, cause I am going to be me, no matter what. If I am wrong, it is my fault. But, yeah, there are times I don't want to answer in front of them. Like if those people from my English [class] were in my science class, my hand would up and no matter, and I would be working harder and I would try and react more because I know how they are already. In this class, it is Chrissy and Teresa, and that's it and we are at separate tables now. So, Aisha and Lindsey sit next to me and we are close, but the rest of the class, I mean, if I ask a question, the whole class looks at me, so I don't know. I don't feel comfortable answering questions in here. (Individual interview, May 15, 2000)

Teresa also expressed awareness about her classmates in science by stating,

> Well, it is kind of because I basically don't know, I still don't know half of the people's names and I have been with them the whole year. It is like they are not even in my class. I don't even talk with them, so it is like, I don't know. They are still all new to me because I don't even talk to those people. Magnet, I don't talk to them; I only have several friends in that class that I am pretty good with. (Individual interview, May 16, 2000)

The girls enrolled in the regular science track also expressed an awareness of the differences they perceived between themselves and their classmates. When Ms. Mulligan allowed Coni and Sophie to work together, they always chose to, usually with three other girls from their English language learning class. Erica, who came to the United States as a toddler and had never been enrolled in English learning classes, chose to work with a group of African American girls, never working with the girls who took English language learning, the only other Latinas in the class. I asked Sophie and

Coni if they ever worked with Erica, and Sophie shared, "No, she only speaks with us when she wants something."

FINDINGS AND IMPLICATIONS

Historically, school science like that at Rockland Middle School favors students whose lives more easily assimilate into the traditional science culture. Costa (1995) found that experiences with school science are relational and are formed between students' worlds of family, peers, and school. Through the voices of Ivette, Maricela, Belinda, Claudine, Teresa, Erica, Coni, and Sophie, I posit that more conversational language use in the classroom and larger school community, whether in English or Spanish, is part of the relationship and oftentimes overlooked. Moreover, students without language that is easily assimilated into their local science classroom are often marginalized from the learning process.

Older science education reform documents (American Association for the Advancement of Science, 1993; National Academy of Sciences, 2011; National Research Council, 1996) advocate for a student-centered hands-on approach to science. The American Association for the Advancement of Science (1993) suggests that school science should include "inquiry projects, individual and group" (p. 286). In Teaching Standard B, the National Research Council (1996) suggests that teachers of science should guide and facilitate science learning through discourse among students. When one considers Ivette, Maricela, Belinda, Claudine, Teresa, Erica, Coni, and Sophie's reticence to talk freely in their science classrooms, we must be particularly cautious when suggesting generic, student-centered approaches as a strategy for meeting the needs of all students. However, at the same time, we must be careful not to plan and implement strategies, whether pedagogical, curricular, or structural, that privilege the already privileged.

More recently, the Next Generation Science Standards (NGSS) (Achieve, 2013) move the science education community away from the more loosely defined inquiry of our older reform documents to a more refined view of science and engineering practices, cross-cutting concepts, and disciplinary core ideas. The intersection of language and science as proposed in the NGSS will hopefully move us away from a more traditional emphasis on science vocabulary to an emphasis on language use for the communication of scientific and engineering practices communication.

The complex learning that is required of science and engineering can challenge all students, but the challenge is greater for English language learners and students with a limited understanding of standard English. The Next Generation Science Standards may hold promise. For example, the practice in the standards is that argumentation from evidence asks students to clarify their thinking through mental and diagrammed models. Students must develop model-based evidence using evidence, logic, and verification. Once model-based evidence is developed, students must develop a rationale in the form of an argument that explains the evidence. This process is language intensive and requires sophisticated classroom discourse. However, with proper classroom supports such as purposeful activities that support meaningful scientific language use (Lee, Quinn, & Valdes, 2013), the science learning and language practices required of the Next Generation Science Standards could offer multiple opportunities for language learning science and engineering practices. As stated by Lee et al. (2013),

> In short, as science classrooms incorporate the discourse-rich science and engineering practices described in the Framework, they will become rich language learning environments as well as richer science learning environments for all students. Engaging ELLs in these practices merits special attention, because engagement can support both science and language learning. (p. 226)

There is precedence for how teachers can change their practices in science classrooms and better engage all students in science learning, and it is through an inquiry model aligned with the tenets of multicultural education. Meyer, Capps, Crawford, and Ross (2012) used a case-study design to show the effectiveness of inquiry, instructionally congruent practice, and the pedagogy of explicit instruction in the nature of science in a middle school classroom, an urban, setting, and including English language learners. The use of inquiry, along with instructionally congruent practice, which includes fostering a diversity of experiences and materials, use of native language, linguistic scaffolding, and sharing of scientific authority, assisted Latino/a students in being engaged in science, better understanding of what scientists do, and helping them to see the relevance of science in their lives, skills, and abilities. Such an approach might have benefited all eight of the Latina girls who worked with me.

In today's educational climate, the role of schools in developing scientific literacy for all students can be immensely challenging. The *Next Generation Science Standards* (Achieve, 2013) encourages school leaders and teachers to meet the science literacy needs of all students, particularly students who have historically been underserved, like Ivette, Maricela, Belinda, Claudine, Teresa, Erica, Coni, and Sophie.

REFERENCES

Achieve. (2013). *Next generation science standards*. Washington, DC: Achieve.

American Association for the Advancement of Science. (1989). *Science for all Americans*. Washington, DC: American Association for the Advancement of Science Press.

Anzaldúa, G. (1987). *Borderlands/la frontera: The new mestiza.* San Francisco, CA: Aunt Lute.

Banquet, N. (1994). Making science meaningful for language minority students. *Equity Coalition, 3*(2), 13–16.

Barry, T. (1991). *Central America inside out: The essential guide to its societies, politics, and economies.* New York, NY: Grove Weidenfeld.

Booth, J., Wade, C., & Walker, T. (2009). *Understanding Central America: Global forces, rebellion, and change.* Boulder, CO: Westview.

Brick, K., Challinor, A. E., & Rosenblum, M. R. (2011). *Mexican and Central American immigrants in the United States.* Washington, DC: Migration Policy Institute. Retrieved February 6, 2012, from www.migrationpolicy.org/pubs/mexcentamimmigrants.pdf

Brown B. A., & Ryoo, K. (2008). Teaching science as a language: A "content-first" approach to science teaching. *Journal of Research in Science Teaching, 45,* 529–553.

Chapa, J., & De La Rosa, B. (2006). The problematic pipeline: Demographic trends and Latino participation in graduate science, technology, engineering, and mathematic programs. *Journal of Hispanic Higher Education, 5,* 203–221.

Costa, V. B. (1995). When science is "another world": Relationships between worlds of family, friends, school, and science. *Science Education, 79,* 313–333.

Economist. (2011). *Central America: The tormented isthmus.* Retrieved July 8, 2013, from http://www.economist.com/node/18558254

Gallard, A. (2009). Dignifying the educational process through conscientização. *Cultural Studies of Science Education, 4,* 733–738.

Hazelwood, C. (1996). *Shaping identities in school science: A narrative study of girls of Mexican American origin.* Unpublished doctoral dissertation, Michigan State University, Lansing.

Humes, K. R., Jones, N. A., Ramirez, R. R. (2011). Overview of race and Hispanic origin: 2010. *U.S. Census Bureau.* Available at http://www.census.gov/ prod/cen2010/briefs/c2010br-02.pdf. Accessed on September 12, 2012.

Lee, O., & Fradd, S. (1998). Science for all, including students from non-English-language backgrounds. *Educational Researcher, 27*(4), 12–21.

Lee, O., Quinn, H., & Valdes, G. (2013). Science and language for English language learners in relation to next generation science standards and with implications for common core state standards for English language arts and mathematics. *Educational Research, 42*(4), 223–233.

Meyer, X. S., Capps, D. K., Crawford, B. A., & Ross, R. (2012). Using inquiry and tenets of multicultural education to engage Latino English-language students in learning about geology and the nature of science. *Journal of Geoscience, 60,* 212–219.

National Academy of Sciences. (2011). *Framework for K–12 science education: Practices, crosscutting concepts, and core ideas.* Washington, DC: National Academies Press.

National Research Council. (1996). *National science education standards.* Washington, DC: National Academies Press.

CHAPTER 4

MATERNAL PERSPECTIVES ON GETTING A DEGREE IN COMPUTER SCIENCE

Does Class Trump Race?

Louise Ann Lyon

Despite successes in some science, technology, engineering, and math (STEM) fields in equalizing representation for women, the field of computer science has remained doggedly inequitable. When we look at bachelor's degree recipients, we find that not only do women lag behind men, but that there has actually been a *decline* in the proportion of women bachelor's degree recipients in the past two decades (National Science Foundation, 2008). Much research has been done on the barriers to women in computer science (for a review, see Cohoon & Aspray, 2006), but researchers have for the most part neglected to explore how the intersection of race, class, and culture may influence women's choices to major in computer science. The numbers suggest that this perspective may be important, as the ratio of females to males is *higher* for each non-White

Girls and Women in STEM, pages 53–69

ethnic group than for Whites in bachelor's degree recipients (National Science Foundation, 2008).

For some time, researchers in many fields have noted that the investigation of social categories such as gender or race alone may misrepresent the lives of particular individuals. Works based on theories from the "double bind" (Malcolm, Hall, & Brown, 1976) to "intersectionality" (Crenshaw, 1991) have attempted to combat this oversight by looking at various categories together to better explain the experiences and outcomes of those who sit at different axes of several social categories. For women poised to major in computer science, expectations for and attitudes about their choice of major may differ based on categories of race, class, and culture, and these pressures must surely influence women in their selection.

Parents can play an important role in the pursuit of STEM fields for young people (Harackiewicz, Rozek, Hulleman, & Hyde, 2012). In particular, mothers are often cast in the role of primary caregivers of children, and they are tasked with the job of passing on culture to their children in ways that can help their children succeed. As the same-sex role model for girls in the family, mothers may influence their daughters in behavior as well as instruction and may provide both supports and barriers to their daughters along pathways to considering a computer science major. Mothers can support daughters in general or specific ways to receive the rigorous foundational academic background necessary to attend college and to major in computer science, for example. Mothers can also instill personal and cultural values and interests in their daughters, which can influence how and why students choose particular majors. In addition, mothers can provide positive or negative role models—both in terms of roles for women and in terms of education—on pathways to a major in computer science.

Positioning theory, proposed by Rom Harré from cultural psychology (Harré & Moghaddam, 2003), suggests that actions available to individuals are constrained both by interactions with others that limit the rights they have to act and by storylines in society that compel individuals to follow expected patterns. If we agree that mothers are significant influences in the lives of their daughters, how are the interactions between mothers and daughters constraining or affording opportunities for the daughters to choose a computer science major, and what storyline patterns are mothers and daughters illustrating and following based on their race, class, and culture? This chapter describes a study in which I explored the attitudes, remembrance of past events, values, and opinions of three mothers whose daughters were considering majoring in computer science and who vary greatly along the axes of race, class, and culture.

MOTHERS AND DAUGHTERS

As part of an ethnographic study centered on women enrolled in a seminar entitled "Women in Computer Science and Engineering" at a large, public university in the Pacific Northwestern part of the United States, three premajor women agreed not only to be interviewed but also to have their mothers interviewed about their interest in and pathways to considering a computer science major. I was interested in discovering how the mothers viewed their daughters' pathways to enrolling in introductory programming, and the values and beliefs of the mothers about education, majors, careers, and the field of computer science. This chapter investigates three cases: "Guadalupe," a remarried migrant farmworker who immigrated to the United States from Mexico with two small daughters; "Teresa," a middle-class Filipina American single mother; and "Ann," a middle-class White elementary school teacher. The three daughters of these women— "Mónica," "Kelsey," and "Erin," respectively—were enrolled in the first or second academic quarter of introductory programming during the time of the study and were considering a computer science major either on its own or as one of a double major. Two of the qualitative interviews with mothers (Guadalupe and Ann) were conducted and videotaped over Skype, with the daughter and me on campus and the mother at home, while the third interview (Teresa) was conducted and videotaped in person on campus without the daughter present.

Guadalupe and Mónica

What came out most strongly in my interview with Guadalupe was her unshakable belief that education and hard work are tickets to better jobs and a better life and her desire for her daughter Mónica to have these things. One way that Guadalupe instilled this message in her children was to insist not only that they complete their homework, but also to require extra reading above and beyond what was necessary for school. Another technique was to have her children work alongside her in the fields picking crops so that they would experience the difficulty of the job in the hopes that it would inspire them to continue their education.

The educational assistance that Guadalupe was able to offer her children was of a general nature, which helped Mónica to have the educational background she needed for college but was not otherwise of great assistance on her path to possibly majoring in computer science. For example, Guadalupe did not require extra math in addition to school requirements that may have helped better prepare Mónica for a computer science major. Now that Mónica is in college, Guadalupe is unable to advise her on choosing a major or a career since she is unfamiliar with the details. For example, when Guadalupe mentioned that Mónica was interested in computer science and I asked if she thought that this would be good for her, Guadalupe answered in the affirmative, reasoning that Mónica was good at creating PowerPoint presentations.

Guadalupe was uneasy about how her daughter would navigate absorbing the beliefs and values of two cultures: the Mexican culture of her parents and the American culture she currently lives in. On the one hand, Mónica must reject the Mexican "machismo" culture in order to become an educated woman, possibly working in a male-dominated field. On the other hand, Guadalupe did not want Mónica to follow the American values of letting boyfriends in the house, parties, and sleepovers, and she was troubled by letting Mónica leaving home at 18 to attend college; according to Mónica, Guadalupe would have been more comfortable with her living at home and attending the local community college. As it turns out, Guadalupe helped her daughter on the path to considering a computer science major by serving as a role model of an independent woman who has insisted on educating herself and on working in "men's jobs."

In talking with Guadalupe, four themes emerged that indicated storylines from both the Mexican and American culture. These themes related to education—*education is the way to a better life* and *the way to success is through hard work*—and to the Mexican culture—*machismo* and *take the best and leave the rest*. For Mónica, these storylines worked together to bring her to a point of being able to choose to major in computer science.

Education Is the Way to a Better Life

When asked about education, Guadalupe emphasized the storyline that *education is the way to a better life*. Guadalupe had experienced the difficulties in being a migrant farmworker, and she had instilled in Mónica the belief that the way out of that kind of life is through education. Guadalupe said, "I told [Mónica] 'You need to work with me. You need to go sometimes with me and check what I am doing. If you don't like this kind of life, you need to study. You need to learn more.'" Mónica concurred that her mother stressed the importance of school, reporting, "I have to say that my mom was very strict on school. She never had education like we did, and so she stressed it on us . . . I thought that helped me a lot." Mónica knew why her mother emphasized doing well in school, as Guadalupe told her, "You're going to go to school; you're going to get a better job than what we had. You have seen what we went through, and I don't want you to go through that." For Guadalupe, "Education is the, how to say, '*principio*,'" or foundation for a better life. When asked about the value of a college education for her daughter, Guadalupe responds that "She gonna be, you know, like, she gonna have better life, she gonna have a better job and she gonna get what she wants. You know? Like more easy than I am. And she gonna be better."

In contrast to the cultural expectations of girls placed upon her while she was growing up, Guadalupe expressed the importance of school to her daughters by requiring them to do their homework before helping her with the housework. She told me, "I told [Mónica] every single day after I came home, I told her 'you need to do your homework. You need to get your thirty minutes...You need to do all of it.'" Guadalupe said that when she was young, her "Mom, she don't care if I have a homework, she wants to see that the stuff clean, the dishes and clothes and I don't like that for my daughters." Mónica reports that her mother would tell her "I don't want you to come help me clean. I don't want you wash the dishes. I want you to go into your room, lock yourself, start doing your homework."

Guadalupe notes that Mónica echoed her valuing of school growing up; in fact, Mónica "don't want to be late. She don't want to miss one class . . . She wants to be better each day." Now that she was in college, Mónica had realized that her schooling was not only important to her, but also to her family and her community. Mónica reported that recently when her grandmother "comes up to me, she never used to this, but when I go to college now, she, '*me opresina*,' how do you say that? She does like a prayer on me, right before I leave." This impressed Mónica, who thinks, "Wow! This is this big thing, not just for me, for my family—my entire family. And so I guess that's what keeps me going."

The Way to Success Is Through Hard Work

Through her words and actions, Guadalupe espouses the storyline that *the way to success is through hard work.* "My idea is I need to tell her how is the real life; how to work for to get money. Because nothing is easy. I teach her work for, if she want something, she need to work for it." Mónica had taken this storyline seriously as she pursued her interest in computer science. In spite of the fact that she didn't know even the basics of computer programming, such as the fact they there are various computer languages ("This guy behind us raised his hand and he asked, 'Oh, so what language is the programming going to be in?' And I turned to my friend and I was, like, 'Well, in English, duh!'"), Mónica put all her effort into succeeding in class. At the start of the academic quarter, Mónica imagined that "this is going to be easy. Simple, right? I can pick up on it. It's computers. OK. It's our generation," but she quickly discovered that "it was a lot more difficult than I thought it was going to be." Her response to the difficulty was to work hard and to seek out help. After performing poorly on a midterm taken immediately after an illness and hospital admittance, Mónica redoubled her efforts and received "100% on the rest of my assignments" during the quarter. Guadalupe can be proud of her daughter's work ethic, as she hoped that what Mónica will learn from her life is that "she needs to work for the things that she wants. You know? Like nothing is free in this life." Guadalupe required reciprocity from Mónica at home; she told Mónica "I don't want to give you everything free and you don't gonna do nothing for me."

Machismo

According to Mónica, her mother had been a big role model in resisting the *machismo* storyline of their Mexican culture. Mónica's stepfather "didn't like the idea of [Guadalupe] going back to school to get her GED," but Guadalupe "kept telling him, like, I'm going to keep going to school, and she would always fight with him." Mónica had found this inspiring, as "seeing my mom succeed in that, seeing my mom break away from all of the obstacles, like, has helped me." She noted that the role model provided by her mother had strengthened her determination to prove that she can succeed in computer science. Guadalupe had also resisted the *machismo* storyline by pursuing what would be considered "men's work." She noted that "I work... like the guys. I'm learned how to drive trucks, and a lot of people said 'No, that job is for mens! Not for girls!' And I said, 'It's a lazy job, I can do it!'" Guadalupe's persistent resistance to the storyline had even brought around her own mother, who Mónica reports used to tell Guadalupe, "You're supposed to be serving your man." Recently, however, Guadalupe's mother had a change of heart, telling her daughter, "[I'm] really proud of you! You have overcome so many things, and you have done so much... You never asked for help from me or from anyone else in the family. You did everything on your own," according to Mónica.

Take the Best and Leave the Rest

Although she rejected aspects of the Mexican culture, specifically the *machismo*, Guadalupe valued other aspects and worried that Mónica would discard her entire cultural background in favor of American culture. In this, Guadalupe hoped that Mónica would follow a storyline of *take the best and leave the rest* in terms of the Mexican and American cultures. Guadalupe reported that, in the way of adolescents, Mónica would come to her mother in high school and say, "'Oh, mom, I want this' or 'I want to go somewhere because this girl, her parents, they let go' and this and that," to which Guadalupe would respond, "This girl is White. This girl has different culture than we are. You know? Like, they have different culture than us. And that's why they think different." In our interview, Guadalupe reported that she had told Mónica to take the *conveniencia*, which Mónica translates for me as "what's good for you. Like, you only take certain things." Guadalupe confirmed this translation, saying that she has told Mónica, "you need to choose the better way; how to make your life happy."

The culture clash that Guadalupe referenced has put Mónica into some uncomfortable positions while trying to navigate a *take the best and leave the rest* storyline. Specifically, Mónica told me, "Like, my mom was saying when I was in middle school, I wanted everything that, like, my friends had, and most of my friends were, like, they were mostly the smart people." This caused tension for Mónica, as befriending the studious kids meant that she was immersing herself in a culture unlike her home culture, as her friends "came from, like, a rich family. And compared to me, like, I was smart, but I was—I didn't come from a rich family." Mónica was successfully able to navigate this tension, as her continued achievements in high school led to receipt of a full-ride scholarship to college, where she socialized with and felt at home with other Latina students. She had absorbed some of her mother's values and beliefs; Guadalupe, for example, reports that "when she was little, I taught her to help when somebody needs help," and now Mónica "want[s] to do something relating to the field [of computer science], but also to help a community. Like, somewhere in destruction. Someone who is suffering."

Teresa and Kelsey

Teresa believes that being a single mom working from home gave Kelsey implicit messages that have influenced her pathway to a major career. Seeing her mother support the family with her work using computers meant that Kelsey did not question that she would one day have a career and that computers could be a large part of that career. Where Teresa found she had to be more explicit with Kelsey was in choosing a major. In our interview, it came across strongly that Teresa not only wanted Kelsey to broaden her options, but that she was instrumental in making sure that she did so. This appeared to be important to Teresa because she believed that Kelsey's future depended both on her innate abilities and also the possibilities open to her. Teresa expected Kelsey to take advantage of opportunities in order to give back to society.

Teresa had been able to help Kelsey along her pathway to considering a computer science major in several ways. Teresa valued education and instilled this in her daughter so that Kelsey had the educational background necessary to continue to college. Having received higher education herself, Teresa was familiar with majors and was able to talk with Kelsey about keeping her options open, exploring majors, and the goals and value of different major choices. With her knowledge of the working world, Teresa was able to help Kelsey match her skills and abilities to possible careers.

Four storylines emerged from Teresa's interview. The storyline that Teresa has been *role modeling* education and career goals for women, the desire for Kelsey to *keep your options open,* the belief that *outcome is a result of possibility plus ability,* and the value to *give back.*

Role Modeling

When talking about her daughter, Teresa spoke of her relationship with Kelsey in a *role modeling* storyline, seeing herself in some cases as a model to imitate and in other cases as a model to oppose. Teresa speculated that she had been a role model for her daughter in Kelsey's interest in a career, saying, "That's all she saw was a woman that, you know, that did, you know, provided for her and, you know, made the way of working and, again, providing for her and just that's what you do," as well as her interest in working with computers. Teresa remembered that Kelsey "could see me from wherever she was in the room when I was working, and I think that kind of set the tone . . . that just part of regular, you know, everyday life is being on a computer."

The importance and value of an education had been part of the *role modeling* storyline since at least the generation of Teresa's parents. Growing up, Teresa found that "education was always a priority. My parents were educators and I'm first-generation born Filipino here." Her parents taught Teresa to "really strive for the best for education," and she noted that her parents "pretty much imbued that in me." Teresa learned from her parents that education was important "for self-worth. And then also for opportunities. But I just think to make yourself a whole person; the best person that you can be to be educated." Now as the adult setting the tone for Kelsey and her sister, Teresa had "tried to give them the best education possible," including letting the two girls choose "different high schools because that's what they wanted to do, and in different parts of town" even though "there are challenges in doing that." Teresa had been a role model for women in higher education, as she was "on the cusp of, you know, definitely women's, you know, graduating from college."

Teresa hoped that Kelsey will forge a new path rather than imitating her mother if she decides to complete a graduate degree. "Sometimes you do graduate, and then you get a job offer and then you are off doing something else, which is what happened to me, so I never went to graduate school, but that may not happen to her." Because of this experience, Teresa had told Kelsey that "it's better to do it [graduate school] now rather than later. It's a lot harder to come back around and do it."

Although Teresa had "definitely" followed the path of what was traditionally expected of her as a woman, she was "really proud" that Kelsey is living a nontraditional life. Teresa found Kelsey's pursuit of an engineering degree and her interest in graduate school both as not following the expected path for women. According to Teresa, Kelsey also felt proud of doing well in male-dominated fields. Teresa noted that Kelsey had received a "pretty good taste" of being underrepresented at work "because last summer she worked at Boeing, and I think she was, like, there was only two other women besides her in this huge department. And so she was kind of proud of that, with its challenges."

Keep Your Options Open

In reference to her ideas about choosing a college major, Teresa was a strong proponent of the storyline *keep your options open*. At the end of Kelsey's high school tenure, Teresa reported that "right off the bat she wanted, you know, to do [major in] graphic design." Teresa, however, was "trying to steer her in the direction of 'Let's see what's out there on the horizon,' and she was fighting a little bit, and I was just trying to, you know, kind of trying to open it up for her." Teresa claimed, "That's kind of how I actually got her interested in pursuing different possibilities."

Teresa believed that a major should be chosen through exploration of many options. When Kelsey enrolled in a programming class, Teresa told her, "This will give you an avenue to . . . explore that and see whether that is something you want to integrate into what you could possible want to do or what you may need to do; . . . you may need to have that skill." When asked what majors Kelsey should consider, Teresa suggested the possibility of double majoring if she were considering "the arts. But I think she's seeing that she can also do that and still, you know, do engineering or have another degree." Teresa did not see computer science necessarily as an end goal, but instead as a way to broaden Kelsey's options. Teresa thought, "It opens up the doors to many other things, because, you know, because I know she will do a lot of different things, you know, going forward. So I think it's a great base for her to have."

Teresa believed that Kelsey's status as an underrepresented candidate would help her to have more options than she would otherwise. Since there are "not that many females in engineering," Teresa thought that there was "a demand for that so . . . that opens up the door for her and her degree . . . opens up the door for possibilities of what she can do. If there's more people pursuing her, it would seem that she would have more offers." Teresa tempered her views by noting that "getting in the working world then going up against a lot of male competition" could be a disadvantage for Kelsey working in a male-dominated field.

Outcome = Possibility + Ability

Teresa believed that the best outcomes are reached not only through keeping your options open but also through natural abilities, or a storyline of *outcomes are based on possibilities plus abilities*. Teresa learned to program many years ago as she "had to have it for my degree," and she believed that Kelsey "has a natural talent for that, or skill" for programming. Although she was surprised when she found that Kelsey was learning to program ("she's doing this and, you know, I didn't really know that she's doing it"), when asked about the qualities Kelsey had that would make computer science a good major choice, Teresa responded that Kelsey is "very detail oriented and very orderly. So she's very good at putting things in sequence, I think. And, you know, and persistent. Which you really definitely have to have to get the, you know, to get it right." Kelsey also "has a really good math background." When Kelsey was younger, Teresa encouraged her in school by telling her to "do her best . . . and to realize that there are certain subjects you're going to do well in and certain subjects that you are not." Teresa believed that Kelsey's natural abilities plus the opportunity to explore programming are what led to her interest in computer science; "I think she just had it in her and had the opportunities early on that kind of gave her encouragement that, you know, 'this is something that I can do.'"

Give Back

When asked what should be considered when choosing a major, Teresa responded with her personal value that you should be able to *give back*. "I think no matter what it is, that [Kelsey] get something that it's giving back, I think, to the community or to society . . . that it's not just kind of self-serving . . . as far as being employed goes." Teresa believed that a computer science major and a computing job "can definitely play in there. Be a big part of it, actually." Kelsey's interests appeared to follow this storyline, as she said, she "really like[s] to do, like, community service" and in her investigation of majors, computer science "has actually become more interesting for me, because I think there's a lot more you can do with it than I thought;" in fact, a group on campus emails her information about a "lot of programming for, like, kind of, like, applications for Third World countries."

Ann and Erin

Since Erin was raised in a two-parent household, Ann's interview referred not only to her beliefs and background but also to those of Erin's father. As an elementary school teacher, Ann valued education immensely, but, interestingly, saw education not only as schooling but also as cultural enrichment and as experiences and interactions with others in the world outside of the classroom. Both Ann and her husband had been role models in gaining a higher education, which they thought improves quality of life. Ann believed that Erin should choose a major and career based on what she loves to do, but she also acknowledged that financial security is important. Ann had great confidence that Erin had a rosy future, while acknowledging the struggles Erin had encountered to prove herself.

Ann and her husband had helped Erin along her pathway to considering a computer science major in both implicit and explicit ways. Erin had followed in Ann's footsteps in her love of mathematics, and it was Ann who helped Erin with her math homework when necessary. When Erin expressed interest in a math major or, more recently, in a computer science major, Ann and her husband repeatedly told her to pursue those interests. Erin had been encouraged to continue her education through the family story about her father's obtaining a college degree after his children were born.

In our interview, six storylines emerged. Erin was raised with the model that *education is not just in the classroom* and Ann and her husband were *role modeling* the importance of education and the fact that *higher education leads to an improved quality of life*. Ann believed that *you can do anything you put your mind to*. Although Ann explicitly stated that, when choosing a major and career, one should *do what you love*, it is also apparent that she believed that *financial security is important too*.

Education Is Not Just in the Classroom

Ann and her husband found that Erin "was a very motivated child to do well in school." Perhaps because of this, Ann and her husband had followed a storyline of *education is not just in the classroom*. Ann did not need to push Erin to excel; instead, "to encourage her, her dad and I would take her to museums or concerts or we would do more family experiences related to learning . . . and just felt like if we opened up [our daughters'] eyes to the world's possibilities they could see more than the four walls of the classroom." This has continued, and Erin "and her dad have developed a great bonding connection where the two of them will just go and spend the day at an art museum or something." At home, traditional roles were reversed, wherein Ann would help Erin with math homework and Erin's father would help with social studies work. Ann reported that they not only "fostered learning through those traditional means and helping with homework and validating what the kids were doing," but that they also encouraged them "to think and to converse with adults and peers about world events and what they were seeing out in the world. And, like I said, those were nontraditional type of learning experiences of going places or doing things."

Role Modeling

When Ann spoke of the importance of education to her and her husband, it appeared that they had been *role modeling* for Erin. Ann, an elementary school teacher, "love[d] school. I have enjoyed it immensely . . . I'm actually a full-time student right now getting my administrative certification. So I just value education a great deal." Ann reported that math was her "favorite subject in school," and Erin seemed to be following in her footsteps, as Ann said Erin has "loved math forever." Ann noted that she and her husband "told our kids from the time they could talk that a college degree was a must," and that her husband served as an example, as he "was not a college graduate when we met, nor when we married, and not when the children were born, and has since gone back and gotten a degree after the fact. So he speaks from experience."

You Can Do Anything You Put Your Mind To

At least in Erin's case, Ann believed a storyline of *you can do anything you put your mind to.* Erin had earned the nickname "Our little Renaissance girl" from her parents due to her eclectic interests. Not only was Erin drawn to "mathematics and things of that nature—and has excelled in all of that—but she also loves art and she paints and . . . loves the idea of learning languages and reading and . . . she loves drama; she's a quite talented actress." Ann believed that Erin could succeed in any field, as she "is extremely gifted and very intellectual . . . most academic endeavors come pretty easily."

In spite of Erin's multifaceted talents, Ann told me that the nature of stereotypes had forced Erin to have to fight to pursue some of her interests. Ann found "that sometimes she is judged harshly because of her looks. And it has happened to her through high school, that she was judged unfairly. And she fights hard to prove herself and to show what she is made of." Ann told me a shocking story that illustrates her point, relating that in high school "in math classes, she had one particular teacher who didn't treat her very kindly. She's a beautiful young girl and came in wearing her varsity cheerleading uniform, and the teacher told her she was in the wrong class." In fact, according to Ann, "There have been several times in her few years in high school that she was judged for her appearance and not her intellect." Ann hoped that she had taught Erin to "stand up for yourself if somebody isn't kind to you. You don't have to put up with it."

Now that Erin was interested in pursuing computer science, Ann anticipated that she would have "a lot of doors to open" since she "is a little bit of an enigma. I think she's a very beautiful young lady, and she's not what people stereotypically think of as a computer person." Ann was aware of the stereotype of computer science majors as "somebody who sits in a room with a wall of computers and never sees the light of day and doesn't have strong social skills, and it's not necessarily a physical appearance, just kind of a behavioral stereotype." Despite her difference from the stereotype, Ann was confident that Erin would be able to "back up her knowledge and her skills" and would "work hard to make sure she makes a name for herself."

Do What You Love

When choosing a major and a career, Ann believed that Erin should follow a storyline of *do what you love.* Ann wanted Erin to "pick something you love," and since Erin had "had a love of things mathematical," Ann and her husband "keep telling her 'stick with the math and the computer stuff!'" as a major.

Erin's love of programming was a recent discovery for her and a surprise to Ann. Ann reported that Erin "took her first computer programming class in fall quarter of this year and loved it. Absolutely loved it! Was excited about the creative part, and she's loved math forever." Because of this, "that's been kind of the direction [Erin] headed, but she would tell me that she felt like with the computer programming she got to take her love of math and apply her creative interest as well." Ann found that when Erin came home during a school break "she got really excited about showing me programs she had written and things she could make the computer do that I thought were weird!" Ann found that "I guess I was a little bit surprised that she was as excited about the computer programming as she was."

Erin's exposure to computer science was serendipitous, according to Ann. Growing up, Erin "didn't really sit around and play on the computer . . . It was a tool and not a toy." Ann felt "like she signed up for computer programming [as] a way to make that big place [the university] feel smaller and more intimate by having classes with friends." Although Erin "never had expressed an interest in it before," once in introductory programming "she just really took to it." Ann had noticed that "we have a very close family friend who is a senior at a different university graduating . . . with a degree in computer science and they've never talked about it. Yeah, it was a surprise that she has a sudden interest."

When Erin was growing up, Ann told her that "she needed to have a job and a career that she enjoyed." Ann believed that "there are too many people who go to work with jobs they hate, and you spend a lot of your life at work, and if you are doing something you love it makes what you do all the better."

. . . But Financial Security Is Important Too

When talking about careers, Ann spoke not only of *doing what you love* but also indicated that *financial security is important*. When asked how a career in computer science might be satisfying for Erin, Ann responded "hopefully financially. But, like I said, I just want her to have a job that she enjoys." In my interview with Erin, she told me that the family story about her father getting a degree after she was born had been important because "he would show us, like, his tax statements for the past couple years and you would able to tell with, like, the jump in salary, like, when he graduated." Ann believed that majoring in computer science would be an advantage to Erin because "computer fields seem to have strong potential for careers and a career path." Ann loved computer science as "an option for her, and I think there's the potential for a well-paying career path. And I would love to see her be an independent person of some means doing something she loves." Similarly, when asked what is important to consider when deciding on a major, Erin mentioned jobs first and enjoyment second; "I mean, the job market is important, but I don't think that should be the absolute deciding factor. If you enjoy doing it, I think, it's the most important."

Ann believed that Erin may have an advantage finding a job in a computer science field, as "many companies are trying to diversify their workforce" by hiring women, and if they hire someone like Erin "who can be a diversity hire, she can prove to anyone that she may be a diversity hire but she can do the job. And so I think that she will have advantages in that regard as well." Ann emphasized that Erin "could potentially get a job based on her gender, but I think she has the ability to prove to people and to become a valuable asset to anybody that would hire her. And could advance in that way."

Higher Education Leads to an Improved Quality of Life

Ann and her husband had emphasized the importance of higher education to Erin because *higher education leads to an improved quality of life*. Ann believes that "the quality of life changes" because "a degree opens doors that are not open to you without that degree, and it buys you often different working conditions. So someone with a college degree is less likely to have to work nights or weekends."

RACE, CLASS, AND CULTURE

Using Positioning Theory, we can see that the interactions between mothers and daughters in these three cases indicate some similar and some differing storylines. For these three mother/daughter pairs, race, class, and culture created storylines in ways that had enabled the daughters to be educationally and socially prepared to consider choosing a computer science major, although there had been struggles along the way. The enthusiasm of the three mothers for education and their conviction that education is the way to a more financially secure and happier life had supported their daughters in navigating the academically rigorous background necessary to have the precollege preparation for a computer science major. All three mothers had served as role models of independently minded, working women who pursue a life outside of the home, which has encouraged their daughters to consider majors, such as computer science, which have strong career outcomes. All three mothers expressed confidence in their daughters' ability to succeed in higher education and beyond.

When we look at the storylines and details of the mothers' points of view, we can see some variations related to race, class, and culture as well as immigration status. For Guadalupe, education is the way to a better life through a less physically demanding and better paying job. Coming from an immigrant, working-class background, Guadalupe was focused on Mónica's ability to improve her class status, and she emphasized to Mónica the value of hard work. In contrast, Teresa and Ann—both middle class, U.S. natives—expressed more concern with the content of the major and career their daughters choose. Teresa wanted Kelsey to keep her options open, to widen the possibilities open to her, and to strive to give back to society. Ann hoped that Erin would do what she loves and would find a career that offers desirable working hours and a better quality of life. In addition, Ann had a broader view of education as cultural exposure and involvement with people of all ages.

Guadalupe felt a cultural and racial tension that neither Teresa nor Ann express. Guadalupe valued her Mexican culture and heritage and was concerned that Mónica would lose some of the morals of her family and culture, such as girls remaining closer to home and family. However, Guadalupe had spent her life fighting against the machismo storyline of her Mexican culture, and she had pushed Mónica to focus on schoolwork and getting a better job instead of the traditional focus for girls on helping in the home. This had enabled Mónica to do well in school and to be academically prepared to consider a computer science major. Guadalupe hoped that Mónica would take the best of her Mexican heritage to combine with what is valuable in her American home culture in the future.

Although Teresa and Ann are different races—Filipina and White, respectively—they do not express large differences in their views of education, majors, and appropriate paths for their daughters. Perhaps the fact that Teresa's parents were educators and that Ann is an educator, their common immersion in American culture from birth, and their middle-class status had given them more commonalities than differences in these areas.

IMPLICATIONS

In order to equalize representation in computer science, we should consider twofold efforts: first, to inform parents of the details and advantages of a computer science major, and second, to provide support, information, and assistance to students that their parents may not be able to provide. Similar to Yang's (2009) findings, this study indicates that middle-class, educated parents of many races are able to help their daughters navigate through the K–16 educational system in a more focused manner than immigrant parents. Daughters of working-class immigrant parents need more information and targeted assistance to better prepare them to choose a major. Girls who do not have parents that emphasize the importance of education and the social capital to succeed in school will not be prepared to consider a computer science major. Informing parents of the details and advantages of a computer science major and career can help them help their daughters make more informed choices, and offering support to students that their parents are unequipped to give can help balance the resources available to students. College counselors can help provide information and assistance to high school students, but perhaps schools also need to reach out to working-class and immigrant communities, assisting in founding parental groups that can provide information and support to parents who wish for their children to succeed in higher education. Groups available in the community during evening or nonworking hours could be self-sustaining once schools provide the initial information and core groundwork.

Although all three mothers indicate that a computer science major and associated career could be an important step toward financial security, Guadalupe, the working-class mother, does not emphasize work enjoyment. Perhaps parents from lower socioeconomic classes understandably do not think as much about job enjoyment as they do monetary gain, but the three daughters in this study indicate that both can be combined. Educators can perhaps fill this gap, particularly in computer science, by introducing the field earlier in the pipeline and in a more interesting manner. None of the three mothers in this study suggested computer science to their daughters, thereby forcing the daughters to find the field by happenstance at the college level. If girls could be introduced to the subject in an enticing manner before graduating from high school, it would be more likely that they would discover and continue in a field that they enjoy while gaining the financial benefits of careers in the field.

Finally, this study indicates that class trumps race in the influence of mothers on their daughters pursuing a computer science major. Teresa and Ann, both from educated, middle-class backgrounds, were able to help their daughters navigate choosing a major in a focused, knowledgeable manner, even though they were different races. Her working-class immigrant background limited the assistance Guadalupe gave to her daughter in emphasizing school and homework. Once her daughter reached college, Guadalupe was unable to provide any guidance or assistance in choosing a major. Because of this, it is important for institutes of higher education to continue to provide information and support to socioeconomically disadvantaged students as they investigate possible majors.

REFERENCES

Cohoon, J. M., & Aspray, W. (2006). *Women and information technology: Research on underrepresentation.* Cambridge, MA: MIT Press.

Crenshaw, K. (1991). Mapping the margins: Intersectionality, identity politics, and violence against women of color. *Stanford Law Review, 43*(6), 1241–1299.

Harackiewicz, J. M., Rozek, C. S., Hulleman, C. S., & Hyde, J. S. (2012). Helping parents to motivate adolescents in mathematics and science: An experimental test of a utility-value intervention. *Psychological Science, 23*(8), 899–906. doi:10.1177/0956797611435530

Harré, R., & Moghaddam, F. M. (2003). *The self and others: Positioning individuals and groups in personal, political, and cultural contexts.* Westport, CT: Praeger.

Malcolm, S. M., Hall, P. Q., & Brown, J. W. (1976). *The double bind: The price of being a minority woman in science.* Washington, DC: American Association for the Advancement of Science.

National Science Foundation. (2008). *Women, minorities, and persons with disabilities in science and engineering.* Retrieved June 29, 2011,

Yang, J. J. (2009). Systems of support: Home and school contexts of Asian and Latino/a high school students. In W. R. Allen, E. Kimura-Walsh, & K. A. Griffin (Eds.), *Towards a brighter tomorrow: College barriers, hopes and plans of Black, Latino/a and Asian American students in California* (pp. 157–180). Charlotte, NC: Information Age.

CHAPTER 5

THE EVOLUTION OF THE CHILLY CLIMATE FOR WOMEN IN SCIENCE

Roxanne Hughes

Over the past 50 years, policies have been implemented to improve women's persistence in the male-dominated fields of science, technology, engineering, and mathematics (STEM) (Carpenter & Acosta, 2005; Robelen, 2010; Rolison, 2003). Women's representation has improved in many fields and at many degree levels—women represent more than half of all bachelor's degrees and over half of all graduate programs (NSF, 2011; Rampart, 2012). Currently, there is relatively equal gender representation in the U.S. workforce, with men representing 52% of the workforce and women 48% (Beede et al., 2011). And yet women's representation in the STEM workforce has remained stagnant over the last decade at 25% (Beede et al., 2011; NSF, 2011). This representation is even less in fields such as physics and engineering (NSF, 2011), and this percentage is even more alarming because, in relation to men, fewer women enter STEM majors as first-year college students. Furthermore, those women with STEM degrees are less likely to move on to STEM careers—moving to education or healthcare professions—compared to their male counterparts. According to Beede et

Girls and Women in STEM, pages 71–92

al. (2011), 1 in 5 women with a STEM degree work in education occupations compared to 1 in 10 men; or put another way 46% of men with STEM degree work in STEM career, compared to only 26% of women.

This underrepresentation of women in the STEM workforce is even more alarming because it is the one sector in which the women make higher salaries and the gender wage gap is the smallest. Women in the STEM workforce earn 33% more than women in non-STEM careers (Beede et al., 2011). The gender wage gap for women in STEM careers is 14% compared to 21% in the general workforce. These gaps are smaller when they are broken down by discipline. For example, in computer and math, the wage gap is 12%, in engineering it is 7%, in physical and life sciences it is 8%, and in general STEM managerial positions it is 9% (Beede et al., 2011). And yet even these positives in wages have not improved the underrepresentation of women in STEM. A recent *New York Times* Room for Debate column brought six experts together to discuss the cultural changes that need to occur to make these policy changes address and improve women's representation and persistence in STEM (Hopkins, Wilson, Berkey, Harper-Taylor, & Lukas, 2012). In this column, one of the authors, Nancy Hopkins, described this change in culture as an affirmative effort in that it should uncover the bias that occurs in hiring, promotion, and compensation for women while also addressing the unconscious bias that continues to prevent women from persisting.

In 1977, after less than a decade of policies aimed at improving women's access to STEM fields, Carole Yee published an essay wherein she discussed the backlash among women in STEM fields toward the women's movement. She argued that "women pursuing careers in technology and science—and benefiting most from women's improved economic opportunities—are probably the least feminist group of educated women" (p. 125). She further discussed how women in these fields focused on equity and access opportunities as the solution to women's underrepresentation rather than the cultural causes for this lack of equitable representation. This perception was surprising to Yee in 1977 after over a decade of work on the part of the women's movement (Anderson, 1995; Friedan, 1963). Sadly, the sentiments and surprise that Yee expressed in 1977 is still echoed by researchers and STEM professionals in the 21st century.

In this chapter, I describe the life histories of three female science faculty members at a large research university in the southeastern United States. These women represent three different generations of women in science. Their experiences highlight both the improvements for women in science fields and the subtle discrimination that continues within the culture of some of these disciplines. In this study, I demonstrate how liberal feminist policies, aimed at improving women's representation in science fields, continue to focus on increased access for women in science as opposed to addressing the overall culture of science that continues to keep women out.

WOMEN IN SCIENCE

Thirty years after Yee's essay, the Committee on Maximizing the Potential of Women in Academic Science and Engineering (an organization that is part of the National Academy of Sciences) convened and concluded that

> Women who are interested in science and engineering careers are lost at every educational transition. More women than men with science and engineering degrees opt into other fields of study; from doctorate to first position, there are proportionately fewer women than men in the applicant pool for tenure-track positions. (National Academies Press, 2007, p. 3)

My study focuses on female faculty in science fields, with STEM faculty defined as individuals who hold PhDs in their fields, conduct research in their respective fields, and teach the next generation of STEM professionals. STEM careers, particularly in research, are some of the highest-paying fields in American society, and they are crucial to America's technological and economic advancement (Beede et al., 2011; Chang, 2009). Women continue to be underrepresented among STEM faculty, and many within these fields are beginning to question the culture of STEM and its role in this underrepresentation (McGrayne, 2005; Wertheim, 2006; Wyer, 2001).

Women's experiences within STEM fields have often been described with one word, *chilly* (Shakeshaft, 1995). Although the representation of women in STEM fields has improved over the last century, there is still a significant underrepresentation of women in most STEM fields, and there is still evidence that women experience subtle discrimination (Hopkins et al., 2012; Lemke, 2001; Mau, 2003; Wyer, 2001). In 1889, only six women received doctorates in science in the United States (Wyer, 2001). By 1900, this number had increased to 36 (Wyer, 2001). According to Wyer's (2001) historical analysis of women in science, this increase marked the beginning of women's entry into the sciences and the "end of men's exclusive claims" to the sciences (p. 40). World War II opened doors to many STEM fields and positions for women, however, this access was taken away once the troops returned. After World War II, women were told to find satisfaction and happiness in the home with their families (Anderson, 1995; Friedan, 1963). Colleges and universities set quotas for the number of women accepted to degree programs to create more space for returning troops. By 1954, the number of women receiving science doctorates had increased to 290, which represented only 6% of the total number of science doctorates (Wyer, 2001).

A well-known example of one woman's exclusion within science occurred during the 1950s. Rosalind Franklin was a chemistry research assistant at King's College in London. Franklin originally discovered and defined the crystallized structure of DNA. However, she was not given credit for her contribution until decades later. The two young male scientists who received the Nobel Prize for the discovery of DNA's structure—James Watson and Francis Crick—used Franklin's data without giving her credit (McGrayne, 2005). Soon after, Watson published a book about the discovery. Although he mentioned Franklin, it was not for her discoveries but rather to complain about her unfeminine appearance and her *difficult* and *belligerent moods* that required her to be *put in her place* (Watson, 1981). Other female scientists experienced similar forms of discrimination in their departments during the 1950s (McGrayne, 2005).

Discrimination continued into the 1960s both within STEM fields and within the working environment as a whole. Women's salaries declined compared to those of men (Anderson, 1995). During the 1950s and 1960s, women made on average 60% of what their male peers made for the same career (Collins, 2009). Some colleges even set higher standards for women or instituted quotas to maintain male dominance in medicine, dentistry, law, and many graduate schools (Anderson, 1995). By the end of the 1960s, women represented 1% of engineers, 2% of dentists, and 7% of physicians. Women were denied jobs based on their gender and were ignored in the government interventions to equalize hiring regulations during the 1960s (Anderson, 1995; McGrayne, 2005).

McGrayne (2005) provided qualitative support for this discrimination in her book in which she shared the individual stories of prominent female scientists from 1900 to 2005, all of whom either contributed toward Nobel Prize-winning bodies of work or received one for their work. According to McGrayne, many of the women in her study were denied tenure at their universities because no university was willing to tenure a female scientist. Presidents and faculty members mentioned maternity leave and women's inability to be both a mother and a scientist as reasons for this discrimination. At least three of the earliest female scientists who received their graduate degrees in the 1920s and 1930s were threatened with losing their job if they married or started a family. Others told stories of not being hired at laboratories because scientists thought they would be a distraction to the men in the laboratory. In two stories, women were permitted to work in their supervisor's laboratory but only during designated times when no male scientists would be present. The laboratory supervisor felt that this would prevent the male scientists from being distracted from their work by the mere presence of women.

In the 1970s, female scientists continued to experience discriminatory actions within the STEM community. According to McGrayne (2005), female scientists who received their degrees during this decade and even later discussed the difficulties they faced in terms of balancing their career and their family. These women believed this was not a concern shared by their male peers and that because of this, family issues were not being addressed by the universities' policies. McGrayne's stories about female scientists from 1950 to 2005 were similar in that each woman had to overcome cultural and organizational gender discrimination within her respective scientific community. The concerns related to the lack of family-friendly policies were an example of the more subtle discrimination that women were facing in the 1970s and 1980s. This lack of policy forced many women to choose between a STEM career and a family (Wyer, 2001).

During the 1980s, women began to recognize and articulate the gender discrimination they were experiencing. For example, in 1980, Ruth Hubbard published a book that highlighted the gender bias in her field of biology (Wyer, 2001). Hubbard explained that previous medical and psychological studies had used only male subjects (Wyer, 2001). She explained that ignoring the uniqueness and different experiences of the female mind and body could be a detriment to women, who were being medically treated based on studies conducted only on men. After Hubbard's book, more female scientists began writing about the gender bias that occurred both in the field and in the classroom. Scientists such as Sue Rosser (2003) published books on female-friendly classroom activities, stressing the bias of the classroom techniques in college courses that privileged men.

As the 20th century ended and the 21st began, women continued to remain outsiders or peripheral observers in the culture of science (McGrayne, 2005; Wertheim, 2006). From 2000 to 2008, Margaret Wertheim interviewed over 30 female scientists and mathematicians and documented the peripheral positions in STEM caused by the chilly climate that women continued to experience. The women whom she interviewed described their constant fight against the cultural idea that women are less suited for math and science. According to Wertheim (2006), certain fields have demonstrated higher levels of discrimination than others: University physics departments were some of the last to accept female professors. Wertheim quoted Gail Hanson, a professor of physics at University of California, Riverside, and the first woman to win the W. K. H. Panofsky Prize in experimental particle physics:

> At this point, there seems to be an acceptance of women in science at relatively junior levels. But once we get to senior levels, a kind of antagonism sets in. Men can tolerate a woman in physics as long as she is in a subordinate position but many cannot tolerate a woman above them. (p. D2)

Engineering is another field in which increases in the representation of women were slower. In a 2011 report, Foud and Singh showed that more women are leaving the engineering field than men, particularly once they are working in their careers (25% of women leave after age 30 compared to 10% of men). This is especially troublesome in engineering, wherein women represented less than 11% of the workforce as recently as 2011 (NSF, 2011).

THE ROLE OF THE WOMEN'S MOVEMENT

As stated, there have been improvements in the representation of women within STEM fields. These improvements are often credited to the work of the women's movement, which helped give women access to many fields in which they had previously experienced discrimination. Most of the policies that have been instituted in response to women's underrepresentation throughout the 20th (and now the 21st) century have been based on liberal feminist theories that women are underrepresented in STEM fields because they have not had access to these fields (Brotman & Moore, 2008; Rosser, 2003; Yee, 1977). The assumption is that once women are given equal access, more women will enter the STEM workforce.

This issue of opening access and ending gender discrimination was first addressed in the United States with the passage of Title IX of the Educational Amendments Act of 1972 (Carpenter & Acosta, 2005). According to the regulations within Title IX, in order for schools or programs to be deemed in compliance and to continue to receive federal funds, they must adhere to one of three options:

- The number of available opportunities for each gender must be proportionate to the number of each gender's interest and numbers,
- The program or institution must show a history of program expansion in response to the interests and abilities of each gender, and
- The program or institution must show that its present programs "fully and effectively" address the interests and abilities of each gender (Carpenter & Acosta, p. 77).

Since 2000, Title IX has entered the political and policy dialogue as a way to address the underrepresentation of women in STEM fields (Rolison, 2003; Rosser, 2003). Despite this increase in access, the number of women entering STEM careers and persisting in these careers has not improved as quickly as expected (NSF, 2011). One of the reasons for this is that these access policies ignore the culture of STEM that continues to prevent women from fully identifying with STEM fields (Brotman & Moore, 2008; Ong, 2005).

Other feminist movements have addressed how culture, particularly the male-dominant culture of STEM, maintains a position of isolation for women (Rosser, 2003). Rosser has argued that the underrepresentation of women in all STEM fields, but particularly technology, continues to affect the number of women who enter these fields as well as how women use the products of these fields. Rosser articulates how various feminist theories frame women's underrepresentation in the STEM workforce along with their use of STEM products. Her articulation of various feminist lenses and their roles in understanding the underrepresentation of women in STEM provided the conceptual framework for my own study.

In her essay, Rosser (2003) described many feminist theories. For the purposes of this chapter, I discuss six, the first of which is liberal feminism, which I have already defined as the basis for current policies aimed at improving women's representation in STEM. The other five theories that I examine in this chapter are socialist feminism, existentialist feminism, psychoanalytic feminism, radical feminism, and postmodern feminism. Rosser examined each of these feminist theories from the perspective of science and technology creators and users. According to Rosser, socialist feminists have argued that since male designers design technology only to meet the needs of men, women tend to not readily use technology because it does not meet their needs. Existentialist feminists have argued that gender differences occur because of the value society places on gender and gender roles; therefore, in the STEM workforce, women are often positioned as helpers, whereas men are positioned as designers with inherent power. Psychoanalytic feminists focused on women as the primary caregivers in society and the role this has on their abilities to fully participate in STEM careers, particularly in a culture that stresses long work hours. Radical feminists have focused on the oppression of women in STEM fields and how this affects their desire to participate in these fields and/or use products from these fields. And finally, Rosser highlighted how postmodern feminists argue that there is no common experience for women. According to these feminists, women's experiences in STEM fields are "fragmented" and "situation-dependent" (p. 50).

These various feminist lenses provided the conceptual framework for the current study of the narrative life histories of three female science faculty members at a large research university in the southeastern United States, which will be referenced herein using the pseudonym State University. These lenses helped me to categorize the views and motivations of these three women and determine how they navigated through the chilly climate of their respective science department cultures throughout their careers. In this study, I demonstrate that the various voices of the feminist movement are still missing from the dialogue of women's underrepresentation, even among women in STEM. The stories of these women show that although improvements have been made through access policies, including many policies that the participants in this study support, these policies are not addressing the underlying culture of STEM.

RESEARCH METHODS

I utilized a narrative life history methodology (Creswell, 2007). The women in this study were selected because of their representation of three different generations within STEM based on ages—they are each on average 10 years apart. (Pseudonyms have been used for all participants). Dr. Sarah Gallagher received her PhD in 1972 in biochemistry and joined the chemistry faculty at State University (SU) in 1977. Dr. Tina Moriarty received her PhD in biology in 1976 but did not join the SU oceanography faculty until 1987. And Dr. Francine Smith received her PhD in physics in 1989 and joined the SU physics faculty in 1994. All three women were involved in programs that aimed to increase women's access to STEM faculty, peers, and research opportunities. Dr. Gallagher started the first chapter of the Association for Women in Science (AWIS) in her state at SU. She later received a 3-year fellowship recognizing her work at SU aimed at increasing the number of female undergraduate STEM graduates. Dr. Moriarty began the Women in Science, Technology, Engineering, and Mathematics (WSTEM) living and learning community at SU in 2001. Dr. Smith began a series of networking sessions for women (both students and faculty) in physics when she first came to SU and then later replaced Dr. Moriarty as the director of WSTEM in 2006. All three women have received awards from the SU administrators for their efforts to improve women's representation in STEM fields.

These women were interviewed between 2008 and 2010. The life history portion was conducted in late 2008, and I remained in contact with each of these women to discuss questions or ideas about their lives in STEM and their opinions related to SU's policies regarding women in STEM. The interviews were transcribed verbatim and sent to the participants as a form of member checking (Creswell, 2007). These transcripts and the email correspondences were analyzed using NVivo software. The analysis was based on codes identified by the conceptual framework and the literature review. In particular, I wanted to understand each participant's experience within the culture of STEM, references to the chilly climate (gender roles, lack of role models, overt discrimination, and subtle discrimination), and their identity as it related to gender and STEM. I also wanted to determine what type of policies they believed were the most successful at improving women's representation (i.e., access and equity). And finally, I coded these responses according to the six feminist lenses identified by Rosser (2003): liberal, socialist, existential, psychoanalytical, radical, and postmodern.

Before I describe my results, it is important for the reader to understand the context of my study, which focuses on faculty members at SU. Universities have their own culture, which can provide either a positive support network or a chilly climate for women faculty in STEM. SU is a large Research 1 university in the southeastern United States. The interviews with each of the faculty members took place between 2008 and 2010. Consequently, I will use data related to SU from that time period to highlight the context and culture. In 2010, SU enrolled an average of 40,000 students. Some 76% of these enrolled students were undergraduates. During the period of this study, STEM majors comprised 15% of the total enrollment. And women represented less than one third of these students. The retention rate for women who entered SU in the fall of 2006 and graduated in the spring/summer of 2010 was 50% (613 women enrolled as STEM majors as first-year students in 2006, and of these, 309 graduated in STEM majors) (Vice President of Undergraduate Affairs at SU, personal communication, August 31, 2010.)

The number of female faculty in each of the STEM departments at SU for 2010 matched the national averages of female faculty in STEM departments as calculated by the NSF (2011). (See Table 5.1, for the total numbers and percentages of female faculty at SU by department.) Similar to national statistics, the department with the highest representation of female faculty was biology, with 29% women (NSF, 2011). The lowest number of female faculty at SU was in the electrical and computer engineering department where there was only 1 female faculty member out of 20. This department was closely followed by the physics department (7%) and the chemical and biomedical engineering department (7%). SU was an adequate representation for the national issues of women's underrepresentation in STEM fields since it mirrored the national statistics for female faculty percentages. Sadly, none of these percentages matched Madill and colleagues' (2007) definition of critical mass, which they define as 30%; and it is this need for a

TABLE 5.1   Female Faculty at State University During the 2009–2010 School Year as Provided by Department Websites

2009–2010 Departments	Number of Full-Time Female Faculty	Number of Total Faculty	Percentage of Women
Biological Sciences	15	51	29%
Chemical Sciences	5	38	13%
Geological Sciences	2	19	11%
Mathematics	9	49	18%
Meteorology	3	16	19%
Physics	3	45	7%
Chemical and Biomedical Engineering	1	14	7%
Civil and Environmental Engineering	3	18	17%
Electrical and Computer Engineering	1	20	5%
Industrial and Manufacturing Engineering	2	15	13%
Mechanical Engineering	2	24	8%

critical mass that has been cited by researchers as a way to improve women's retention in STEM fields (Rosser, 2003; Seymour & Hewitt, 1997).

Women-Only Programs

I selected these three faculty members (Dr. Gallagher, Dr. Moriarty, and Dr. Smith) because they represented three generations of women in STEM. Dr. Gallagher received her PhD and entered her career before Title IX and other antidiscrimination policies were enforced at the higher-education level. Dr. Moriarty graduated 4 years after the signing of Title IX and entered her career at a time when access policies were first being initiated, typically as affirmative action. Dr. Smith received her PhD almost two decades after Title IX, but in a field that has historically had (and continues to have) a significantly small representation of women—physics. All three women also devoted their time to women-only programs, which aimed to improve the persistence of female students and faculty within STEM through exposure to mentors, role models and networking opportunities. In particular, all three women worked (in some form) with the first living and learning community (LLC) devoted to women in STEM at SU: Women in Science, Technology, Engineering, and Mathematics (WSTEM). WSTEM, like other women-only STEM living and learning communities, is a program in which college women who are first-year students at SU live together with other women who have declared a STEM major. The program offers paid research opportunities with faculty members at SU and free tutoring. Participants must also participate in a one-credit, weekly course, which includes a variety of activities: presentations by guest speakers who are scientists in different STEM fields, readings and/or assignments related to women in STEM fields, discussions of current topics in STEM fields, and visits to local laboratories and facilities associated with SU. Both program directors (Dr. Moriarty and Dr. Smith) have encouraged the young women to participate in research and activities beyond the classroom so that they will have more exposure to STEM fields and therefore make more informed decisions regarding STEM careers.

The university administration supports WSTEM and its goal of increasing the number of women in STEM fields. In an e-mail statement, the Vice President of the university said,

> The university attempts to encourage women to major in the STEM fields and follows up on this in a number of ways. First, it developed WSTEM. Second, it asks about the status of women in the STEM-related Quality Enhancement Reviews. And third, the Provost discusses this issue with relevant Deans in his annual evaluation. (Vice President of Undergraduate Affairs at SU, personal communication, August 31, 2010)

This support from the university emphasizes the university's policy—and the supportive climate at SU—of increasing the number of women in STEM fields.

RESULTS

All three of these women expressed an intrinsic love for science and learning that first sparked their interest in their eventual STEM career. Dr. Gallagher said that she "fell in love with learning" at an early age and is "still in love with it." Dr. Moriarty explained that she "loved science" beginning in elementary school. Dr. Smith explained that her interest in physics stemmed from her perception that physics focused on the *basis of all sciences*. All three of these women recognized women's underrepresentation in STEM fields throughout their careers and were motivated to improve this through various access policies that they instituted.

The Chilly Climate Then and Now

Despite the love for learning and science that each of these women described, they each encountered some aspect of the chilly climate when they entered their faculty positions, if not before. Dr. Gallagher described her most vivid experience with the chilly and sexist culture of science when she began interviewing for faculty positions in 1972. At this point, there was little enforcement of Title IX or antisexual harassment policies in the workplace. As a result, during one of her interviews with the chemistry department chair at one university, Dr. Gallagher described the following experience: "After I gave my presentation, the department chair came up and pinched me on my bottom." She reported the incident to the dean of the college but only knew that the man involved in the sexual harassment incident kept his job. She explained that during that time period, there "was a lot of discrimination, and men were really reluctant to open the door and to even be supportive [of women]." This discrimination continued even when she became a faculty member at SU. She explained a situation wherein she was denied an authorship:

> There was one faculty member who I shared a grant with. When it came time to write the publication, I had helped the graduate student during the whole thing. He [the graduate student] had never used this technique. And we did the whole thing and then when he [the faculty member] wrote it up, I was not a coauthor. They credited me for my technical assistance. And that was in 1982. So I was not yet tenured and that's really when you need the papers, I mean you need them any time. But I talked to him and he said no. And I

said, "You don't even know what it [the technique I had taught the graduate student] is." And I went to my department chair, but you can't make people [add your name to the paper]. I was furious. That was discrimination, and he would have never of done that to a man.

During this experience and others, Dr. Gallagher could not be sure if her commitment was undervalued because she was a woman or simply because of the personality of the principal author. This led to her sense of feeling isolated within her department, even after earning her tenure.

Similarly, Dr. Moriarty described this sense of isolation and the overall chilly climate early on in her career. As a high school student in the late 1960s, she indicated that the typical choice for girls who were interested in biology was to teach high school. She described her first experience observing a high school class after which she became more motivated to stay in science and pursue a research career since research was her passion. After earning her PhD, she worked as a researcher at a private oceanographic research facility. She described her first experience with overt discrimination there:

I had just gotten my first grant. I was discussing it in the faculty lounge and there was this guy [in the room]. I explained that I was so proud to have received this grant and his response—and this was a colleague who was actually in a more senior position than I—and he said, "Oh, what did you do, sleep with the program director?" and I just sort of stood there dumbfounded.

Because of this experience with sexual harassment, Dr. Moriarty, like Dr. Gallagher began to doubt her overall abilities and question her accomplishments. Dr. Moriarty described another experience that added to her doubts:

I remember I had gotten a grant and we were all waiting to hear from NSF, and a colleague said something like, "Oh, well you're going to get it, you're a woman." There was a notion that, "Oh well, we've got to fund women," so it really didn't matter what the quality was.

Both Dr. Moriarty and Dr. Gallagher felt that their abilities were dismissed or called into question because of their gender. They also felt isolated due to the fact that at the time of their entry into academia, they were the only women in their departments. The isolation and constant questioning of their abilities in STEM that both of these faculty members felt was further exacerbated by their perception that reaching out to other women or women's organizations would be viewed negatively.

Both of these women entered their respective departments at a time when affirmative action policies that were aimed at increasing access actually caused them to doubt their own abilities in terms of grant awards. In addition, the low number of women present in STEM departments (Dr. Gallagher was the only female faculty member in her department) made it difficult to seek advice. Actually, Dr. Moriarty approached Dr. Gallagher during her interview at SU because Dr. Gallagher was in charge of the Association of Women in Science (AWIS) chapter at SU. Dr. Moriarty expressed her desire to maintain ties to this organization as a faculty member since she had been involved as a graduate student and researcher. However, once Dr. Moriarty joined the oceanography department, she found it hard to find time for AWIS and also cited her sense that her participation might negatively affect her tenure.

During this time (1980s), Dr. Smith was completing her PhD in physics. Despite earning her PhD over two decades after Dr. Moriarty and Dr. Gallagher, she also discussed overt discrimination:

> As a graduate student, I worked in a lab, and whenever I would have to go back into the tech area, it would be plastered with pictures from *Hustler*. I said something about it and the response was, "Well, just don't go back there." And I had to decide, how much do I want to rock the boat? When you're a graduate student, you don't want to rock the boat, so I didn't push any more after that. Now when I think back, I think, "Well, you should have because it was wrong." But part of me thinks that I just wanted to fit in. Another example was how I dressed. It sounds dumb now but when I was an undergraduate working at [a national research] lab, I thought about what I wore. I did not want to look like a secretary. That was so important to me.

This comment highlights two issues that women in science have historically raised: the lack of recourse when encountering discrimination and the sense of not fitting in. All three women experienced some sort of overt discrimination. Dr. Smith and Dr. Gallagher actually reported the discrimination to their superiors, but nothing was done to alleviate the discrimination or reprimand those involved. Neither woman pushed the issue further because they did not want to hurt their chances of finding a faculty position or, as Dr. Smith put it, they did not want to be accused of *rocking the boat.*

All three women also described their internal belief that they did not fit in with their chosen career. Dr. Moriarty and Dr. Gallagher both described this sense of not fitting in as isolation. But Dr. Smith described it in terms of the gender roles of society. She did not want to dress in a feminine manner because she felt that she would be seen as a secretary and not a scientist. She felt that dressing like *a secretary* would negatively affect her ability to move forward in STEM.

Later, as a faculty member, Dr. Smith described other examples of not fitting in:

> A senior faculty member who had been there long before I was hired said something about how I was hired because I was a woman. Another colleague explained that I was their first choice, but I still felt stunned. I should have said something to the senior faculty member but instead I avoided him. But I should have said something and I didn't. I didn't want to stand out; I just wanted to fit in.

And yet, despite this sense of not fitting in, she expressed in her interview that as an undergraduate, she would never have sought out an organization like WSTEM to find women to fit in with because she would have seen that need as a weakness. "I would look at it and think, I don't need that help, I have to learn to deal with the men. But now I wish I knew more women. I just don't associate with all that many women."

These women's stories all share similarities. First, they all encountered overt discrimination that they could not solve through any institutional recourse. Second, because of the lack of female role models, there were few women to turn to who could give them advice regarding how to deal with discrimination. Third, each woman was wary of joining women's organizations because they did not want to have that seen as a weakness that might negatively affect their tenure. Yet each of these women persisted in their chosen field because of their intrinsic love for their research, and once all three earned their tenure, they became actively involved in programs and policies that aimed to improve both female student and faculty's experiences in STEM.

This work can be seen through the story of WSTEM's origins and current status as one venue aimed at providing a safe space for female STEM students. In 1993, Dr. Gallagher wrote a proposal regarding the need for a residency hall where women who were interested in math and science could live together as a way to improve women's interest and persistence in these majors. Dr. Gallagher claimed that her original motivation for starting the floor was her own experience as a woman in science for over 30 years.

> It was very hard, coming into the South and being the first woman to do research like the men. This was 1977. It's tough enough now, but it was very tough [then]. The men were always wondering if I would do anything.

Her experiences in science departments within academia made her realize the importance of having a support group of other women who could help each other through their courses and guide each other through the chilly climate that existed within the sciences. Dr. Gallagher explained, "I thought it was a good idea to have support, people with common interests, so you weren't so isolated." Her efforts to improve women's experiences in the sciences, including her department, began once she earned tenure at SU.

The original hall, which began in 1994 with Dr. Gallagher's help, had a very small budget. The women simply lived on the same floor, with no mentoring, research opportunities, or colloquium sessions. One of the members of the committee who reviewed the living and learning communities each year was Dr. Moriarty. She proposed the idea of a formal living and learning community aimed at women in STEM fields. After submitting a formal proposal to the Vice President of the university, she was given the position as director. She became the official director in 2000, and the program began in the 2000–2001 school year.

She spoke of her knowledge of other living and learning programs nationally and how she envisioned creating a similar program at SU:

> I've always thought it [living and learning communities for women in STEM] was important, and I had noted that there were a number of programs at universities designed to promote the participation of women in science. There were a few programs that had been developed that were in the residential aspect with peer support. And I felt there was a value to that, especially at a large university.

By the time Dr. Moriarty took over the director position of WSTEM, she had been in science fields for over 20 years. She knew of the research on the improvement of women's persistence in STEM fields, claiming that she was "well aware of a lot of data on participation, women and minorities in science, and aware of some of the studies indicating what mattered, like role models, internships, and things like that."

Like Dr. Gallagher, Dr. Moriarty had a history of supporting women in science throughout her career based on her own experiences as a woman in a male-dominated field. "I've always been interested in promoting the participation of women and minorities in science. I saw that there was a lack, and I thought it was important. I think things have greatly improved today, but they're not completely gone." Dr. Moriarty recognized the value of having other women to talk with about these issues and pressures through her participation in AWIS and other organizations. This networking and support group were two of the goals for WSTEM as well. She described this concept of support by comparing it to her own undergraduate experience:

> For me, I never would have succeeded at a university this size [SU]. I'm a pretty shy person. I went to a small undergraduate school. So to me, that is one of the benefits of WSTEM and other LLCs; they provide small college attention within a large university along with all the benefits that a large university offers.

In the fall of 2005, Dr. Moriarty took over an administrative position at SU. She knew this position would not allow her to give the necessary attention to WSTEM. As a result, the provost of the university approached Dr. Smith regarding her interest in the position of director of WSTEM. Dr. Smith took over this position in October of 2005. Her first full year in charge of the program was the 2006–2007 academic year. Dr. Smith had been a member of WSTEM's advisory board since 2000, so she was familiar with the original program and its goals. One of the major changes that Dr. Smith instituted was paid research opportunities for WSTEM participants. She felt that paid research would increase the number of professors who would be willing to take on WSTEM participants (since the program would pay for the student and each individual department would not have to). She also felt that the paid portion of the research would increase the number of WSTEM participants who chose to participate. Her choice to institute paid research was based on her personal experience with research and its positive impact on her interest and persistence in physics.

Like both Dr. Moriarty and Dr. Gallagher, Dr. Smith used her own experience to determine how she wanted to shape WSTEM:

> I think research is valuable for them. I think having access to the research and having somebody push them to do the research is really important. I mostly brought in my own experience about what I thought would be useful or what I wished I had had.

Beyond research, Dr. Smith also felt that networking was an important goal of WSTEM:

> I mean, my basic idea is still that they have a community of women. That idea doesn't seem important to them when they're 18, but when they're 38, then they'll know more women, professional women anywhere around the country, people who are at the same career level and going through about the same things even if they're not in the same field. So that's a big part of it. Then they need to get involved in research because once they start doing research they'll see that its fun. And they will see that they can do research. Many of them think that it will be too hard or that they can't do it, but that is just not the case. I explain that they can do it, they just have to work at it really hard. And then I also provide tutors for those who need them.

Another component of WSTEM that Dr. Smith continued were the weekly colloquium sessions—weekly 1-hour classes with the entire WSTEM cohort. Some aspects of these colloquium sessions that Dr. Moriarty originated were continued by Dr. Smith, including guest speakers, laboratory visits, and social outings. She also added some other portions. For instance, she had students read a book about scientific inquiry or women in science that they discussed and then wrote a short reflection on. For at least four sessions during the year, she scheduled female STEM guest speakers. She and her graduate assistant planned social outings for the students twice a month each semester. Dr. Smith also scheduled once-a-semester meetings with each of the participants to discuss their courses and any issues they were having with their major. But Dr. Smith believed that the real success stories of persistence regarding WSTEM and its effects came through participation in research.

> Very few kids have the opportunity to see scientists involved in research, which prevents them from seeing it as a career path. I want to give them these opportunities. I want to open the possibilities and encourage them to take advantage of it.

She described personal stories about WSTEM participants to highlight the importance of research.

> There was one woman who was a math major and wanted to be an optom-etrist. She got involved in research in the math department and helped de-velop a new algorithm. And then she went to work in biology dissecting zebra fish eyes. You should see her talk about it; she lights up, it's great to watch. When I first met with her, she told me that she wanted to be an optometrist so that she could help people to see. I explained that working as a researcher, she could actually help more people than a single optometrist, for example if she found the cure for river blindness, she would help more people than any individual optometrist. After her research experiences, she decided to go to graduate school to do eye research.

All three of these women discussed the discrimination that they en-countered as part of different generations in science. All three agreed that currently, overt discrimination appears to be gone in STEM departments; however, subtle forms still exist, and because of the subtlety, it is hard to determine the underlying cause. In explaining the subtlety, Dr. Smith, said, "That's the big problem; you don't know if the discrimination is be-cause you're a woman or if it's because you're not quite good enough." The unique experiences of each of these women affected their goals for WSTEM and its precursor dormitory hall. Dr. Gallagher's experience as the only female faculty member in her department influenced her goal of creating a residence hall where women with the same interest (STEM) could live together and not feel isolated. Then Dr. Moriarty's experience as a woman in science and her knowledge of factors that improve women's retention in STEM fields affected her decision to create WSTEM as a living and learning program that could provide peer support and networking for students. Finally, Dr. Smith's experience in a later generation showed the slight changes that occurred in STEM fields. Dr. Smith claimed that the discrimination was subtler for her. Despite being one of few women dur-ing her STEM education and career, she felt that research was the most beneficial to her own retention in STEM. Consequently, she tried to get more WSTEM participants into research by providing funding. She also believed that the networking was important to success in STEM fields, but not as important as the paid research opportunities.

The Role of Feminism

All three of these women were motivated to work with WSTEM and other programs because of their beliefs in access policies (liberal feminism). Each of these women believed that access to research and networking would improve women's persistence in STEM fields. All three women believed that bringing in more qualified female faculty to serve as possible role models to female students could improve persistence. Despite the idea that opening access and providing a support network would improve persistence; all three women acknowledged the role raising a family has on female STEM faculty as opposed to male faculty (existentialist feminism and psychoanalytic feminism). Dr. Moriarty summarized this situation best:

> As a woman in science, or just as a woman in the workforce, you know all the issues affecting women, like childcare and flexible time, and you know if you want the full participation of women in the workforce, you'd better come up with some kind of model that enables women to have children. That's certainly one of the issues in science: as you get your degree, your childbearing years are right there at the beginning stages, forcing women to make choices about having children. To me, those are some of the bigger issues today. The discrimination that went on, it still exists, but I fortunately think it's not as bad.

All three acknowledged that the policies for family leave had improved in favor of female faculty, but they still saw the underrepresentation of women among their faculty peers. Only Dr. Smith acknowledged how the culture of STEM could be to blame for the underrepresentation of women:

> I think the reason why the science culture is the way it is, is because it's been populated by men for so long. Men by themselves behave very differently than they do when they are in cogendered environments. So I think the culture will probably change as more women enter the field. And I think that there are more women entering, but the number is not large enough yet. And most of us have figured out a way to adapt ourselves to what is here.

Notice here that she begins to hint at ideas expressed by radical feminists—the culture exists because it has been so male focused; however, she reverts back to liberal feminism as the solution, wherein increasing the number of women will end the historical male dominance.

Sadly, these women also experienced an antifeminism backlash that Yee referenced in 1977. Dr. Moriarty and Dr. Gallagher described female faculty members who refused to discuss or acknowledge programs that focused on women in STEM because "they made it the hard way and other women should make it the hard way." Dr. Smith actually saw an antifeminist standpoint among younger generations of women in STEM:

> They [younger generations of women in STEM] see feminists as sort of bra-burning women and they don't want to be like that. There were some of them who are very antifeminist. They don't seem to realize that they are able to do what they want to do because of the women who came before them. And they think everything's OK now. Even at the graduate level, I've had comments like, "Everything's OK, I get paid the same as guys do." Well that's because there are rules in place that all graduate students get paid that much. Those rules were put into place after I was a graduate student.

All three women seemed surprised by this reaction, particularly since they were part of the many generations of women who had to fight for the rights that their younger counterparts enjoy.

CONCLUSION

In this study, I focused on the stories of three women who represented three different generations of women in STEM fields. Their individual stories show the discrimination that women encountered in STEM fields throughout the 1970s, 1980s, and 1990s (Rosser, 2003). This discrimination echoes historical literature of this time period. However, these individual experiences also affected the ways in which each of these women chose to address discrimination and how to solve the continued problem of subtle discrimination. Each of these women supported liberal feminist policies that opened access for women and exposed them to female role models. They succeeded in STEM and were able to find motivation to persist despite overt discrimination. So it makes sense that they would conclude that if this overt discrimination is removed and women are given more opportunities, then more women would persist. Yet the national numbers of women are increasing in only a few STEM fields (e.g., biology and chemistry). In other fields, like physics and engineering, these numbers remain stagnant, and some others, like computer science, are actually decreasing. This raises the issue of the culture of STEM and the feminist lens utilized by those addressing that culture to improve women's representation in STEM fields.

For instance, the participants briefly discussed aspects of the existentialist feminist and psychoanalytic lenses in that policies for faculty who are parents, particularly women who choose to have families, need to be improved at the university level. These participants discussed that the policies tend to reward men in that they have more time to work on publications during family leave, whereas women either choose to or are forced to spend more time recovering and caring for children during this family leave time. By viewing this issue from an existentialist and/or psychoanalytic lens, one can see that the policies will continue to result in inequities based on gender if the underlying culture dictating who provides primary care for children or simply the acknowledgement of the physical recovery of pregnancy is not addressed. The participants also briefly referenced a radical feminist aspect of STEM in that many of the STEM fields have been dominated by men. The resulting underrepresentation of women lowers their motivations to join these fields. This perception led the participants to conclude that opening access for women would improve their motivation and persistence, which does not fully address the cause of this lack of persistence and the cultural aspects affecting men's dominance in these fields.

None of the participants mentioned a socialist feminist or postmodern feminist lens. The socialist feminist perspective could begin to explain the cause of women's underrepresentation, that is, that men have dominated STEM fields resulting in research that focuses on stereotypical male interests (e.g., Rosser's discussion that medical studies before the 1980s studied male subjects and therefore could not explain complications or medical experiences for women.) But this lens also assumes that women, particularly women in STEM, have similar experiences. The postmodern feminist lens acknowledges that there is not a common experience for women. If policy responses to subtle discrimination and STEM culture incorporate individuals' varied experiences, then they might reach more women than the current liberal feminist policies.

The issues concerning culture and the stagnating affect that access policies are having is further exacerbated by the antifeminist backlash that my participants described in 2010 and Yee discussed in her 1977 essay. Women within their respective STEM cultures are often afraid to support feminist policies or policies that provide special services to women because they do not want to appear affiliated with special treatment. Or these women feel that this special treatment is unnecessary and that equity exists in STEM cultures—a sentiment that the women in my study described when referring to younger generations. This study adds to the current literature that says that equity does not exist in these fields; rather, women suffer from subtle discrimination, which in some cases is caused by the affirmative action policies put in place to help them. Women are still affected more in terms of tenure because of family planning issues. And there has not been a movement to aggressively change the culture and resulting policies and attitudes that continue to leave women out.

The women in my study persisted because of their intrinsic interest in their respective STEM field; and at SU, 50% of the female undergraduates at the university are able to persist most likely because of intrinsic interest and access policies. However, women are still encountering a chilly climate over 40 years after access policies were initiated to alleviate this problem. Consequently, I, along with other researchers, have demonstrated that other feminist lenses may help in addressing women's continued underrepresentation in STEM.

REFERENCES

Anderson, T. H. (1995). *The movement and the sixties.* New York, NY: Oxford University Press.

Beede, D., Julian, T., Langdon, D., McKittrick, G., Khan, B., & Doms, M. (2011, August). Women in STEM: A gender gap to innovation. *U.S. Department of Commerce, Economics and Statistics Administration.* ESA Issue Brief #04-11. Retrieved from http://www.esa.doc.gov/sites/default/files/reports/documents/womeninstemagaptoinnovation8311.pdf

Brotman, J. S., & Moore, F. M. (2008). Girls and science: A review of four themes in the science education literature. *Journal of Research in Science Teaching, 45*(9), 971–1002.

Carpenter, L. J., & Acosta, R. V. (2005). *Title IX.* Champaign, IL: Human Kinetics.

Chang, K. (2009, November 23). White House pushes science and math education. *The New York Times.* Retrieved from http://www.nytimes.com

Creswell, J. W. (2007). *Qualitative inquiry and research design: Choosing among five traditions* (2nd ed.). Thousand Oaks, CA: Sage.

Collins, G. (2009). *When everything changed: The amazing journey of American women from 1960 to the present.* New York, NY: Little, Brown.

Fouad, N. A., & Singh, R. (2011). *Stemming the tide: Why women leave engineering.* Milwaukee: University of Wisconsin-Milwaukee. Retrieved from http://studyofwork.com/files/2011/03/NSF_Women-Full-Report-0314.pdf

Friedan, B. (1963). *The feminine mystique.* New York, NY: Norton.

Hopkins, N., Wilson, J., Berkey, D., Harper-Taylor, J., & Lukas, C. L. (2012, September 30). Breaking the bias against women in science. *The New York Times.* Retrieved from http://www.nytimes.com

Lemke, J. L. (2001). Articulating communities: Sociocultural perspectives on science education. *Journal of Research in Science Teaching, 38,* 296–316.

Madill, H., Campbell, R., Cullen, D., Armour, M., Einsiedel, A., Ciccocioppo, A. . . . Coffin, W. (2007). Developing career commitment in STEM-related fields: Myth versus reality. In R. J. Burke & M. C. Mattis (Eds.), *Women and minorities in science, technology, engineering, and mathematics: Upping the numbers* (pp. 210–241). Nortampton, MA: Edward Elgar.

Mau, W. (2003). Factors that influence persistence in science and engineering career aspirations. *The Career Development Quarterly, 51,* 234–243.

McGrayne, S. B. (2005). *Nobel prize women in science: Their lives, struggles, and momentous discoveries* (2nd ed.). Washington DC: Joseph Henry.

National Academies Press. (2007). *Beyond bias and barriers: Fulfilling the potential of women in academic science and engineering.* Retrieved from http://www.nap.edu/openbook.php?isbn=0309100429&page=R1

National Science Foundation (NSF). (2011) *Women, minorities, and persons with disabilities in science and engineering* (NSF11-309). Arlington, VA: Author.

Ong, M. (2005). Body projects of young women of color in physics: Intersections of gender, race, and science. *Social Problems, 52,* 593–617.

Rampart, C. (2012, September 28). Enrollment drops again in graduate programs. *The New York Times.* Retrieved from http://www.nytimes.com

Robelen, E. W. (2010, January 7). Obama unveils projects to bolster STEM teaching. *Education Week, 29*(18). Retrieved from http://www.edweek.org/ew/articles/2010/01/07/18stem_ep.h29.html?tkn=OOZFMX%2FPkhA0%2BgD5yyafJA8RPCvYg%2F3%2FYLVv&intc=es

Rolison, D. R. (2003). The back page: Can Title IX do for women in science and engineering what it has done for women in sports? *American Physical Society News, 12*(5). Retrieved from http://www.aps.org/publications/apsnews/200305/backpage.cfm

Rosser, S. V. (2003). Attracting and retaining women in science and engineering. *Academe Online, 89*(4). Retrieved from http://www.aaup.org/AAUP/pubsres/academe/2003/JA/Feat/Ross.htm

Seymour, E., & Hewitt, N. M. (1997). *Talking about leaving: Why undergraduates leave the sciences.* Boulder, CO: Westview.

Shakeshaft, C. (1995). Reforming science education to include girls. *Theory Into Practice, 34,* 74–79.

Watson, J. (1981). *The double helix: A personal account of the discovery of the structure of DNA.* New York, NY: Norton.

Wertheim, M. (2006, October 3). Numbers are male, said Pythagoras, and the idea persists. *The New York Times.* Retrieved from http://www.nytimes.com

Wyer, M. (2001). *Women, science and technology: A reader in feminist science studies.* New York, NY: Routledge.

Yee, C. Z. (1977). Do women in science and technology need the women's movement? *Frontiers: A Journal of Women Studies, 2*(3), 125–128.

PART TWO

INTERVENTIONS ON BEHALF OF GIRLS
AND WOMEN PURSUING STEM FIELDS

CHAPTER 6

THE EFFECT OF ALTERNATIVE ASSESSMENTS IN NATURAL SCIENCE ON ATTITUDES TOWARD SCIENCE IN GRADE 8 GIRLS IN SOUTH AFRICA

Nicole N. Wallace
Annemarie Hattingh

INTRODUCTION

Attitudes toward science and school science have long been studied because of a desire to keep students in science-related subjects and science-related careers. In South Africa, little research has been done to identify what interventions would encourage students, especially girls, to continue in the sciences. This study focused on the implementation of an alternative assessment in Natural Science in grade 8 at an all-girls independent school. Students were given an open-ended questionnaire at the beginning and end of the school year to determine their choices for their favorite and hardest parts of Natural Science. These choices acted as a proxy of their attitude toward science. They also completed three sections of the Relevance

Girls and Women in STEM, pages 95–138

of Science Education (ROSE) questionnaire in June after the alternative assessment was completed. From this data, three conclusions were made. First, the students had a positive attitude toward the alternative assessment. Second, the students had a positive attitude toward science and showed evidence of the impact of alternative assessments on this attitude. Third, the alternative assessment did not show long-term effects on the students' attitude toward science.

This study investigated the relationship between alternative assessments in the Natural Science classroom and attitudes toward science and school science. There is a desire to increase the number of girls in the fields of science, and this formed the rationale behind investigating what efforts could encourage girls to remain in science subjects at school and beyond. Alternative assessments are a type of intervention that has become more common in classrooms around the world, and their efficacy and effect in the South African context has not yet been determined. This study will investigate their effect on attitudes toward science in grade 8 girls.

BACKGROUND AND RATIONALE

Why Is It Important to Consider Attitudes Toward Science?

Attitudes toward a subject can affect the choices that individuals make. Some researchers argue that we should be concerned with attitudes toward science because the more people who engage with science, the more innovation and development nations will see. Below is an excerpt from a report by the National Science Board (NSB), which is a part of the National Science Foundation in the United States (2010).

> The Nation needs STEM innovators—those individuals who have developed the expertise to become leading STEM professionals and perhaps the creators of significant breakthroughs or advances in scientific and technological understanding. A key component of innovation is the development of new products, services, and processes essential to the Nation's international leadership. (p. 1)

In this report, the NSB suggests that the best way to do this is to give students the best education possible and identify and foster talent from a young age. This would potentially lead to more individuals choosing studies and then careers in STEM areas.

South Africa is trying to improve the economy and increase the number of jobs available. President Jacob Zuma has said in his State of the Nation address year on year that there needs to be more effort to increase job opportunities in the country and details how and where in the economy this should be done (South African Government Information., 2011, 2012). The areas mentioned in the last two speeches are in STEM-related areas such as manufacturing and mining (South African Government Information., 2011, 2012). Increasing the innovators within these sectors (a direct result of the fostering of innovation during their education) will increase jobs in these sectors.

Why Girls?

There is an African proverb that says "If you educate a boy, you educate a man. If you educate a girl, you educate a family." This proverb speaks about a basic education, but when looked at through the lens of science education for the informed citizen, it takes on a different meaning. In an increasingly technological world where individual members of society are called upon to engage with socioscientific issues, it has become increasingly important to focus on science education (Kolsto, 2000), and through the lens of this proverb, it becomes even more important to focus on the science education of girls.

The problems within the science education of girls have long been documented (Acker & Oatley, 1993; Brotman & Moore, 2008; Carlone, 2003, 2004; Jesse, 2006; Scantelbury & Baker, 2007; Thom, 2011). Acker and Oatley (1993) report on continued negative instances that girls must face while engaging with or trying to get into science or science-related fields, such as inequality with regard to textbook writing or bursaries for further study. Jesse (2006) states that often when boys are not achieving in science and math, the system is blamed, but when girls are not achieving in science and math, the girl is blamed.

Many, like former Harvard President Lawrence Summers, believe that there is a biological difference between men and women that prevents women from actually succeeding in science-related fields (Holmgren & Basch, 2005). However, Jesse (2006) states that although there is a difference in brain function between the sexes, there is no difference in problem-solving ability. Therefore, what is creating the difference in job searches and subject choices?

Carlone (2003) argues that girls are often fighting against the "powerful sociocultural legacy of science," which is often enacted in the classroom without the teacher realizing it (p. 308). She shows through a discourse analysis of the teaching practices and interviews with a male physics teacher, that the male-dominated and elitist view of traditional physics is what is delivered, even though the course content is innovative and alternative (Carlone, 2003, 2004). Aschbacher, Li, and Roth (2010) also investigated the reasons that girls were dropping out of the pipeline of science, engineering, and mathematics (SEM) courses in high school (p. 564). They found that these same male-dominated and elitist views were not only being enacted at school, but they were also being repeated at home. Female students who stayed in SEM courses had had an affirming relationship with something (zoo, aquarium, science center, etc.) or someone (family member, teacher, researcher, etc.) that encouraged or enabled them to pursue this course.

Economically, there is a strong argument for encouraging girls to stay in and pursue careers in STEM fields. One in every two households in South Africa is headed by a single parent, and 50% of these households are headed by women (Ellis & Adams, 2009). The alarming part of the statistics regarding women-headed households is that they are on the rise in South Africa. In 1998, these women comprised only 42% of the households in South Africa, whereas in 2008 they formed greater than 52% of all households (Ellis & Adams, 2009). Many of these heads will be less likely to have a job, more likely to have less education, and more likely will struggle to feed their children due to unemployment or low wages (Ellis & Adams, 2009; Kinyondo & Mabugu, 2009).

As markets shift and productivity in the work place changes, women will need to be resistant and resilient to these changes. Kinyondo & Mabugu (2009) reflect on the realization that women with the same skillset are often passed over in favor of their male counterparts for semiskilled and skilled positions. As a result, these women are then required to take a position that is considered unskilled or one with a lower salary. Jobs in STEM sectors are historically more stable and have a higher wage (Kinyondo & Mabugu, 2009). The authors, therefore, suggest that by improving the education of women in the science- and math-related fields, they would increase their chances for employment in STEM sectors (Kinyondo & Mabugu, 2009).

The same trends are seen on an international scale as well. Lopez-Claros and Zahidi (2005) investigated the gender gap in 58 countries based on five criteria, including economic participation and economic opportunity. With regard to economic participation, they found that women earn less than 78% of what equally qualified men earn. The economic opportunities that women have are generally in low skill and low wage areas or are in sectors deemed "female," such as nursing or teaching (Lopez-Claros & Zahidi, 2005, p. 3). These jobs often do not have movement up in terms of administration or opportunities. The opportunities that do exist for women often do not offer them "family-friendly" benefits such as maternity leave. As a possible result, Lopez-Claros and Zahidi also found "49% of high-achieving women to be childless, as compared with only 19% of their male counterparts" (p. 4).

With regard to education, Lopez-Claros and Zahidi (2005) called it "the most fundamental prerequisite for empowering women" (p. 5). Education within South Africa has been a long-contested system. Robert Morrell (2000) outlined the findings of the South African Gender Equity Task

Team with regard to the education of girls and the plea for more single-sex schools within South Africa. He stated that girls were often not provided with a safe environment in which they could learn. This was with regard to both academic performance and general emotional safety. In a single-sex school, Morrell also argued that girls will often take more "boy's" subjects and perform better. He also stated that girls-only schools have less sexual harassment and have more positive female role models for the students. Therefore, girls within a coeducational school are having to struggle with issues far greater than their subject choice and may therefore choose easier subjects or fewer "boy's" subjects as a result.

Regardless of Morrell's (2000) case for opening more girls-only schools, South Africa currently has a higher percentage of girls graduating from high school (60%) than many other African countries (Ellis & Adams, 2009). The Further Education and Training (FET) phase and tertiary sector of education have had higher percentages of women since 2007 (Council for Higher Education, 2009; Molebatsi, 2009). And yet in the STEM courses at universities (especially in the advanced degrees), women are consistently underrepresented. Therefore, it is important to determine the points in the secondary education of girls at which they are encouraged or discouraged to continue in the sciences.

Why Innovate?

Innovation stems from the need for change within a system. In the educational system, it can be sparked by a number of different emergent factors, such as technology (Dooley, 1999), philosophy of education (Singh, 2002), or pedagogical theories (Montessori, 1912). Innovation can also be sparked by internal factors, such as high-stakes testing results or participation in a subject (Couling, 2011). Hannan, English, and Silver (1999) reviewed the reasons that higher education institutions were innovating and discovered that some educators are forced by the management of the school into innovative teaching practices while others will try new methods to improve their students' learning willingly and independently. Regardless of its source or *raison d'etre*, innovation is a way that teachers and academics are attempting to change the outcome of one part of the pedagogy in a schooling system and improve the education of the students (Wilkes & Bligh, 1999).

Within this context, there is a drive to increase the number of girls in STEM courses and careers. This is happening globally, from educational to corporate to government interventions (Office of Science and Technology Policy, 2011). These interventions seek to increase access for girls to interact with scientists (Nagaraja, 2012), change the focus of assessments to be more gender-neutral (Chilisa, 2000), and improve attitudes of girls through curriculum changes (Carlone, 2003).

Why Educational Innovation?

Dooley (1999) quoted Rogers' 1995 definition of innovation: "an idea, practice, or object that is perceived as new by an individual or other unit of adoption" (p. 36). This meaning is broad and can be applied to many different points in Bernstein's "Pedagogic Device" (Singh, 2002) of education. It is important to recognize at what point in this process the innovation is taking place as this will determine who will be responsible for the evaluation of the effect of the innovation.

Innovation is useful only when evaluated in light of the criteria or outcomes desired. Who is evaluating the innovation will also determine the evaluation criteria (Wilkes & Bligh, 1999). For example, if the question is about student performance, the results on summative assessments would most likely be collected to determine the effectiveness of the course. The evaluation criteria can be very broad or rather narrow (Wilkes & Bligh, 1999). However, it is through the evaluation process that innovations may be adopted, changed, or discarded. Without this step, innovations often fall away as being too difficult (Dooley, 1999).

However, it is within the evaluation and assessment process of innovation teaching and learning methods that skeptics raise issues. The evaluation process often fails to take into account the entire situation of the student (the whole program or social environment of the student). When asked to evaluate a number of innovative medical curricula, Friedman et al. (1990) noted that it is difficult to determine how one aspect of a program can be credited with the changes in knowledge, skills, or behavior of the candidates. It is important to view the effect of the entire program on the candidate, and this also requires a long-term view (potentially up to 10 years with medical students) (Friedman et al., 1990). Therefore, when reviewing educational innovation within one institution or classroom, it is also important to view the whole picture of the student rather than take a narrow focus on one innovative aspect.

What Are Alternative Assessments?

Alternative assessments have been characterized by Herman, Aschbacher, and Winters (1992). These types of assessments have five basic characteristics in common: (a) asking students to perform, create, produce, or do something; (b) tapping higher-level thinking and problem-solving skills; (c) using tasks that represent meaningful instructional activities; (d) involving real-world applications; and (e) using human judgment to do the scoring (as cited in Corcoran, Dershimer, & Tichenor, 2004, p. 213).

These assessments often provide a more holistic view of a student's progress or understanding (Century, 2002). Lawrenz, Huffman, and Welch (2001) presented their findings that these alternative assessments can also be fairer to lower-achieving students, therefore giving a teacher a more realistic picture of what all the students in the class understand. This definition of alternative assessment fits into the understanding of assessment *for* learning instead of assessment *of* learning. This view of assessment is alternative in itself as it brings the assessment into the middle of the learning process instead of being removed from the learning process altogether.

21st Century Skills and Alternative Assessments

A new buzz phrase in education is "21st century skills." Many educators and policymakers are promoting the idea that education needs to take another angle in this "knowledge economy." Since the knowledge (content) that the students need is often at their fingertips now via the Internet, teaching and learning have become less about a transfer of knowledge and more about an evaluation and synthesis of knowledge, which are classified as more higher-order thinking skills. The workplace of the next generation will not look like it does today, and the question often asked is how will we educate students for a world of work that we don't recognize? The answer many educators now give is through skills. The Partnership for 21st Century Skills (P21) developed a framework for the skills necessary for expected success in the workplace. These include the *4Cs* for learning and innovation, which include collaboration, communication, critical thinking and creativity, in no particular order (Partnership for 21st Century Skills, 2012).

Science is an extremely collaborative subject. Just a quick glance at *Science Daily* (an Internet-based science news site) will show a large percentage of collaborative projects. A short conversation with academics at any university will reveal that many projects are done with a variety of people, all of whom bring a different skillset to the table and without whom the project would not have been a success. Therefore, it begs the question, Why are we not promoting this kind of collaboration at a school level?

Innovation and creativity are seen as the key to an improvement in the global economy as well as independent country economies. In the United States, there is a move to identify and support young people (and through them, educators) who are showing innovative talents. These talented young people need to be nurtured and developed in order to become the next innovators (as discussed above). It is through these alternative assessments in classroom settings at a young age that these talented young people will be inspired to continue with STEM courses.

In any country, girls are needed to increase the human capacity of innovators, engineers, researchers, and developers so that the economy can continue to positively grow. Therefore we need to address the early attitudes of girls toward STEM courses and careers. Within the secondary school education of girls in South Africa, there is a need for innovative practices in the science subjects to encourage girls to remain in these subjects. Alternative assessments may be the tool used in schools to affect girls' attitudes toward STEM courses and careers.

CONCEPTUAL FRAMEWORK

The conceptual framework examines the intersection of attitudes, alternative assessments, and the learning styles of girls. Each will be discussed with regard to their working definition for this study as well as current literature about each topic. However, it is the intersection of these three constructs that formed the central theme of this study. Information in Figure 6.1 illustrates the intersection of these three concepts.

Attitudes Toward Science

What Is an Attitude?

Mager (1968) defines an attitude as "a general tendency of an individual to act in a certain way under certain circumstances" (p. 14). Century (2002) defined it as an individual's prevailing tendency to respond favorably or unfavorably to an object, person, or group of people, institution, or event. Attitudes can be changed over time (Eagly & Chaiken, 1993; Mager, 1968)

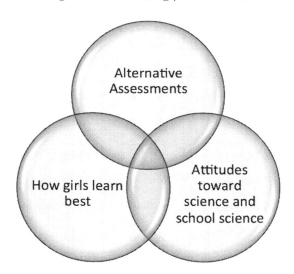

Figure 6.1 Framework showing the intersection between attitudes toward science, learning styles, and alternative assessment.

and are influenced by everything around the individual—teachers, media, classmates, parents, family members, or friends (Mager, 1968). It can be as easy as a teacher reflecting on one's own school experiences and determine points that lead one into a specific field or, conversely, away from a specific field. This is also true for many adults. Bauer (2002) identified specific things that college-level chemistry students remembered about their high school chemistry classes, such as the frequency of practicals or demonstrations, how well the teacher could explain challenging concepts, and how well the teacher could relate the subject of chemistry to everyday life. Eagly and Chaiken (1993) identified the three components of an attitude as being cognitive, affective, and behavioral. These three aspects can be seen as responses of an attitude or as influences toward an attitude.

The affective aspects of an attitude are the emotions that a person would attach to the thing or idea (Eagly & Chaiken, 1993). When a student is asked if science is fun or hard or challenging, these words help a researcher to construct the emotions that students have around the construct of science. An emotive response might be as simple as feeling angry or happy when presented with the subject in any form. Some students have commented that they feel happiest when they see science is next on their timetable. Other students are excited about the time when they can "give up" science after grade 9 (the point in a South African student's education after which science classes become an elective subject). This emotive response will lead to different kinds of behavioral responses, another aspect of a student's attitude. Behavioral responses are the seen effect of the student's attitude toward an attitude object (Eagly & Chaiken, 1993). If students have a positive attitude toward science, they are more likely to choose science-related subjects or books or television shows. These "moving toward" responses (Mager, 1968) would indicate that the student in question is choosing these things based on a positive attitude toward science. Cognitive aspect of attitude refers to the individual's belief about the subject or thing (Eagly & Chaiken, 1993). An individual's interaction with a subject will lead to specific beliefs about it, such as a belief that they are good at the subject or that the subject has inherent value.

The purpose of studying student attitudes toward science is the effect it will ultimately have on their choices, specifically academic and career choices. As stated before, there is a large need for students to continue to study STEM courses in South Africa for economic, social, and academic reasons. If students maintain a positive attitude toward science, they may be more likely to continue in a science-related field past grade 9 and into tertiary education. Cherian and Shumba (2011) investigated the attitudes toward science in a sample population of grade 12 Northern Sotho students in the Limpopo province of South Africa. In their findings, boys exhibited a more positive attitude toward science than girls, and their findings showed a small effect with regard to age; the older girls or women (> 20 years old) had less of a positive attitude than those under 20 (p. 293). George (2006) looked at the change of attitudes in high school students over a 5-year period to determine the trend in attitude change over high school. While there was a strong correlation between a positive attitude toward science and a positive attitude toward the utility of science (defined as the usefulness of science for society), students had a general decline in attitude toward science over the 5 years (p. 585). It is important to determine what is causing the change in attitudes within a schooling system and potentially what can be done to continue to maintain a more positive attitude toward science, regardless of their future field of study.

How Have Attitudes Toward Science Been Measured Before?

Student attitudes toward science, school science, and assessment have long been studied (Osborne, Simon, & Collins, 2003). It is important to differentiate between attitudes toward science, attitudes toward school science, and scientific attitudes (Osborne et al., 2003). The first is science as a construct in society, the larger idea that is science. The second refers to science as a subject at school level. The last idea refers to specific behaviors and characteristics that would define a scientific person (Osborne et al., 2003, p. 6). In this study, attitudes toward science and school science were discussed and investigated. Students were asked about a potential future for themselves in science, but this was not be regarded as "scientific attitudes" as Osborne et al. (2003) referred to, but it was used as a proxy to discuss the relationship between their attitudes and school science.

Since attitudes have been studied for more than 30 years, many tests have been designed to this end. The following are examples of the kinds of tests developed. The final one was the test used in this study.

The Test for Science Related Attitudes (TOSRA) was developed by Fraser in 1978 to assess high school student attitudes in Australia (Welch, 2010). It contained seven dimensions of attitudes toward science originally discussed by Klopfer in 1971 (Welch, 2010). Fraser developed 10 statements for each dimension and used a 5-point Likert scale as the method for answering. This questionnaire investigated affective, cognitive, and behavioral aspects of attitudes toward science, seen as "enjoyment of science lessons" to "normality of scientists" to "leisure interest in science" (Welch, 2010, p. 188). The sections could stand alone or be used together to get individual or whole pictures of a student's attitude toward science. TOSRA has been subsequently used for attitude research worldwide, across age groups and intervention types (Farenga & Joyce, 1999; Khalili, 1987; Lyons & Quinn, 2010; Ouyang & Hayden 2010).

Simpson and Troost designed an attitude questionnaire in 1982 (STAQ), with the first look at a rising dropout from science-related subjects at school

(Owen et al., 2008). This test consisted of statements that participants had to rank on a 5-point Likert scale and investigated the relationship between attitudes toward science and specific influences like peer groups and family groups. Their questionnaire has been used a number of times in the last 30 years to determine the attitudes of certain populations toward science (Nasr & Soltani, 2011; Owen et al., 2008).

The Relevance of Science Education (ROSE) questionnaire was developed by Schreiner and Sjøberg (2004) to investigate what students want to study as well as how they relate to specific areas of science (such as technology or the environment). The questionnaire, like the two above, consists mainly of statements that participants responded to using a 4-point Likert scale. There was also the inclusion of one open-ended question in which student voice could be heard as the responses were individual and personal. Unlike other surveys, the ROSE questionnaire was developed to be cross-cultural. The panel that developed the questions represented 10 countries with languages and educational systems very different from each other (Schreiner & Sjøberg, 2004). As a result, there is a high degree of validity when using the test in different cultures, which has led to many researchers using it (more than 20 full texts are available at http://roseproject.no/?page_id=39).

Regardless of the tool used, the trend has been that girls exhibit less-positive attitudes toward science (whether school science or science as a whole) than boys (Bennett, Lubben & Hogarth, 2006; Farenga & Joyce, 1999; Smith & Matthews, 2000; Weinburgh, 1995) and that on the whole, attitudes toward school science and science as a whole decline through the middle school and high school years (George, 2006; P. D. Morrell & Lederman, 1998; Sorge, 2007). For this reason, it has become necessary to examine different populations of students around the world with regard to the relationship between different variables (assessments, other subjects, teachers, parents, age, ethnicity, etc.) and attitudes toward school science and science as a whole.

Intersection of Attitudes and Alternative Assessments

While many studies look to investigate the intersection of attitudes with specific criteria (such as peer group influence, nonclassroom science interventions, achievement, or family interactions), only recently have people looked at the interaction of alternative assessments and attitudes toward science.

Bennett et al. (2006) conducted a meta-analysis of studies that linked attitudes toward science and specific types of alternative assessments. These assessments were classified as context-based or science-technology-society (STS) approaches. Their research concluded that while these approaches improved attitudes toward school science, it did not conclusively translate into an improvement of attitudes toward science.

Smith and Matthews (2000) were able to see an improvement in 15-year-old girls' attitudes toward science as a result of similar science, technology, and society (STS) approaches in the classroom. They were also able to see a shift in their subject choices after the intervention of STS teaching. Students also showed a change in their rationale behind choosing specific subjects, showing more interest in a subject rather than a need to study it for a career.

Kirikkaya and Vurkaya (2011) were able to set up a control versus experimental group within three schools in Turkey. In this study, attitudes and academic achievement were monitored pre- and postassessment during a unit on "Electricity in our Lives." There was a more positive attitude toward science postassessment in all schools, indicating that the alternative assessment was the cause of the change in attitude. It was also seen that in all three schools, there was a significant difference between the achievements of students in the experimental groups versus the control groups. This would indicate that the assessment method was the reason for this improvement in their marks. This study was a small sample size, but gives a good comparison between experimental and control groups within the same setting (same school).

Alternative Assessments

What Is an Alternative Assessment?

Within a study that focuses on alternative assessments, it is also important to distinguish these from traditional assessments, since this underpins any inferences from this study. Traditional assessments are generally one-time measures in which the questions asked have one correct answer. They are generally a paper-and-pencil test, worksheet, or comprehension activity wherein a specific body of knowledge, removed from a real-world context, is recontextualized for the purpose of determining a student's performance in a determined amount of time. These assessments tend to be culturally separated from many of the students that take the assessments because the teachers are not consulted in the construction of these tests. Traditional assessments are designed for large-scale use, national reporting, or statistical analysis (SEDL, 2012; State of New Jersey, 2010). All of these points are in opposition to the five characteristics of alternative assessment tasks described (State of New Jersey, 2010).

Alternative assessments are designed to engage a student's higher-order thinking skills as well as engage them in real-world contexts, lending themselves to problem-solving. The scoring of these tasks depends on the immediate teacher's judgment, which can bring in cultural context and situational bias. Alternative assessments are also underpinned by a constructivist theory of learning. Students have freedom of choice within the context of the assessment, which leads to ownership of the ideas created and social interaction to create the ideas and products (Janich, Liu, & Akrofi, 2007). These assessments are often received in a positive manner, with students being able to reflect not only on the subject matter but also how they have approached the assessment (Janich et al., 2007). Waters, Smeaton, and Burns (2004) found other positive effects of alternative assessments like collegiality and creativity within the classroom, with a decrease in off-task behaviors. Researchers and teachers alike have seen the benefits of using alternative assessments to improve both achievement and attitudes in students (Kirikkaya & Vurkaya, 2011).

Previous Research in and of Alternative Assessments
In order to understand alternative assessments, it is necessary to review some of the current literature as the topic is considered highly contextual. Each of the studies below highlights different reasons for the alternative assessments and the effect that it had on the context. It is important to note that in many cases, there was a positive relationship between the implementation of the alternative assessment and the improvement of attitudes in the students toward that subject.

Couling (2011) conducted action research with her General Chemistry students in grade 10 to investigate how to curb cheating on homework and improve results on solo tests. She did this through a 3-cycle approach to research, in which each cycle contained an intervention and an evaluation. Through each cycle, she monitored cheating on homework and recorded solo test results. Collaborative units tended to decrease cheating on homework as it allowed the students to set and mark their own homework assignments. This led to improvements on solo tests, which is very relevant to the South African framework of high-stakes testing. Without intending to, Couling also noted a change in their attitudes toward chemistry as a result of the interventions. The attitudes of most students had improved as a result with more of them saying, "I can do chemistry."

Archer et al. (2010) created a 5-year longitudinal study in which they studied students in five different schools in the London area. The sample represented a large diversity of schools and students, since their question was based on the identity the students were creating for themselves. The main question that the researchers were trying to answer was the link between "doing science" and wanting to "be a scientist" in the eyes of middle school and high school students. They reviewed student interviews for clues about the enjoyment of doing science and learned that many of the students enjoyed participating in science at school level. They concluded that doing science in elementary school does not equate to students wanting to be a scientist after high school.

Carlone (2004) researched the effect that an innovative teaching method had on the attitudes and achievement of the students in the class. The class of Active Physics students at Sunnyglen High included both boys and girls and was taught by a male teacher. The teacher employed a problem-based learning approach to the subject of physics based on a national curriculum called Active Physics. Carlone (2004) found that even though the method of instruction was innovative and alternative to the regular (or traditional) physics class at the same high school, the students had the same attitudes toward physics and science at the end of the investigation. She witnessed instances within the enacted curriculum that historical views of women in science were portrayed by the male teacher. Traditional values of science and scientists were the norm, even though the curriculum was innovative. Girls were never seen as naturally gifted, whereas boys in the class were. As a result, fewer girls had a positive attitude toward physics at the end of the investigation. This is important, as it denotes the importance of the teacher in the benefits of alternative and innovative education.

Since alternative assessments are considered contextual, as effort was made to investigate other research into alternative assessments in South Africa, but no formal research was found. However, from discussions with other teachers at this school and others, a few vignettes were noted about the effects that alternative assessments can have on attitudes toward school subjects and alternative assessments.

In the grade 4 class at this school, the teachers were told that the incoming class did not enjoy reading and could not work together. Therefore, the teachers designed a unit around a set book that incorporated different kinds of group work as the assessments throughout the unit. The assessments involved creating new story lines for the main character, drawing these stories, narrating them into a movie, creating new buildings within the fantasy land of the book, and teaching others about the story. The qualitative feedback from the students after the unit was finished was that they enjoyed reading more and felt that they had accomplished a lot through this project. The feedback from the teachers was that the students were more capable collaborators and could solve group problems better. They also commented that the reading logs of these classes had increased by the end of the project. They were able to compare these results to a traditional assessment in the following term. The individual marks were lower on average and the students did not respond with the same enthusiasm for the assessment.

From these examples, one can determine that alternative assessments can have a positive effect on the attitudes of the students toward science and school science as well as their achievement within these subjects.

How Girls Learn Best

If one reviews the definition above of alternative assessments by Herman et al. (1992), cited in Corcoran et al. (2004), it is clear that these points would fit within the paradigm of how girls learn best. The following is a discussion about the optimal learning conditions for girls.

Problem-solving skills are noted as one of the characteristics of alternative assessments. In order to develop this skill, students need to be able to understand the complexity of problems and develop solutions. They also need to be able to express their ideas in a common language to the group. According to Gurian and Stevens (2004), girls develop the "verbal-emotive functioning" parts of their brain more than boys at a similar age (p. 22). A girl's brain is more likely to revert to using these aspects of her brain than the "spatial-mechanical functioning" that boys have (p. 23). This could indicate that girls will more likely use their ability to dialogue with each other in order to find solutions to problems rather than independently create solutions. Therefore they will want to work together.

Thom (2001) discusses the differences between boys and girls with regard to their optimal learning environments. She states that girls will generally benefit from working collaboratively, whereas boys will work better independently and competitively. Brotman and Moore (2008) quoted previous research that indicated that girls were more collaborative and less competitive than boys. Honigsfeld and Dunn (2003) investigated the relationship between learning styles in high school students across eight different countries. Within their results, they were able to highlight a few characteristics of how girls learn versus boys. Across cultures, girls learned better in a system that allowed for varied sociological mixtures, such as independently, in pairs, in groups, or even with the teacher, as compared with classrooms that focused on one style of mixing students (such as often in pairs or often independently). Bonomo (2010) stated that girls can work better in groups because they are more able to multitask and can listen and differentiate sounds better.

Since Gurian and Stevens (2004) say that "children will naturally gravitate toward activities that their brains experience as pleasurable" (p. 22), one can infer that girls will gravitate toward situations in which they are able to discuss possible solutions in a common language, usually one that includes everyday words rather than complex scientific terminology. This conclusion would indicate that for girls, group work and problem-solving should be significant factors when designing assessments.

For both alternative assessments and girls' preferences in learning, real-world context and everyday language have appeared in many studies. In a German physics classroom, Stadler, Duit, and Benke (2000) investigated the differences between how boys and girls responded to a practical investigation of the limited predictability of a chaotic system. Within the coed group, girls were more likely to use discussion as a way to reach an answer. Girls were more prone to using everyday language to express their ideas as well as trying to relate the concepts to daily contexts. This is consistent with the alternative assessments being those that are placed in a real-world context and represent meaningful instructional activity. Girls should respond more positively to assessments that give a connection to their daily lives or assessments that allow them to make these connections.

With these concepts in mind, it was predicted that girls' attitudes toward science will improve if they are provided with opportunities to learn through problem-solving and real-world contexts and given assessment tasks that allow them independence compared with projects that encourage regurgitation of facts or comprehension-based questions.

PURPOSE OF THIS STUDY

This study investigated the intersection of three aspects of research—how girls learn, the effect of alternative assessments, and student attitudes toward science. If students are given situations in which they are placed in optimal learning environments, they will presumably have a more positive attitude toward that subject. If a student has a more positive attitude toward that subject, it may lead to further choices in science and science-related fields ("moving toward" responses; Mager, 1968). Thus, it is hypothesized that with the presence of an alternative assessment within a curricular year, students would show a positive attitude toward the subject matter by choosing to continue studying it past high school in a theoretical context as well as an overall positive attitude toward science.

RESEARCH METHODOLOGY

Research Design

There are a variety of ways in which researchers can mix their qualitative and quantitative methods, mainly based on their desired outcomes (Creswell, 2009). Through an investigation into these desired outcomes, the mixed methodology often emerges. This study has used a number of methods for reasons that are explored below.

A quasi-experimental design was used to try to identify a change in attitudes in the sample. Specifically, an equivalent time-samples design was used (Tuckman, 1994). This allowed for a qualitative questionnaire at the beginning of the year to determine a baseline for attitudes toward natural science, followed by the alternative assessment, followed by another qualitative questionnaire midyear, and a final qualitative questionnaire at the end of the school year. Additionally, there was a quantitative questionnaire completed concurrently at the midyear point. This was determined by the sequentially exploratory design (mixed methods approach) described by

Creswell (2009). The beginning of year questionnaire highlighted themes that were used to determine the sections of the ROSE questionnaire used. The purpose of the ROSE questionnaire was to use an internationally recognized and validated attitude survey to which to compare these students.

Qualitative Approach

The questions asked at the three different times of the year were open-ended. This kind of questioning allows the subjects to create their own answers. This allows for specific themes to emerge naturally and improves the validity of their answers because they are not guided by the question itself (Creswell, 2009, pp. 15–16).

The January (beginning of the year) and December (end of the year) questionnaires contained two questions that were open-ended in order to identify their favorite and hardest parts of Natural Science. Bennett et al. (2006) stated that "subject choices…and/or career aspirations are important indicators of attitude to the subject" (p. 363). By identifying these, students were indicating their attitudes toward specific parts of the subject of science by classifying their answers under the headings of *favorite* and *hardest* part.

In June (midyear) and December (end of the year), the open-ended questions were slightly different. The final question from the ROSE questionnaire asked the students to think about the future and assume that they had become a scientist. They were then asked to identify what they would study and give a reason why they would study this area of science. Continuing with the rationale given by Bennett et al. (2006), one can determine the attitudes of the students toward the subject of science based on their career aspirations. This question guided their answer to provide more detail about their career aspirations. It also included their rationale for choosing a specific topic. This gave insight into how and why the students responded as they did. This question was used twice to determine if their career aspiration or rationale had changed over the second half of the year.

Quantitative Approach

Quantitative data was also collected midyear for purposes of identifying larger patterns within the attitudes of this nonrandom sample of students toward science. The addition of this survey of attitudes was in line with a "sequential exploratory design" as described by Creswell (2009, p. 209). In this design, the qualitative data collection and analysis informed the choices of the quantitative data collection method. A total analysis of the data followed at the end. Within this study, however, the data analysis has included all the qualitative data collected and the quantitative data collected, as they have informed each other.

The statements given in the ROSE questionnaire were closed questions. This kind of question identifies that kind of information or answers that the researcher is interested in collecting (Creswell, 2009). These statements covered two different topics—Science, Technology and Me, and Me and My Science Classes. These all included statements that the students had to rank using a Likert scale in terms of importance to them (from Not Important to Very Important) or in terms of agreement (from Strongly Disagree to Strongly Agree). These sections were chosen from the ROSE questionnaire because of the themes that emerged from the beginning-of-the-year questionnaire. These two sections also allowed for the measurement of attitudes toward science and school science. There were six other sections of the ROSE questionnaire that were not used. Three of these sections dealt with topics that students may want to learn about. One section dealt with experiences that students have out of school, another with the number of books in a student's household. The last two sections were concerned with the kind of job the students want in the future and how they relate to environmental challenges (Schreiner & Sjøberg, 2004). These sections were not used because they did not fit with the purpose of the study, as they did not relate directly to attitudes toward science or did not allow the analysis to link back to alternative assessments.

Sampling Method

The grade 8 class of the school was chosen for this study. The reason that grade 8 was chosen as a year of study was threefold: there are new girls introduced into the school at this stage, so that the histories of the students with regard to Natural Science were all different; this is the first year in the high school within this school; and it is the grade in the middle of a phase within the GET, which gave a good historical point at which to collect this kind of data. A nonrandom sample was chosen for this study. This was in line with the quasi-experimental design. Since there were only 68 students in the grade, and this number was large enough to assess and large enough to use as an appropriate sample size, all the students were chosen to receive the alternative assessment. The number of students in the sample was therefore regulated by the total number of students in the grade 8 class at this school.

This "critical case sampling" (Palys, 2008) was chosen to give insight into the attitudes of girls in a privileged environment. The privilege indicated that the school (and by association, the students) did not have any barriers toward learning taking place (e.g., all girls were well-fed and had equal access to computers, desks, books, etc. at school).

Research Participants

The school in which this study took place is an all-girls, faith-based school from grades 00 to 12. The school is over 140 years old and maintains many traditions, both religious and secular. As a faith-based school, girls are exposed to regular religious instruction and ceremonies. The school is also a part of the Round Square conference of schools. This organization, founded by Kurt Hahn, is underpinned by six IDEALS: Internationalism, Democracy, Environmentalism, Adventure, Leadership, and Service. These themes are expressed inside and outside of the classroom environment. Recently the school was chosen to be a supermentor school for Microsoft Partners in Learning. This international program strives to recognize educators and schools who value and embrace innovation in education through the incorporation of 21st century skills within their classrooms and school environment. This is a testament to the innovative teaching and learning practices that are at work within all sections of the school.

The classrooms are all equipped with a computer, which has Internet and intranet access, and most have a projector that the teachers use on a regular basis. More than half of the classes have interactive white board technologies. There are two classrooms that have a small bank of computers, one being the science classroom. There are two computer rooms (each with 25 computers) and a large bank of computers for student use in the library. Information technology (IT) forms a large part of student life at the school. There is an intranet where teachers post work and links relevant to their subjects, and each student has an email address for communication in and out of the school. Girls have IT as a subject from grade 1 to grade 9 and in the Senior Phase (grades 7–9), and they study to complete their International Computer Driving License (ICDL).

There are many extracurricular activities offered. One school sport is mandatory at grade 8 level. Many girls also participate in cocurricular activities such as debating or community partnerships or pottery. The school also hosts a variety of extracurricular activities as a whole. These include guest speakers (such as Lewis Pugh) or theme days (such as Africa Day). These days increase awareness about issues from within their communities and extend to the continent. The school also has a Barraza meeting each term, when the girls listen to a speaker or watch a movie and then break into small discussion groups from grades 8–12 to discuss the meaning and impact of the presentation on their lives. These are student driven and led.

There are about 50 teachers in the Senior School, who also come from a variety of backgrounds and socioeconomic classes. Many are international or have spent a significant amount of time in another country (either living or teaching or both). Therefore, the viewpoint that they bring to the class is broad and varied.

In terms of academic results, the school has had a 100% pass rate for the last 10 years. The school has appeared in the top 10 schools in their province during this period and often had students who are the top student in specific subjects in the province or the nation. Therefore, the drive to succeed academically is strong among the student body.

There are just over 800 students in the school, with about 330 in the Senior School (grades 8–12). Each grade has an average of 70 students. Students come from a variety of backgrounds and socioeconomic classes, but the majority are from a top socioeconomic class. In grade 8, about 66% of the class is accepted from the Preparatory School and about 33% are new students from a variety of schools. Therefore, the experiences of the girls up to this point are different. Due to the lack of a concrete curriculum in Natural Science at this point in time, the topics covered in their previous schools are also different.

With regard to the numbers of science students in the FET phase, a decade ago, there was one class of Physical Science that had fewer than 20 students at the grade 12 level. Therefore, less than 30% of the matric class was taking Physical Science. In 2012, a total of 41 students (54%) in grade 10 class registered for Physical Science, and 41 students (54%) registered for Life Science. Out of 76 students in the grade, 31 students (40%) registered for both Life and Physical Science; two students (3%) registered for Life Science, Physical Science, and Geography; and only 12 students (16%) did not register for either Life or Physical Science. Therefore, there has been an increase in the number of students who want to study science courses and who believe that they *can* study these subjects. This number may change over the course of the year due to students changing subjects, but the matric science classes of 2014 will still be the largest that the school has seen in 10 years. Because of the increase in students choosing science-based subjects at grade 10 level, it was decided that the impact of these alternative assessments driving the GET phase Natural Science curriculum at this school needed to be investigated.

Research Instruments and Analysis

Development of the Alternative Assessment

To determine the effect of an alternative assessment on attitudes, there must be a process by which an assessment is qualified as alternative. An alternative assessment was drawn up by the researcher and her colleagues to cover the topic of sustainable energy and renewable resources. This alternative assessment formed part of an alternative education week at the end of Term 1 (near the end of March). Within this week, the students investigated the theme of "Our Big Issues," a community-focused, hands-on approach to learning, concentrating on a number of subjects (Natural Science, Life Orientation, English, and Mathematics). No traditional classes were held during this week, and regular class groups were mixed across the grade. For Natural Science, the "big issue" covered was that of sustainable energy and renewable resources.

Sustainable energy and renewable resources was a topic in both grade 7 and 8 within the National Curriculum Statement (NCS). Therefore, at least some of the students had covered the topic in some detail. A twofold quiz game was used to refresh their memory or teach them some content about sustainable energy practices and renewable energy sources. The students were split into teams of four and given four 10-question quizzes that they had to discuss and answer. There were prizes for the first to complete the questions and the team with the most correct answers, so accuracy and efficiency were rewarded. After the teams had completed this, each team nominated a member to participate in a knockout round of single questions. This quiz formed the part of the time dedicated to content acquisition for the alternative assessment, but did not form any part of the marks.

When changes to the assessment task were being made, the criteria quoted by Corcoran et al. (2004) were kept in mind. With the first criteria in mind ("to perform, create, produce, or do something"), the students were asked to create a survey, collect data from the survey, collate this into a presentation in which they discuss their findings, and then develop an educational video about one aspect of their research. Students completed a unit in the same term, which focused on these skills; therefore, this was an application of previously learned skills. With the second criteria in mind ("tapping higher-level thinking and problem-solving skills"), students were asked to evaluate questions for the survey as well as the data that they had collected. They were further asked to evaluate information to determine its educational value. With the third criteria in mind ("using tasks that represent meaningful instructional activities"), students learned a variety of skills that would be applied throughout their other subjects, such as data collection and manipulation, collaboration, time management, and skilled communication. They also learned about sustainable energy and renewable resources and awareness by asking their own questions and collecting their own data rather than reading about data from another source. With the fourth criteria in mind ("involving real world applications"), students had to involve the real world and real people in both collecting data and during the movie. The movie had to include an interview with a person who was relevant to their topic. This included parents, siblings, professionals, and like-minded strangers. With the fifth and last criteria in mind ("using human judgment to do the scoring"), a rubric was drawn up for each step of the project. This allowed the students to know the criteria beforehand as well as understand that they were being evaluated by their teacher, as opposed to a machine (as with standardized, multiple choice tests).

Moderation of the Alternative Assessment

A moderation rubric was drawn up according to these criteria, and the student assignment was moderated by five colleagues in Natural Science.

This group represented internal and external colleagues from both secondary and tertiary institutions. They all agreed that the task fit the criteria completely. This independent analysis supports the construct validity that the assessment was alternative.

Informed Consent and Authenticity of Work

Since Natural Science is a compulsory subject at this level, the assessment was carried out with all grade 8 students at the school (67 in total). The headmistress gave informed consent for the school's students to be used. Some 60 students and their parents also gave informed consent that their work would be used and anonymity preserved. Seven students and parents did not reply or give consent. All tasks were collected (surveys, PowerPoint presentations, presentation rubrics, movies, and movie rubrics). These formed a part of the authenticity validity to show that the work was the work of the students.

Beginning-of-the-Year Questionnaire

At the beginning of the school year before any teaching took place, the students were asked to complete a written questionnaire that asked them to identify their favorite and hardest parts of Natural Science. Based on Mager's (1968) idea of "moving towards" responses and the link to positive attitudes, choices that students made in response to these questions indicated what parts of science and science classes they were the most attracted to or dissuaded from. This idea was supported by Bennett et al. (2006), who stated that the choices students made for further study was an indication of attitudes toward the subject. The more students chose to participate or study specific areas, the more of a positive attitude they would associate with these subjects.

The students were given as much time as they required to complete this form. The words they used were chosen by them. There were a few suggestions given to start their process, and these words were varied between skills and topics, such as "what we do in class" or "what topic you enjoy the most." Because there were no limits or choices given for these questions, there was an implicit trust in the validity of their answers as authentic. This information was collected and classified: first between skills and topics, and second into specific kinds of skills and topics. Within the topics, the words that the students wrote were used to determine the classification system. The topics were then classified into Biological Sciences, Physical Sciences, or Other. This formed a baseline for the interests in and attitudes toward science.

Reflections of the Alternative Assessment

Each student was asked to write a one-page, open-ended reflection of the assessment during the alternative education week. Reflections by all learners of the assessment were collected and were linguistically analyzed. A classification system for the comments was created based on the affective data in the reflections. This system was used to code the reflections of the students to determine their attitude toward alternative assessments.

The ROSE Questionnaire

The Relevance of Science Education (ROSE) questionnaire was developed in 2004 for an international survey of student attitudes toward science education. This 9-part, closed question (except for Section I) survey was originally developed for an international group of academics to investigate the relevance of science education to 15-year-olds (Schreiner & Sjøberg, 2004). The validity of the survey was determined through its rigorous development process with academics from nine countries and can therefore be used internationally. It has a specific coding scheme and marking scheme that was used. However, only specific sections of the 9-part questionnaire were used for the following reasons. Section F (my science class) was used to see how important they rank classroom instruction. Section G (my opinions about science and technology) was used to understand how they view the relationship between themselves and technology, especially since the project delved into sustainable uses of energy. Section I (myself as a scientist) was used as it is an open-ended question to give the students a chance to reflect on what they can see themselves doing in the future. Through communication with Sjøberg, it was accepted that only some of the sections of the attitude survey could be used as they were developed to stand alone from each other (S. Sjøberg, personal communication, April 10, 2012).

Upon completion of the assessment, the students were given an electronic version of the ROSE questionnaire using SurveyMonkey (an online survey tool) and asked to complete it. The students were brought to the computer lab and given unlimited time to complete the questionnaire. The girls were given instructions, including not to discuss their answers with each other, but there was no adult present in the room to potentially influence their results. Results were compiled and analyzed based on the coding and marking schemes originally developed by the authors. To determine the percentage of positive responses, the total Agree and Strongly Agree responses were added together and a percentage of the total was calculated. The coding question 3 about "If I were a scientist" was coded using the original researchers coding scheme, and percentages of the totals were calculated.

The End-of-the-Year Questionnaire

At the end of the school year, the students were given a final set of reflection questions. They were asked again about their favorite and hardest part of Natural Science as well as the open-ended question from the ROSE questionnaire. The reason to ask these questions again was to determine the long-term effect of the alternative assessment on their attitude toward specific topics or skills in science. The girls hand-wrote these responses. The results were analyzed in the same manner as before.

RESULTS

The results will be presented in the following order:

- Reflections on the alternative assessment
- Results from the ROSE questionnaire
- Results from the open-ended questions regarding the favorite and hardest parts of Natural Science
- Results from the "If I were a scientist" questionnaire

These results from each bullet have been grouped per instrument instead of chronologically, because it made the description of the results easier. In each section, relevant results are given and reported upon, but in certain cases, extra data can be found in the Appendices at the end of the document.

Reflections of Students Regarding the Alternative Assessment

At the end of the first day of the alternative education week in which the students had to complete the quiz, create the survey, and begin collecting data, the students were asked to write a one-page reflection on their experiences. The day also included a different activity linked to Life Orientation (another subject at school). Therefore, the reflections contained information from both activities. Students were able to demonstrate what they had learned from the activities and assessment at this point, described in Figure 6.2. Students showed a positive attitude toward the activities and assessment rather than a negative one. A total of 42% of the comments were classified as "fun, interesting, exciting, enjoyable, or helpful" as compared to 3% being classified as "tedious, uninteresting, not exciting, unenjoyable," found in Figure 6.3.

Student Responses From the ROSE Questionnaire

The ROSE questionnaire used contained four sections of statements to which students responded on a 4-point Likert scale. Question 1 dealt with

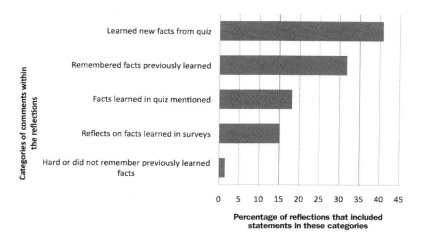

Figure 6.2 Percentage of reflections that included comments about facts from the quiz and survey.

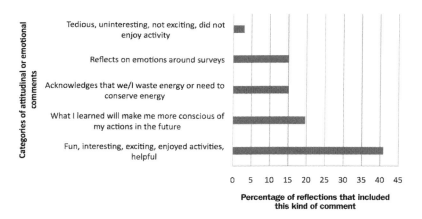

Figure 6.3 Percentage of reflections that included an attitude or emotional comment.

specific details of "My Science Classes" and question 2 dealt with specific details of "My Opinions of Science and Technology." The Likert scale associated with these two questions was a 4-point scale that ranged from Strongly Agree to Strongly Disagree. Results for the survey consisted of adding the two categories of Agree and Strongly Agree to determine the percentage of students who had a positive response to the statement. Certain relevant data are reported here.

With regard to school science, students had an overwhelmingly positive response, finding the subject interesting (92%), important for our way of living (85%), and helpful for their everyday lives (71%). The data suggest that students find this subject linked with the world around them in concrete, obvious ways. Compared to the results from Schreiner & Sjøberg (2010), the students were above the international average in their responses to these statements (pp. 11–14), thus exhibiting a very positive attitude toward their science classes, as indicated in Figure 6.4.

With regard to their future paths in science however, students were not as positive. Only 20% stated that they would like a job as a scientist and 22% stated that they would like a job in technology. Within 1 year, these students would make a choice about their subjects to study at school level, and only 39% stated that they would like to take as much science at school as possible, as reflected in Figure 6.4. This dichotomy is concerning because it means that although they find their science classes interesting, they do not link this interest with something that they would want to pursue in future studies. This was in line with results from Schreiner & Sjøberg with regard to the more developed countries in their survey. This indicates a similar future problem with recruitment into science careers that many developed countries are currently experiencing (Schreiner & Sjøberg, 2010, p. 26).

With regard to their opinions of science and technology, students believed that science and technology are important for society (92%) and that it will give future generations more opportunities (90%), as illustrated in Figure 6.5. There was a general optimism about science and technology, but this was juxtaposed

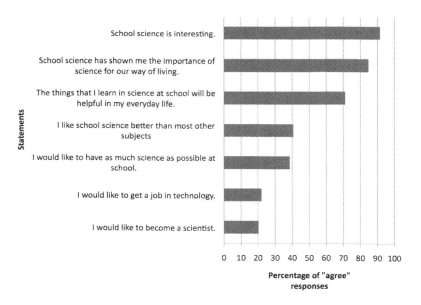

Figure 6.4 Responses to my science classes.

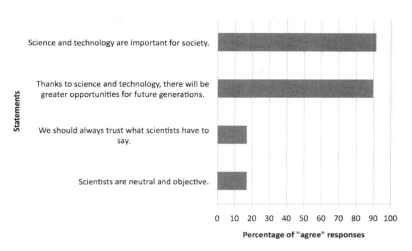

Figure 6.5 Responses to my opinions about science and technology.

against skepticism about the stability and trustworthiness of science and technology. Students believed that scientific theories are developing and changing all the time (88%). When presented with the statements "we should always trust what scientists have to say" and "scientists are neutral and objective," few students agreed (17% each), as noted in Figure 6.5. These results bear an interesting comparison to the results of Schreiner & Sjøberg (2010). In their findings, it was the students of more-developed countries that had a positive attitude but more skepticism than students of less-developed countries (p. 7).

Students' Favorite Part of Natural Science

Beginning-of-the-Year (January) Reflections

In January, the students preferred both skills and topics in Natural Science, as reflected in the data in Figure 6.6. The only skill mentioned was experimentation. In Harwell (2000), in an open-ended interview, grade 7 girls also mentioned experimentation specifically and chose "active learning strategies" as their preferred method of learning science (p. 229). Other than skills and topics, there was a small mention (2%) of the teacher. Schibeci (1982) had previously identified "Science Teacher" as one of the eight stimuli that students would react to when forming an attitude toward science (p. 566). This is why it is interesting that this presented itself as a factor to a very small percentage of students, but it was not an overwhelming factor mentioned. In terms of the topics preferred, there was a preference for Physical Science (31%) over the Biological Sciences (12%). Within the Physical Sciences, there were a variety of topics mentioned, from Astronomy (22% of

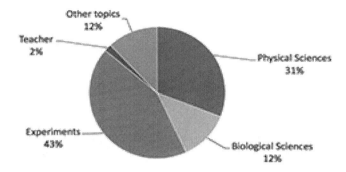

Figure 6.6 Students' favorite parts of Natural Science in January.

Physical Science topics) to General Chemistry (22% of Physical Science topics) and Electricity (11% of Physical Science topics). Within the Biological Science topics, students mentioned Animals, Human Body, Biology, Genetics, and Plants. There were other topics mentioned at this time, such as the range of topics covered and conservation (both classified as Other Topics).

End-of-the-Year (December) Reflections

In December, the students chose more topics than skills in Natural Science (see Figure 6.7). There was a marked increase in the number of Biological Sciences topics that appeared at this point (34%). There was also not a significant change in the number of students who chose a Physical Science topic (29% now as opposed to 31% in January). Topics under Physical Science included Astronomy (32% of Physical Science topics mentioned), Light (32%), Gases (12%), and General Chemistry (8%). Skills and processes were much more varied at this time. Experimentation was listed 50% of the time for skills. Other skills and processes included games for learning and review, projects (including the alternative assessment on sustainable energy and

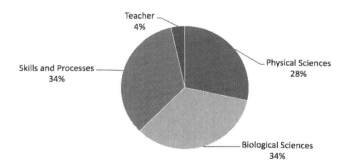

Figure 6.7 Students' favorite parts of Natural Science in December.

renewable resources), how work was approached, the logical order of learning science, and the random conversations that took place between topics.

Changes From January to December
Changes were also noted from January to December. As one can see in Figure 6.8, students had a drastic change in their favorite topic, favoring the Biological Sciences in December.

Students' Hardest Part of Natural Science

Beginning-of-the-Year (January) Reflections
In the beginning of the year, there was a fairly even split between skills and topics that the students found difficult, as reflected in Figure 6.9. There were three major skills and processes that students found extremely challenging: memorizing things, organizational skills, and writing. Other things listed included paying attention, creating and interpreting graphs and diagrams, the mathematical side of science, projects, and tests. The Physical Science topics mentioned were Astronomy, Chemistry, the Periodic Table, and Electricity. The Biological Science topics mentioned were Biology, Body Systems, Classification, Dissecting, and Plants. Other topics mentioned were scientific names and seasons. Two students mentioned that they did not find anything hard about Natural Science thus far.

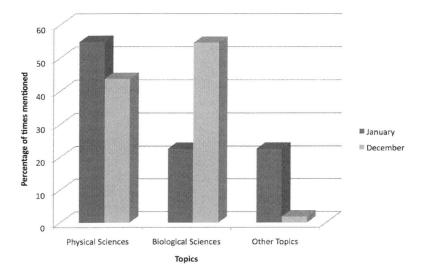

Figure 6.8 Chart showing the changes in favorite topics from January to December.

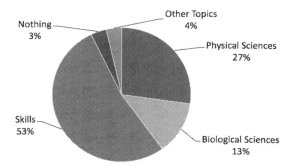

Figure 6.9 Students' hardest parts of Natural Science in January.

End-of-the-Year (December) Reflections

In December, students were more descriptive about what they found challenging in Natural Science, as described in Figure 6.10. In terms of skills and processes, the largest category was Key Issues (a skills-based, month-long unit on environmental problem-solving done at the very beginning of the year). Memorizing things was the second most common thing mentioned. Other skills and processes mentioned were keeping answers concise, creating surveys, creating graphs, the Expo project (a personally designed scientific experiment on any topic), the large amount of work, learning things on their own, the pace of work taught, and tests and examinations.

In terms of the topics that students found hard, there was also an increase in the number of students who found a Biological Science topic challenging (24%, as compared to 13% in January).

Changes from January to December

As one can see in Figure 6.11, the students found Biological Sciences and Physics more challenging as the year progressed, but they found Astronomy and Chemistry less of a challenge. In these results, Physical Science was

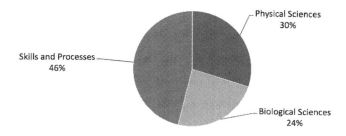

Figure 6.10 Students' hardest parts of Natural Science in December.

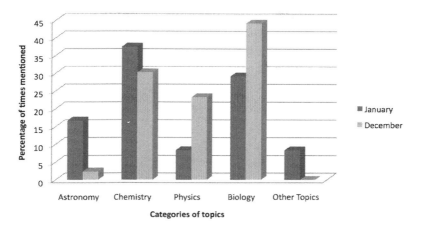

Figure 6.11 Chart showing the changes in topics perceived as hard from January to December.

divided into these three subsubjects because of the significant shift within Astronomy and Physics. However, when combined, there is no noticeable shift in Physical Sciences from January (27%) to December (30%), as illustrated in Figures 6.9 and 6.10.

Responses to "If I Were a Scientist" Open-Ended Question

Midyear (June) Responses

In June, the students preferred to study Biological Sciences over Physical Sciences or other sciences (such as Environmental or Paranormal Science), found in Figure 6.12. Within the Biological Sciences, the most commonly

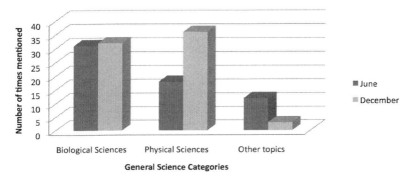

Figure 6.12 Categories of topics chosen to study if they were a scientist.

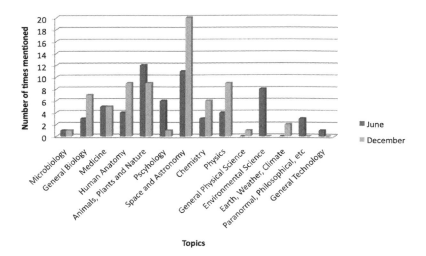

Figure 6.13 Number of times that students chose this topic to study if they were a scientist.

chosen category was "Animals, Plants and Nature," as identified in Figure 6.13. This category included all answers that involved some aspect of this category.

End-of-Year (December) Responses

In December, there was a marked change in the choice of a Physical Science topic to study. The main category mentioned here was "Space and Astronomy," which is illustrated in Figure 6.13. There was also a decrease in topics that were not covered by the Natural Science syllabus. The categories of "Paranormal, Philosophical, etc.," "Environment," and "General Technology" decreased to zero times mentioned.

Changes From June to December

The data in Figure 6.13 reflect the changes in individual categories from June to December. Z-values were determined for the data samples of June and December. There were two significant changes between the samples. The category of "Animals, Plants and Nature" decreased in standard deviations from the mean from 2.02 to 0.71. The category of "Space and Astronomy" increased in standard deviations from the mean from 1.75 to 2.67. No other category changed more than one standard deviation from the mean. This statistically shows a meaningful change in the numbers of times these categories were mentioned in their choices of what science to study, as reflected in Table 6.1.

TABLE 6.1   Z-Values for Two Topics That Significantly Changed in Preference

TOPIC	Number of Times Mentioned in June	Z-Values	Number of Times Mentioned in December	Z-Values
Animals, Plants, and Nature	12	2.02484	9	0.71226
Space and Astronomy	11	1.75991	20	2.67098

Changes From June to December With Regard to "Why" They Would Study This Topic

There was a shift from June to December with regard to the reasons why they would choose specific subjects, as outlined in Figure 6.14. In June, students responded with big-picture, worldview-style answers. For example, one student responded with the following answer: "I want to make the planet greener and enjoy the green planet. Let our chidren's children see what we are seeing today" [*sic*].

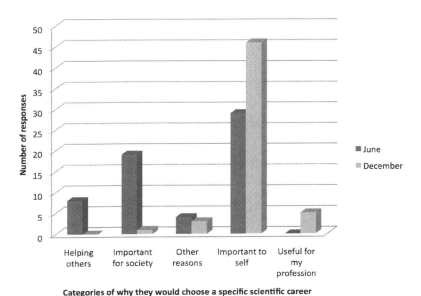

Figure 6.14   Attitude responses to why students would choose a specific scientific career.

In December, student answers were much different, focused more on individual motivation rather than global or future thoughts. Five students were even able to specify that they would study something because it would benefit a specific job (i.e., being an environmental conservationist or a doctor). The length of student answers were also much shorter than in June, most probably because they were using a computer in June and hand-writing answers in December.

CONCLUSION

Students found the alternative assessment enjoyable and felt that they had learned something or refreshed their previous knowledge. Through the ROSE questionnaire, students said that they enjoyed science classes, but few said that they wanted to continue into a job in science or technology. Students also indicated a dichotomy in their attitudes toward science and technology, revealing that although they found it important, they were wary about the trustworthiness of science and scientists. Students showed a change in their favorite subjects from January to December, showing an increase in the Biological Sciences. This same change was also seen in the comparison from January to December with regard to the hardest part of Natural Science. Students showed a significant change in the career aspirations from June to December, the largest changes being between the Animal, Plants, and Nature and Astronomy categories. Their rationale behind these career aspirations also changed from June to December from helping people or finding the topic important to society to wanting to study a subject because of personal reasons (interest or career).

DISCUSSION

The hypothesis stated that with the presence of an alternative assessment within a curricular year, students would show a positive attitude toward the subject matter by choosing to continue studying it past high school in a theoretical context as well as an overall positive attitude toward science. While the results were reported on in groups according to the instrument, this analysis will be cross-instrumental and cover three of the intersections from the original conceptual framework, as seen in Figure 6.15. This discussion will examine the following relationships, found in Figure 6.15. The intersection of "Alternative Assessments" and "How girls learn best" will be discussed first. The intersection of "Alternative Assessments" and "Attitudes toward science and school science" will be discussed second. Finally, the overall relationship between the three variables will be discussed

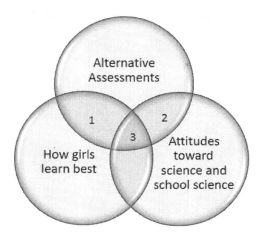

Figure 6.15 Analysis of the intersection of alternative assessments, learning styles of girls, and attitudes toward science.

third. The final intersection of "How girls learn best" and "Attitudes toward science and school science" will not be discussed, as the tools used did not aim to collect or report on this relationship.

REFLECTION ON ALTERNATIVE ASSESSMENTS

The assessment was developed in line with the criteria given in the introduction by Herman et al. (1992) (as cited in Corcoran et al., 2004). The assessment was then moderated by peers and found to be alternative based on the five criteria outlined. When the students were given the assessment, they reflected that the assessment was fun, enjoyable and interesting, indicating a very positive attitude toward the assessment. This is in line with international studies that have identified positive student responses to alternative assessments (Couling, 2011; Janich et al., 2007; Kirikkaya & Vurkaya, 2011). As stated previously by Gurian & Stevens (2004), "children will naturally gravitate toward activities that their brains experience as pleasurable" (p. 22). A positive attitude toward the assessment would indicate that this assessment was in line with how these girls enjoy learning.

Reflection on the Relationship Between Alternative Assessments and Attitudes Toward Science and School Science

After the alternative assessment was completed, students completed the ROSE questionnaire, which highlighted their attitudes toward science and school science. The responses to the statements under the question of "My Opinions about Science and Technology" reveal their attitudes toward science. When reviewing the results in Figure 6.5, there seems to be a dichotomy within their answers. They showed a positive response to the statements, which indicated the importance of science, such as "Science and technology are important for society." But they also showed a low agreement with statements about the trustworthiness of science and scientists, such as "The benefits of science are greater than the harmful effects that it could have" and "Scientists are neutral and objective." This dichotomy does not reveal a negative attitude toward science but rather highlights the critical thinking and evaluation skills that the alternative assessment purports to teach. It stands to reason that if students are taught to critically evaluate information, then they would not agree with these last two statements. Therefore, there is a possible positive effect of the alternative assessment on their attitudes toward science, however without a pretest to which to compare these results, it not possible to positively link these two concepts.

The responses to the statements under the question of "My Science Classes" highlighted the students' attitudes toward school science. Students found their classes interesting and important, which was very much above average for the international survey. But when compared to other subjects, students exhibited average responses (41% said that they like science better than most other subjects). This was followed by a low desire to remain in science subjects and even lower desire to continue into science or technology as a career path. The results of this questionnaire highlight that while students found their science classes interesting, it was not enough motivation for students to think about remaining in science subjects or picture themselves in these career paths. These results are in line with the findings of Bennett et al. (2006). Their meta-analysis concluded that while similar assessments and approaches improved attitudes toward school science, there was little conclusive evidence that these positive attitudes would translate into further study or career paths in science. This is also in line with the findings of Shamai (1996), who tracked students from grade 6 to grade 11 to determine if there was a relationship between their attitudes in grade 6 and their course of study in grade 11. Regardless of gender, there was no significant relationship between a student portraying a positive attitude toward science in grade 6 and choosing to study science in grade 11.

Reflection on the Intersection of Alternative Assessments, Learning Styles, and Attitudes Toward Science and School Science

It was proposed that if girls were presented with an opportunity for learning that was developed in line with how they learn best (i.e., the alternative assessment), then they would exhibit positive attitudes toward the subject matter by choosing to continue studying it past high school in a theoretical context as well as an overall positive attitude toward science. When reviewing the data collected from the January, June, and December open-ended questions, two points of analysis emerge: there is a difference between the attitudes of these students toward specific science subjects compared with international norms, and there does not seem to be a long-term effect of alternative assessments toward students' attitudes toward science.

Discussion of Attitudes Toward School Science

To discuss the positive attitudes of the students toward specific school science topics, it is important to compare these students with international literature. Gender and attitudes toward specific subjects in science have been positively correlated (Baram-Tsabari & Yarden, 2011; Britner, 2008; Osborne et al., 2003; Schreiner & Sjøberg, 2010). In most studies, girls have a more positive attitude toward Biological Sciences (Biology, Ecology, and Health) than Physical Sciences (Chemistry and Physics) (Baram-Tsabari & Yarden, 2011; Reigle-Crumb, Moore, & Ramos-Wada, 2011). In this grade 8 class, there was a very different profile throughout the year. In January, girls exhibited a more positive attitude toward the Physical Sciences than Biological Sciences by choosing these topics more often in the initial questionnaire. This was upheld in the June questionnaire as the majority of the topics chosen to study were categorized as Physical Sciences. In December, however, there was a shift from Physical Sciences to Biological Sciences in terms of the students' favorite parts of Natural Science, but when the topics chosen for future study were analyzed, students still preferred Physical Science topics. This cohort of students therefore, goes against the internationally recognized perception that girls prefer the Biological Sciences.

This difference from international norms is interesting because these students come from a number of different primary schools, so the education within the Preparatory School of this school cannot be held solely accountable for the results. However, most of the students within this grade 8 class have a background in a single-sex school. Carter (2005) found that more girls in single-sex schools were choosing to take sciences in the grades 10 to 12 phase in her study of South African schools. An avenue for further research would be to follow these students through high school and monitor their subject choices and attitudes throughout the next 4 years to see if there are changes and investigate possible causes of these changes.

Discussion of the Effect of the Alternative Assessment on Attitudes Toward Science

To determine the effect of the alternative assessment on attitudes toward science, one must compare the results across all the open-ended questionnaires throughout the year. In January, 9% of the students mentioned that Energy was their favorite topic in Natural Science. In June, 6% of the students chose to study sustainable energy or renewable resources if they were a scientist. These terms are important as they are in line with the topic of the alternative assessment and show they have internalized what they learned from the assessment. However, in December, no students mentioned either energy, sustainable energy or renewable resources as a favorite topic or a topic they would study as a scientist. Two students (2.3%) mentioned the movie aspect of the alternative assessment as their favorite part of Natural Science, but this could have been because they enjoyed this form of assessment rather than the topic.

If Mager's (1968) concept of positive attitudes as "moving towards" responses is applied here, then there was no long-term effect of the alternative assessment on the students' attitudes toward science. Bennett et al. (2006) stated that "subject choices ... and/or career aspirations are important indicators of attitude toward the subject" (p. 363), and it is clear that there was a change in their career choices over the course of the year, indicating a change in their attitude toward science. This does not reflect a negative attitude now, but it does mean that their positive attitude toward Energy was replaced by a more positive attitude toward a different topic.

This change in positive attitudes could have been because of an internal shift within the students. When the rationale behind their answers is analyzed, one can see a shift from external rationale in June to an internal rationale in December with regard to their career choices if they were scientists. This shift indicates that students are choosing a career now based on interest rather than its importance to society or other people. Five students went as far as to say that they would choose to study a subject because it is in line with their actual career goals (i.e., they want to become a doctor or environmental conservationist). This shift could indicate that although students may still think that studying sustainable energy and renewable resources is important, it is not something that they find interesting enough to study themselves.

Smith and Matthews (2000) also found a shift in the rationale behind the subject choices of 15-year-old students in Ireland. After a science, technology, and society (STS) approach in the classroom, more students were choosing science subjects because they were interested in the subject matter. This could be because STS and other alternative approaches allow for open-ended research, discussion, and assessments, which allow for creativity and freedom of expression. This allows students to critically explore and develop their own interests and therefore understand the rationale behind their choices. This internal shift is important, as it highlights the time that students are beginning to understand and value the choices about their future, which means that a study of career options and career guidance could be more effective at this stage rather than later on in high school when most career guidance takes place (mainly grades 9 and 12).

The change in their positive attitudes could have also been because of a limitation of the study. The open-ended questionnaires were designed to have little or no input from the teacher as to the words or topics that students may use, thus validating their answers as authentic. However, it has been noted that students may have struggled to remember the entire year's work in such a short amount of time without prompting. This may have led students to choose topics or skills that were in the second half of the year, especially since they had just completed an examination on this material and these topics and skills were fresh in their minds.

Overall, there were no long-term effects of alternative assessment on attitudes toward science based on the results from this study. Evidence exists that students exhibit a positive attitude toward science from the ROSE questionnaire results and that the skills honed by the alternative assessment may give rise to the positive attitude toward science. However, when looking at the subject choices over the year as an indicator for positive attitudes toward science, there is no obvious relationship between the alternative assessment and attitudes toward science.

Limitations of the Study

Sample Population
The limitations of this study are that the student population represents a small microcosm of South African society, and therefore extrapolation to the larger South African population of high school students is very limited. Correlations may be seen with similar schools in similar urban settings, but a larger sample size from varied urban environments would be needed before reliable comparisons could be made.

Methodology
To improve the results, a ROSE questionnaire could have been completed before the alternative assessment took place. This would have enabled another layer of comparison and analysis of their attitudes toward science based on the alternative assessment.

With regard to the open-ended questionnaire in December, the students may have struggled to remember the entire year's work on their own. Therefore, it may have altered the results if a list of topics and skills was provided for them so that they could choose their favorite and hardest parts of Natural Science. Also, the format of the January and December questionnaires was written, and this may have discouraged some students from embellishing their reasons behind their choices, especially in December after examinations, when students are less likely to write prolifically. To improve this, using a computerized version of the questionnaire (such as via SurveyMonkey) may have encouraged them to be more descriptive in their answers.

CONCLUSION

To conclude, an investigation into the effect of alternative assessment in Natural Science on attitudes toward science in grade 8 girls was completed over one school year. Data was collected via open and closed questionnaires at three points in the year. Through an analysis of this data, three conclusions can be drawn. First, the students showed a positive attitude toward the alternative assessment. Second, students showed a positive attitude toward school science, but this positive attitude did not directly indicate a desire to continue in the fields of science or technology. Third, by analyzing their subject choices over the course of the year, there is no long-term effect of the alternative assessment on their attitudes toward science.

REFERENCES

Acker, S., & Oatley, K. (1993). Gender issues in education for science and technology: Current situation and prospects for change. *Canadian Journal of Education, 18*(3), 255–272.

Archer, L., Dewitt, J., Osborne, J., Dillon, J., Willis, B., & Wong, B. (2010). "Doing" science versus "being" a scientist: Examining 10/11-year-old schoolchildrens' constructions of science through the lens of identity. *Science Education, 94,* 617–639.

Aschbacher, P., Li, E., & Roth, E. (2010). Is science me? High school students' identities, participation, and aspirations in science, engineering and medicine. *Journal of Research in Science Teaching, 47*(5), 564–582.

Baram-Tsabari, A., & Yarden, A. (2011, June). Quantifying the gender gap in science interests. *International Journal of Science and Mathematics Education, 9*(3), 523–550.

Bauer, C. (2002). What students think. *The Science Teacher, 69*(1), 52–55.

Bennett, J., Lubben, F., & Hogarth, S. (2006). Bringing science to life: A synthesis of the research evidence on the effects of context-based and STS approaches to science teaching. *Science Education, 91,* 347–370.

Bonomo, V. (2010). Gender matters in elementary education: Research-based strategies to meet the distinctive learning needs of boys and girls. *Educational Horizons, 88*(2), 257–264.

Britner, S. (2008). Motivation in high school science students: A comparison of gender differences in life, physical, and earth science classes. *Journal of Research in Science Teaching, 45*(8), 995–970.

Brotman, J., & Moore, F. (2008). Girls and science: A review of four themes in science education literature. *Journal of Research in Science Teaching, 45*(9), 971–1002.

Carlone, H. (2003). Innovative science within and against a culture of "achievement." *Science Education, 87*(3), 307–328.

Carlone, H. (2004). The cultural production of science in reform-based physics: Girls' access, participation, and resistance. *Journal of Research in Science Teaching, 41*(4), 392–414.

Carter, T. A. (2005). *The effect of single-sex schooling on girls' achievement in physical science*. Unpublished manuscript, University of South Africa Pretoria, South Africa.

Century, D. (2002). *Alternative and traditional assessments: Their comparative impact on students' attitudes and science learning outcomes: An exploratory study*. (Unpublished dissertation). Temple University, Philadelphia, PA.

Cherian, L., & Shumba, A. (2011). Sex differences in attitudes toward science among northern Sotho speaking learners in South Africa. *Africa Education Review, 8*(2), 286–301.

Chilisa, B. (2000). Towards equity in assessment: Crafting gender-fair assessment. *Assessment in Education, 7*(1), 61–81.

Corcoran, C., Dershimer, E., & Tichenor, M. (2004). A teacher's guide to alternative assessment: Taking the first steps. *The Clearing House, 77*(5), 213–216.

Couling, J. (2011). "I can do chemistry": A move towards alternative assessment in high school chemistry. Unpublished MA, Pepperdine University, Malibu, CA.

Council for Higher Education (2009). Higher education monitor 7: Postgraduate studies in South Africa—A statistical profile. Retrieved November 3, 2013, from HYPERLINK "redir.aspx?C=JDEGt8kBpEmzbRqSk3N_sl6IqlW-Pr9AIU520GFZGKpthDIIAVc0mZITl3S–uUm69CzEMR7JLOQ.&URL=htt p%3a%2f%2fwww.che.ac.za%2fmedia_and_publications%2fhigher-educa-tion-monitor%2fhigher-education-monitor-7-postgraduate-studies"http:// www.che.ac.za/media_and_publications/higher-education-monitor/ higher-education-monitor-7-postgraduate-studies

Creswell, J. (2009). Research design: Qualitative, quantitative, and mixed methods approaches (3rd ed.). Thousand Oaks, CA: Sage.

Dooley, K. (1999). Towards a holistic model for the diffusion of educational technologies: An integrative review of educational innovative studies. *Educational Technology & Society, 2*(4), 35–45.

Eagly, A. H., & Chaiken, S. (1993). *The psychology of attitudes*. Orlando, FL: Harcourt Brace Jovanovich College.

Ellis, C., & Adams, W. (2009). *Towards a 10-year review of the population policy implementation in South Africa (1998–2008): Families, households and children*. South Africa: Department of Social Development.

Farenga, S., & Joyce, B. (1999). Intentions of young students to enroll in science courses in the future: An examination of gender differences. *Science Education, 83*(1), 55–75.

Friedman, C., de Bliek, R., Greer, D., Mennin, S., Norman, G., Sheps, C. . . . Woodward, C. (1990). Charting the winds of change: Evaluating innovative medical curricula. *Academic Medicine, 65*(1), 8–14.

George, R. (2006). A cross-domain analysis of change in students' attitudes toward science and attitudes about the utility of science. *International Journal of Science Education, 28*(6), 571–589.

Gurian, M., & Stevens, K. (2004). With boys and girls in mind. *Educational Leadership, 62*(3), 21–26.

Hannan, A., English, S., & Silver, H. (1999). Why innovate? Some preliminary findings from a research project on "innovations in teaching and learning in higher education." *Studies in Higher Education, 24*(3), 279–289.

Harwell, S. (2000). In their own voices: Middle level girls' perceptions of teaching and learning science. *Journal of Science Teacher Education, 11*(3), 221–242.

Herman, J. L., Aschbacher, P. R., & Winters, L. (1992). A practical guide to alternative assessment. Alexandra, VA: Association for Supervision and Curriculum Development. Retrieved from http://www.cse.ucla.edu/products/guidebooks/APractical.pdf

Holmgren, J., & Basch, L. (2005). *Encouragement, not gender, key to success in science.* Stanford, CA: Carnegie Foundation for the Advancement of Teaching.

Honigsfeld, A., & Dunn, R. (2003). High school male and female learning-style similarities and differences in diverse nations. *The Journal of Educational Research, 96*(4), 195–206.

Janich, C., Liu, X., & Akrofi, A. (2007). Implementing alternative assessment: Opportunities and obstacles. *The Educational Forum, 71*(3), 221–230.

Jesse, J. (2006). Redesigning science: Recent scholarship on cultural change, gender, and diversity. *Bioscience, 56*(10), 831–838.

Khalili, K. (1987). A crosscultural validation of a test of science-related attitudes. *Journal of Research in Science Teaching, 24*(2), 127–136.

Kinyondo, G., & Mabugu, M. (2009). The general equilibrium effects of a productivity increase on the economy and gender in South Africa. *South African Journal of Economic and Management Science, 12*(3), 307–326.

Kirikkaya, B., & Vurkaya, G. (2011). The effect of using alternative assessment activities on students' success and attitudes in science and technology course. *Educational Science: Theory & Practice, 11*(2), 997–1004.

Kolsto, S. D. (2000). Scientific literacy for citizenship: Tools for dealing with the science dimension of controversial socioscientific issues. *Science Education, 85,* 291–310.

Lawrenz, F., Huffman, D., & Welch, W. (2001). The science achievement of various subgroups on alternative assessment formats. *Science Education, 85,* 279–290.

Lopez-Claros, A., & Zahidi, S. (2005, December). *Women's empowerment: Measuring the global gender gap.* Cologny/Geneva, Switzerland: World Economic Forum.

Lyons, T., & Quinn, F. (2010). Choosing science. Understanding the declines in senior high school science enrollments. Armidale, NSW, Australia: University of New England.

Mager, R. F. (1968). *Developing attitude toward learning.* Palo Alto, CA: Fearon.

Molebatsi, K. (2009). *Towards a 10-year review of the population policy implementation in South Africa (1998–2008): Gender equality and equity.* South Africa: Department of Social Development.

Montessori, M. (1912). *The Montessori method* (A. E. George, Trans., 2nd ed.). New York, NY: Frederick A. Stokes.

Morrell, P. D., & Lederman, N. G. (1998). Students' attitudes toward school and classroom science: Are they independent phenomena? *School Science and Mathematics, 98*(2), 76–83.

Morrell, R. (2000). Considering the case for single-sex schools for girls in South Africa. *McGill Journal of Education, 35*(3), 221–244.

Nagaraja, M. (2012). NASA G.I.R.L.S. *Women @ NASA.* Retrieved from http://women.nasa.gov/nasagirls/

Nasr, A. R., & Soltani, K. A. (2011). Attitude towards biology and its effects on student's achievement. *International Journal of Biology, 3*(4), 100–104.

National Science Board (NSB). (2010). *Preparing the next generation of STEM innovators: Identifying and developing our nation's human capital.* Arlington, VA: National Science Foundation.

Office of Science and Technology Policy. (2011, November 30). Retrieved from http://www.whitehouse.gov/administration/eop/ostp/library/docsreports

Osborne, J., Simon, S., & Collins, S. (2003). Attitudes towards science: A review of the literature and its implications. *International Journal of Science Education, 25*(9), 1049–1079.

Ouyang, Y., & Hayden, K. (2010). A technology infused science summer camp to prepare student leaders in 8th grade classrooms. *Proceedings of the 41st ACM Technical Symposium on Computer Science Education,* pp. 229–233.

Owen, S., Toepperwein, M., Marshall, C., Lichtenstein, M. J., Blalock, C., Liu, Y. . . . Grimes, K. (2008). Finding pearls: Psychometric re-evaluation of the Simpson–Troost attitude questionnaire (STAQ). *Science Education, 92*(6), 1076–1095.

Palys, T. (2008). Purposive sampling. In L. M. Given (Ed.), *The Sage encyclopaedia of qualitative research methods* (pp. 697–698). Thousand Oaks, CA: Sage.

Partnership for 21st Century Skills. (2012). *Partnership for 21st century skills: Overview.* Retrieved April 21, 2012, from www.p21.org

Reigle-Crumb, C., Moore, C., & Ramos-Wada, A. (2011). Who wants to have a career in science or math? Exploring adolescents' future aspirations by gender and race/ethnicity. *Science Education, 95*(3), 458–476.

Scantelbury, K., & Baker, D. (2007). Gender issues in science education research: Remembering where the difference lies. In S. K. Abell & N. Lederman (Eds.), *Handbook of research on science education* (pp. 257–285). Mahwah, NJ: Lawrence Erlbaum.

Schibeci, R. A. (1982). Measuring student attitudes: Sematic differential or Likert instruments? *Science Education, 66*(4), 565–570.

Schreiner, C., & Sjøberg, S. (2004). *Sowing the seeds of ROSE. Background, rationale, questionnaire development and data collection for ROSE (the relevance of science education)—A comparative study of students' views of science and science education.* (No. Acta Didactica 4/2004). Oslo, Norway: Department of Teacher Education and School Development, University of Oslo.

Schreiner, C., & Sjøberg, S. (2010). *The ROSE project: An overview and key findings.* Oslo, Norway: University of Oslo.

SEDL. (2012). *Comparing traditional and performance-based assessment.* Retrieved October 20, 2012, from http://www.sedl.org/loteced/comparing_assessment.html

Shamai, S. (1996). Elementary school students' attitudes toward science and their course of studies in high school. *Adolescence, 31*(123), 677–689.

Singh, P. (2002). Pedagogising knowledge: Bernstein's theory of the pedagogic device. *British Journal of Sociology of Education, 23*(4), 571–582.

Smith, G., & Matthews, P. (2000). Science, technology and society in transition year: A pilot study. *Irish Educational Studies, 19*(1), 107–119.

Sorge, C. (2007). What happens? Relationship of age and gender with science attitudes from elementary to middle school. *Science Educator, 16*(2), 33–37.

South African Government Information. (2011). *State of the nation address by his Excellency Jacob G Zuma, President of the Republic of South Africa, at the joint sitting of parliament, Cape Town.* Retrieved from http://www.info.gov.za/speech/DynamicAction?pageid=461&sid=16154&tid=27985

South African Government Information. (2012). *State of the nation address by his Excellency Jacob G Zuma, President of the Republic of South Africa on the occasion of the joint sitting of parliament, Cape Town.* Retrieved from http://www.info.gov.za/speech/DynamicAction?pageid=461&sid=24980&tid=55960

Stadler, H., Duit, R., & Benke, G. (2000). Do boys and girls understand physics differently? *Physics Education, 35*(6), 417–422.

State of New Jersey. (2010). *Rethinking assessment.* Retrieved October 20, 2012, from http://www.state.nj.us/education/frameworks/worldlanguages/chap6.pdf

Thom, M. (2001). Young women's progress in science and technology studies: Overcoming remaining barriers. *NASSP Bulletin, 85*(628), 6–19.

Tuckman, B. W. (1994). *Conducting educational research* (4th ed.). Orlando, FL: Harcourt Brace College.

Waters, F., Smeaton, P., & Burns, T. (2004). Action research in the secondary science classroom: Student response to differentiated, alternative assessment. *American Secondary Education, 32*(3), 89–104.

Weinburgh, M. (1995). Gender differences in student attitudes towards science: A meta-analysis of the literature from 1970–1991. *Journal of Research in Science Teaching, 32*(4), 387–398.

Welch, A. G. (2010). Using the TOSRA to assess high school students' attitudes toward science after competing in the FIRST robotics competition: An exploratory study. *Eurasia Journal of Mathematics, Science & Technology Education, 6*(3), 187–197.

Wilkes, M., & Bligh, J. (1999). Evaluating educational interventions. *British Medical Journal, 318*(7193), 1269–1272.

CHAPTER 7

THE ROLE OF OUT-OF-SCHOOL TIME IN ENCOURAGING GIRLS IN STEM

Merle Froschl
Barbara Sprung

INTRODUCTION

Despite significant advances in recent years, girls and young women continue to be underrepresented in STEM degrees and careers (NSF, 2011). According to the U.S. Department of Commerce, women comprise 48% of the U.S. workforce, but are just 28% of STEM workers (Beede et al., 2011). As a result, women are missing opportunities to participate in the nation's most highly paid and fastest growing occupations. By 2018, upwards of 63% of all jobs will require skills in STEM (U.S. Congress Joint Economic Committee, 2012).

There are a number of reasons why girls and women do not persist in the STEM pipeline, including lack of early preparation and insufficient course preparation in high school, lack of parental support, and lack of role models and mentors (Sax, 2001). In addition, stereotypes about "appropriate" roles for women still play a large part in lowering girls' aspiration for science and engineering careers (AAUW, 2010).

Girls and Women in STEM, pages 139–152
Copyright © 2014 by Information Age Publishing
All rights of reproduction in any form reserved.

Out-of-School Time (OST) programs (afterschool, Saturdays, and during the summer) offer unique opportunities to address these issues and help increase girls' interest and participation in STEM. Research has shown that effective OST programs can promote girls' achievement in STEM through fostering engagement and self-identity and creating a greater confidence in science ability (Afterschool Alliance, 2011; Calabrese Barton, Tan, & Rivet, 2008). They increase STEM knowledge and skills, further persistence in the STEM pipeline, increase interest in and improve attitudes toward STEM careers, change course-taking behavior, and change perceptions of who can do science (Clewell & Darke, 2000; Afterschool Alliance, 2011). In addition, OST programs provide an opportunity to reach girls and other groups currently underrepresented in STEM in large numbers since afterschool programs serve low-income and minority children at a greater rate than the general population (Afterschool Alliance, 2009; California Tomorrow, 2003).

Over the past 15 years, there has been a dramatic expansion in the range of engaging learning opportunities through high quality afterschool and summer learning programs (Peterson, 2013). There is now a sizeable infrastructure of programming and support (e.g., the U.S. Department of Education's 21st Century Community Learning Centers initiative) focused especially on serving young people from groups typically underrepresented in STEM fields (Krishnamurthi, Ottinger, & Topol, 2013). This chapter addresses the role that OST can play in facilitating girls' success and draws upon firsthand examples from successful programs such as Great Science for Girls, a national project that built the capacity of OST programs to provide gender-equitable STEM; and the Science Mentoring Project, a program in New York City that provided girls with authentic science experiences.

WHY OST PROGRAMS ARE IDEAL SETTINGS

The three primary characteristics that support girls' STEM participation are engagement, capacity, and continuity (Jolly, Campbell, & Perlman, 2004). Girls must be engaged, that is, have the awareness, interest, and motivation toward science. They also must have the capacity in terms of knowledge and skills needed to advance in STEM disciplines. The third factor, continuity, means that girls must have the opportunities and resources to support their advancement. All three factors need to be present to produce success in STEM coursework and careers.

OST can play a critical role in providing girls with these critical factors of engagement, capacity, and continuity. Without the constraints of in-school mandates, OST programs can provide the time needed for exploration and engagement—the place that girls can be encouraged to explore without fear of giving a wrong answer, to take the risks that lead to scientific discovery. They can expose girls to a wide variety of careers and to dispel stereotypical notions of who does science and to become connected to role models and mentors who look like them and have already chosen a STEM path. For example, many hands-on science and technology centers train diverse youth as "explainers" (also called "helpers" or "docents") who guide students through museum exhibits. These young museum staff members become "real life" examples that a future in STEM does not belong to the stereotype of an elderly White male with wild hair, a lab coat, and a pocket protector full of pens, ala Albert Einstein. Also, OST programs are typically staffed by young people who reflect the diverse profile of the students they serve. When they have been trained to facilitate STEM curricula, OST staff can become another source of inspiration as role models and mentors— they are interested in youth development, they are in college, they are competent in STEM. Being in frequent contact with young female adults whom they can emulate gives a tacit message to girls that "I can do it too."

Further, the experiential, hands-on nature of the learning provides experiences that help girls make a personal connection to science (AAUW, 2004; Freidman & Quinn, 2006; Froschl, Sprung, Archer, & Fancsali, 2003). The close ties between staff and young people that are integral to OST programs and the focus on the "youth voice" make this environment particularly conducive to inquiry learning experiences (Froschl et al., 2003; Walker, Wahl, & Rivas, 2005). STEM is put in a different context; one that offers social and psychological supports that help overcome obstacles to participation in STEM careers (Walker et al., 2005).

OST programs also provide opportunities for families to be involved in their children's learning in informal unschool-like settings that some parents find less threatening. Parents who are involved in OST programs report greater appreciation of their children's talents and increased attention to their schooling (Horowitz & Bronte-Tinkew, 2007). This is important to encouraging girls' interest in STEM, since research has shown that parents play an important role in their children's later involvement in STEM activities (Goldman & Booker, 2009), and that fathers in particular have a major impact on the degree of interest their daughters develop in STEM (University of Michigan, 2007).

Fostering Engagement, Identity, and Confidence

OST programs can improve attitudes, enthusiasm, and self-identity as potential math or science professionals (Afterschool Alliance, 2011; Calabrese Barton et al., 2008). This is particularly important for girls since one of the most critical barriers to girls' persistence in STEM is work/life balance (Sax, 2001). Gender identity and STEM identity do not come together for many girls, and researchers have begun to explore how to address identity as a critical pathway to the STEM pipeline for girls. The importance of starting to create a STEM identity early is borne out by research conducted at the University of California, which indicates that students who start college with a strong STEM identity are more likely to have STEM identities in the future (Eagan, Sharkness, & Hurtado, 2010).

A number of researchers are exploring issues of gender and science learning, conducting research that focuses on urban girls in high poverty areas. In a series of case studies, Tan and Calabrese Barton (2007) documented that girls, especially minority girls, need to create "identity in practice" in science classes by combining knowledge from their in-school and out-of-school worlds. The ability to see oneself as a "master practitioner" is formed through a classroom community of practice created by a teacher who provides space for students to bring knowledge from their social worlds to their study of science (Calabrese Barton et al., 2008; Tan & Calabrese Barton, 2007). The small group and project-based work that is the hallmark of OST programs can help girls develop STEM identities by providing opportunities to showcase unique skills.

Identity leads to engagement (Tan & Calabrese Barton, 2007) and, as discussed earlier, engagement is a critical element in keeping girls in the STEM pipeline. Robert Tai, a researcher at the University of Virginia, also views engagement as the first rung of a ladder leading to a STEM career. His research demonstrates that students who express early interest in STEM and an expectation of following a STEM career have a higher rate of follow-through than students who score higher on mathematics but do not express interest in a STEM career (Tai, Qi Liu, Maltese, & Fan, 2006). Combining knowledge from in-school and out-of-school experiences can help girls create "identity in practice" (Tan & Calabrese Barton, 2010).

Turning Research Into Practice

The research clearly points to what works for girls: collaborative learning with an emphasis on practical applications and teaching of science in a more holistic and social context (Campbell, Holly, Hoey, & Perlman, 2002; Koch, 2002; Wenglinsky, 2000) and the combining of hands-on activities, role models, mentoring, internships, and career exploration (Campbell & Steinbrueck, 1996; Ferreira, 2001). The challenge is to turn research into practice by developing gender-equitable STEM programming that will broaden and sustain girls' interest in STEM. OST presents just such an opportunity.

In 2003, Educational Equity Concepts (EEC), the Academy for Educational Development (AED), and the American Association for the

Advancement of Science (AAAS) hosted a conference on Science, Gender, and Afterschool to develop a research-action agenda to enhance the role of afterschool education in increasing girls' participation in STEM courses, majors, and careers. The resulting agenda focused on three areas: (a) access, recruitment, and persistence; (b) program content, approaches, and strategies; and (c) staff and professional development. Since that time, EEC (now Educational Equity at FHI 360) has been engaged in projects that address this agenda.[1] Two such projects that illustrate the agenda—the Science Mentoring Project and Great Science for Girls—are described below.

The Science Mentoring Project[2]

During spring 2003 and 2004, EEC developed an informal science education model in collaboration with the River Project, a Hudson River marine biology field station located on Pier 26 in New York City, and the Henry Street Settlement afterschool program, located at PS 20 on the Lower East Side of Manhattan. The population of the school was low-income children, 99% were eligible for free lunch, and 10% came from recently immigrated families whose first language was not English. Most of the children were Latino/a and African American, with a small number of Pacific Islanders; 51% of the children met the standards for English Language Arts, and 65% met the standards for math. The school was a caring place with a dynamic principal and a dedicated teaching staff.

In their afterschool program facilitated by a teacher from the day program, 5th-grade students were engaged in a series of hands-on, inquiry-based activities from EEC's After-School Science PLUS curriculum (AS+), which was designed to develop higher-order thinking skills such as decision-making, problem-solving, and creative thinking. In addition to hands-on experiences, AS+ students learned about diverse scientists and options for science careers. For the field experience, 5th-grade students from PS 20 were paired with high school student mentors who were recruited by the River Project. The River Project provided training to the mentors on the skills they would need to conduct their experiments with the afterschool students, and EEC provided training in equity issues and mentoring techniques. The 5th-grade students used the skills they'd learned—observation, data recording, and model-making—to serve as junior research assistants to their mentors, taking part in actual research projects such as tracking and mapping the movement of water, restoring oyster beds in the Hudson River, evaluating the relative importance of environmental pollutants on fish, studying the effect of invasive crab species, and collecting data on plankton ecology.

Students participated in six, 2-hour weekly sessions at the River Project's Marine Biology site at Pier 26 on the Hudson River. Topics covered during the 6 weeks included water quality (students tested air and water temperature, salinity, dissolved oxygen and PH), oyster restoration, plankton ecology, and fish ecology. Students worked in small groups with their mentors, making observations; recording, graphing, and plotting data; and presenting their data to peers and mentors. Back at their school, they presented their data boards at a school fair. The 5th-graders were the "experts," sharing knowledge gained by their participation in the River Project with teachers, administrators, and parents.

A number of gender-equity issues were observed during the first year of the project. For example, there was a difference in the way the 5th-grade boys and girls interacted with the mentors. Boys were more often encouraged to do hands-on activities than their female counterparts, volunteered more frequently, and were called upon first. While they also sat mostly in the back, boys moved to the front to view certain procedures when it was to their advantage. Female mentors offered to handle the fish for girls during messy procedures, although they did not do so for the boys, and male mentors often handed the data sheets over to female mentors so that they could do the recording. Observing this behavior, EEC staff arranged a special training session on gender awareness for mentors. As a result, by the end of the program, the girls began to assert themselves more, mentors were more aware of their own behavior in terms of male/female stereotypes, and mentors were appropriately intervening to ensure a more equitable environment for boys and girls.

Based on the lessons learned, in the second year, more of the mentor training was dedicated to equity issues with a focus on gender equity. Activities helped to create an awareness of the issues, equity issues from last year were discussed, and mentors developed proactive strategies to address the issues. As a result, the mentors appeared to be much more aware of gender stereotyping issues. For example,

- Mentors were careful to ensure that students all had an opportunity to do the hands-on work each week. When one of the 5th-grade girls was reluctant to check traps in the river because the rope was slimy, her mentor (a male) encouraged her to participate in several ways, including recruiting a female mentor to demonstrate the process. When even this was unsuccessful, he brought a pair of rubber gloves for the following week, and she then checked the traps.
- Each week, groups tended to sit in the same seats. When the visiting researcher did the plankton study and video microscopy, there was an advantage to sitting in the front. The boys immediately took these seats (this was an identical behavior to the group in the first year). The mentors were quick to point out the unfair advantage of switching seats at this point and asked the students to take their usual seats.

Throughout the 2-year duration of the Science Mentoring Project, the mentors were extraordinarily conscious of their responsibility to the younger students. They were careful to explain instructions, review the science, encourage students during activities, and urged them to continue science in school and afterschool.

In summary, the Science Mentoring Project fulfilled the goals for successful and gender-equitable STEM based on the literature and set out by the Science, Gender, and Afterschool Research Action Agenda. The project

- Provided hands-on, inquiry-based and authentic activities both in the afterschool setting and at the field site. Collaboration and small group work were key elements.
- Created mentorship for students and training for mentors. The focus on equity in the training was of benefit to both students and mentors, and the fact that the mentors were just a bit older than the preteen 5th-graders made an interest in STEM seem "cool." Mentors reported that their female mentees became more eager to touch sea creatures and to go out on the floating dock.
- Exposed elementary school students to diverse female and male scientists working in the environmental sciences and provided a rich partnership between school and a science-rich resource.
- Gave students opportunities as "experts" and provided a showcase to convey what they had learned.

Great Science for Girls (GSG)

Extension services for gender equity in science through afterschool programs was a 5-year STEM initiative led by Educational Equity at FHI360 and funded by the National Science Foundation Program for Gender in Science and Engineering (NSF/GSE). NSF/GSE envisioned the extension services model as a way to address the vast and persistent underrepresentation of girls and women in STEM education and careers by creating a cadre of "agents" who use research-based approaches to increase the participation of girls and women in STEM.

GSG worked with 13 intermediary organizations to build their capacity and, in turn, the capacity of the afterschool centers they served to deliver high quality STEM programming that would broaden and sustain girls' interest and persistence in STEM. Key components of GSG included site-based Professional Development Institutes; ongoing technical assistance and reboot sessions on request; evidence-based, girl-friendly curricula; all-site meetings in person and online to share strategies and develop a GSG Community of Practice; and development of an interactive GSG website and program tools that would sustain the work beyond the grant period. From 2006 to 2011, GSG was implemented in 150 afterschool centers reaching over 8,000 students underrepresented in STEM—59% were girls and 70% were African American or Latino/a.

The guiding principal of the program was the GSG Unified Program of Change—a way to provide OST STEM education built around the three critical areas identified by Jolly et al. (2004). Researching girl-friendly curricula that fostered STEM skills and confidence, opportunities for exploration and discovery, role models and mentors, and information about future education and career opportunities was a key element of GSG. A rigorous 14-point set of criteria was used to identify curricula that had been professionally evaluated and had shown positive outcomes in relation to girls and STEM. Curricula developers collaborated with GSG throughout the initiative by participating in planning and providing training and technical assistance as centers implemented the curriculum of their choice. The seven evidence-based curricula are

1. *After-School Science PLUS (AS+)*: 11 inquiry-based core activities, suitable for OST programs serving students ages 6–14, using low-cost and found materials and including brief biographies of diverse scientists as role models. A comprehensive evaluation using a pre/post design revealed that after participating in AS+, student attitudes about science became more positive and less stereotyped (Campbell, Bachmann, & Hoey, 1999).
2. *Afterschool Universe*: A hands-on astronomy program for middle school girls, which takes them on a journey through the universe beyond the solar system. In a pre/post survey, girls reported an increase in positive attitudes, interest, and understanding that science has "real world" applications (Cornerstone Evaluation Associates, 2012).
3. *Girls at the Center (GAC)*: Community-based and museum workshops for girls ages 6–14 and an adult partner that fosters active science investigation. A comprehensive 5-year evaluation using written questionnaires, face-to-face and telephone interviews, and focus groups showed that girls participating in GAC activities multiple times reported an increase in science interest, consistently enjoyed experiences with science, shared their experience with others, and were more likely to aspire to science-related careers (Adelman, Dierking, & Adams, 1999).
4. *Girls Inc./Operation SMART*: An approach to engaging girls and young women in inquiry-based science through hands-on, minds-on experiences. Results show that the more a girl participates in Operation SMART, the more favorable is her attitude toward studying science and math. An independent evaluation showed that after participating in SMART, 75% of girls ages 6–11 had a positive attitude toward science (LeCount, 1990).

5. *SciGirls*: 14 standards-based STEM activities for girls ages 6–13, including life, physical, earth, and space science suitable for camps, clubs, science centers, museums, and afterschool centers. Summative evaluation found that the curriculum increased girls' confidence to participate in science, deepened their understanding on the inquiry process, and increased their awareness of and interest in science careers and/or showed them that science can be fun and exciting (Knight-Williams, 2008).

6. *Techbridge*: A science and engineering OST program for girls ages 10–18 featuring teamwork and problem-solving, role models, and career information. Eight years of evaluation demonstrated that participation results in development of technical skills and aptitude, increased self-confidence, and promotion of career interest in technology, science, and engineering (Ancheta, 2008).

7. *Wonderwise 4-H*: A series of learning kits for girls ages 8–12 featuring contemporary women scientists as role models as they do their laboratory and field work and at home with their families. Each kit contains a video profile of the scientist, a virtual field trip, and activity sheets. Findings suggest that girls were more likely than boys to imagine a women scientist with positive intellectual/work-related and personality traits. Results also show that students increased their understanding of what science is, broadened their view of scientists and their work, became more confident and capable, and saw the possibility of a science career (Spiegel, 2003).

From the beginning, GSG envisioned a unified program of change in which intermediary organizations would recruit afterschool centers to join the initiative expanding their reach over time, provide turnkey professional development to the centers they served, and engage in community outreach to spread the word to businesses, media, schools, and parents about the importance of STEM equity for girls and other underrepresented groups. Ongoing third-party evaluation was conducted over the 5-year grant period. A brief overview of outcomes follows (Bat-Chava & Abruzzo, 2011).

- Intermediaries reported that GSG influenced the organization's focus on quality, their awareness of gender equity, and their ability to provide technical assistance around gender-equitable STEM to the afterschool centers within their networks.
- Afterschool centers participating in GSG increased their gender-equitable and inquiry-based STEM program offerings, and observations showed that these centers received high scores for promoting gender equity and for conducting engaging inquiry-based activities.

- Afterschool educators who participated in GSG became more interested in science and aware of its importance, and more sensitive to classroom and career gender bias and stereotyping.
- Afterschool students who participated in GSG reported a change in their interest in science, opinions about science, and opinions about women in science. Girls reported a greater change than boys in these three areas.
- Over 70% of surveyed youth agreed that through the GSG programs they learned new things about science, gained new skills, and had fun.
- Over 90% of surveyed youth reported their interest in science increased as a result of their participation.

In order to ensure that the concept of gender-equitable STEM in OST continued well beyond the grant period, GSG developed a set of sustainability tools that are available and downloadable free of cost from the GSG website (www.greatscienceforgirls.org), which is designed as a virtual support system for current and future implementers of gender-equitable STEM programming. They are Starter Kits for intermediary organizations and afterschool programs, including basic information needed to start a GSG program; the GSG Program Quality Tool, a low-stakes gender/STEM assessment tool suitable for personal or group use; and Gender Equitable STEM Strategies: Stories from the Field, a guide based on the direct experiences of GSG implementers.

CONCLUSION

This chapter began with the fact that despite gains in recent years, girls and young women continue to be underrepresented in STEM degrees and careers. As the *New York Times* recently reported, on an international science test given to 470,000 15-year-olds in 65 countries throughout Europe, Asia, and the Middle East by the Organization for Economic Cooperation and Development, girls generally outperform boys in science; but not in the United States, where boys consistently score higher than girls. According to this report, perception, expectations, and gender-stereotyped roles in occupation appearing as early as age 4 still seem to be barriers that limit how girls view their future options (Fairfield, 2013).

This chapter has also demonstrated that we know how to change the picture for girls and that when provided the opportunity, girls can become engaged, gain self-confidence, and consider STEM as a career path. In addition to the two interventions described, there are myriad successful OST programs taking place in summer camps, museum settings, youth serving organizations, and afterschool centers. However, OST programs cannot do it all. STEM education within the school day and the school building also must step up to the plate. Science and math in the typical classroom are still textbook and pencil-and-paper subjects that offer little in the way of inquiry, hands-on experience, or awareness of gender equity. They are also in-school subjects wherein boys often take the lead.

One area of potential change for gender-equitable STEM within schools is in the current trend toward expanded learning time. In 2011, the Wallace Foundation, a major supporter of summer learning and extended-day programs, convened "Reimagining the School Day: A Forum on More Time for Learning," which brought together 70 thought leaders from around the country to discuss how the concept of an expanded school day and school year could benefit students, especially those who did not have opportunities for enrichment outside of school. Many conference participants made the point that an extension of the school day should not be more of the same, but activities that extend learning in more creative and engaging ways. The extended school day should not be used for the same delivery of content and instructional methods as the school day, but to provide all students with opportunities for academic enrichment and to develop other interests with peers in a safe, supervised environment (Stonehill, Donner, Morgan, & Lasagna, 2010). Lucy Friedman, a leader in the expanded learning time movement also sees using the expanded time as a way for community organizations to partner with schools to give students a wider range of opportunities to learn. As she states, "We can help 21st Century learners prepare to succeed in the information age by using the learning hours to engage, support, and challenge all students more effectively" (2013).

The expanded-day movement presents a challenge and an opportunity to bring what research and practice has taught us about gender-equitable STEM to a much larger population of students. In the extended day, in-school teachers and afterschool staff can interact and share strategies from both perspectives for the benefit of both girls and boys. We know from research and practice how to make STEM a subject in which girls can excel. Now we need to go to scale—in school, in OST, and in expanded learning time.

The United States cannot afford to lag behind the rest of the world in STEM education. We need the perspective of girls and women from all ethnic and racial groups in all STEM fields. Attracting and retaining more women in STEM starts with capturing and retaining girls' interest and persistence. The authors believe that women in STEM will bring innovation, creativity, and a much needed different perspective to the field. As First Lady Michelle Obama eloquently stated at the National Science Foundation Family-Friendly Policy Rollout in September 2011, "If we're going to out-innovate and out-educate the rest of the world, we've got to open doors for everyone. We need all hands on deck, and that means clearing hurdles for women and girls as they navigate careers in science, technology, engineering, and math."

NOTES

1. In 2005, Educational Equity Concepts merged with the Academy for Educational Development (AED), becoming the Educational Equity Center at AED. In 2011, Family Health International acquired the assets of AED, and the Educational Equity Center became Educational Equity at FHI 360.
2. This section is based on evaluation reports prepared by Dr. Cheri Fancsali and her article, "The Science Mentoring Project: How Student-to-Student Mentoring can Encourage Motivation, Participation and Inquiry," in Afterschool Matters (Corwin Press, 2008).

REFERENCES

AAUW. (2004). *Under the microscope: A decade of gender equity projects in the sciences.* Washington, DC: American Association of University Women Education Foundation. Retrieved from http://www.aauw.org/learn/research/upload/underthemicroscope.pdf

AAUW. (2010). *Why so few: Women in science, technology, engineering and mathematics.* Washington, DC: Author.

Adelman, L., Dierking, L. D., & Adams, M. (1999). *Summative evaluation year 3: Findings for Girls at the Center. The Franklin Institute Science Museum & Girl Scouts of the U.S.A. technical report.* Annapolis, MD: Institute for Learning Innovation.

Afterschool Alliance. (2009). *American after 3pm: The most in-depth study of how America's children spend their afternoons.* Retrieved from http://www.afterschoolalliance.org/documents/AA3PM_National_2009.pdf

Afterschool Alliance. (2011, September). *STEM learning in afterschool: An analysis of impact and outcomes.* Retrieved from http://www.afterschoolalliance.org/STEM-Afterschool-Outcomes.pdf

Ancheta, R. (2008). *Report on quantitative longitudinal evaluation of Techbridge.* San Francisco, CA: Rececca Ancheta Research.

Bat-Chava, Y., & Abruzzo, G. (2011, November). *Evaluation of Great Science for Girls: Extension services for gender equity in science through after-school programs, Year 5: September 1, 2010–June 30, 2011.* Brooklyn, NY: Comprehensive Research and Evaluation Services.

Beede, D., Julian, T., Langdon, D., McKittrick, G., Khan, B., & Doms, M. (2011, August.). *Women in STEM: A gender gap to innovation.* ESA Issue Brief #04-11. Retrieved from http://www.esa.doc.gov/Reports/women-stem-gender-gap-innovation

Calabrese Barton, A., Tan, E., & Rivet, A. (2008). Creating hybrid spaces for engaging school science among urban middle school girls. *American Educational Research Journal, 45*(1), 68–103.

California Tomorrow. (2003). *Pursuing the promise: Addressing equity, access, and diversity in after school and youth programs.* Oakland, CA: Author.

Campbell, P., & Steinbrueck, K. (1996). *Striving for gender equity: National programs to increase student engagement with math and science.* Washington, DC: American Association for the Advancement of Science.

Campbell, P., Bachmann, K. A., & Hoey, L. (1999, June). *Playtime is Science Plus: Final evaluation report.* Groton, CT: Campbell-Kibler Associates.

Campbell, P., Holly, E., Hoey, L., & Perlman, L. (2002). *Upping the numbers: Using research-based decision making to increase the diversity in the quantitative disciplines.* Newton: MA: Education Development Center.

Clewell, B., & Darke, K. (2000). *Summary report on the impact study of the National Science Foundation's programs for women and girls.* Washington, DC: Urban Institute Education Policy Center.

Cornerstone Evaluation Associates. (2012, August). *Afterschool universe: Bringing astronomy down to earth 2010–2012, Final Evaluation Report.* Pittsburgh, PA: Author.

Eagan, M. K., Sharkness, J., & Hurtado, S. (2010, June). *Developing a science identity: Long-term effects of first-year experiences that matter.* Poster presented at the International Conference on the First-Year Experience, Maui, HI.

Fairfield, H. (2013, February 5). Clues to a troubling gap. *The New York Times.*

Fancsali, C. (2008). The science mentoring project: How student-to-student mentoring can encourage motivation, participation, and Inquiry. In S. Hill (Ed.), *Afterschool matters: Creative programs that connect youth development and student achievement.* Thousand Oaks, CA: Corwin Press.

Ferreira, M. (2001). The effect of an after-school program addressing the gender and minority achievement gaps in science, mathematics and engineering. *ERS Spectrum.* Arlington, VA: Educational Research Service.

Friedman, L. (2013). Reinventing the learning day: How ExpandED schools blend the best of school and afterschool through community partnerships. In T. K. Peterson (Ed.), *Expanding minds and opportunities: Leveraging the power of afterschool and summer learning for student success.* Washington, DC: Collaborative Communications Group. Retrieved from http://www.expandinglearning .org/expandingminds/article/reinventing-learning-day-how-expanded-schools-blend-best-school-and

Friedman, L., & Quinn, S. (2006). It's never too early: Promoting college prep in middle school after school programs. *The Evaluation Exchange, 12*(1).

Froschl, M., Sprung, B., Archer, E., & Fancsali, C. (2003). *Science, gender, and afterschool: A research-action agenda.* New York, NY: Educational Equity Concepts and AED.

Goldman, S., & Booker, A. (2009). Making math a definition of the situation: Families as sites for mathematical practices. *Anthropology & Education Quarterly, 40*(4), 369–387.

Horowitz, A., & Bronte-Tinkew, J. (2007). Building, engaging, and supporting family and parental involvement in out-of-school time programs. *Research-to-Results Brief,* Child Trends Publication #2007-16.

Jolly, E. J., Campbell, P. B., & Perlman, L. (2004). *Engagement, capacity and continuity: An overview of a trilogy for student success.* Fairfield, CT: GE Foundation.

Knight-Williams. (2008, April). *Summative evaluation report: Dragonfly TV SciGirls Grantee Outreach Program.* Sacramento, CA: Knight-Williams Research Communications.

Koch, J. (2002, April). *Gender issues in the classroom: The past, the promise and the future.* Paper presented at the annual meeting of the American Educational Research Association.

Krishnamurthi, A., Ottinger, R., & Topol, T. (2013). STEM learning in afterschool and summer programming: An essential strategy for STEM education reform. In T. K. Peterson (Ed.), *Expanding minds and opportunities: Leveraging the power of afterschool and summer learning for student success.* Washington, DC: Collaborative Communications Group. Retrieved from http://www.expandinglearning.org/expandingminds/article/stem-learning-afterschool-and-summer-programming-essential-strategy-stem

LeCount, J. M. (1990). *Evaluation report: Operation SMART.* Indianapolis, IN: Girls Inc.

National Science Foundation (2011). *Women, minorities, and persons with disabilities in science and engineering.* Arlington, VA: Author.

Peterson, T. K. (2013). Introduction: The importance of and new opportunities for leveraging afterschool and summer learning and school-community partnerships for student success. In T. K. Peterson (Ed.), *Expanding minds and opportunities: Leveraging the power of afterschool and summer learning for student success..* Washington, DC: Collaborative Communications Group. Retrieved from http://www.expandinglearning.org/expandingminds/introduction

Sax, L. J. (2001). Undergraduate science majors: Gender differences in who goes to graduate school. *The Review of Higher Education, 24*(2), 153–172.

Spiegel, A. N. (2003, May). *Wonderwise 4-H: The trial testing process, evaluation report.* Lincoln, NE: Center for Instructional Innovation.

Stonehill, R., Donner, J., Morgan, E., & Lasagna, M. (2010). *Integrating expanding learning and school reform initiatives: Challenges and strategies.* Policy Brief from Learning Point Associates and the Collaborative for Building After-School Systems.

Tai, R. H., Qi Liu, C., Maltese, A. V., & Fan, X. (2006). Planning early for careers in science. *Science, 312,* 1143–1145.

Tan, E., & Calabrese Barton, A. (2007). *From peripheral to central: The story of Melanie's metamorphosis in an urban middle school science class.* doi:10.1002/sce.20253

Tan, E., & Calabrese Barton, A. (2010). Transforming science learning and student participation in 6th grade science: A case study of an urban minority classroom. *Equity & Excellence in Education, 43*(1), 38–55.

U.S. Congress Joint Economic Committee. (2012, April). *STEM education: Preparing for the jobs of the future.* Retrieved from http://www.jec.senate.gov/public/index.cfm?a=Files.Serve&File_id=6aaa7e1f-9586-47be-82e7-326f47658320

University of Michigan. (2007, June 25). How dads influence their daughters' interest in math. *ScienceDaily.* Retrieved from http://www.sciencedaily.com/releases/2007/06/070624143002.htm

Walker, G., Wahl, E., & Rivas, L. (2005). *NASA and afterschool: Connecting to the future.* New York, NY: American Museum of Natural History.

Wenglinsky, H. (2000). *How teaching matters; bringing the classroom back into discussions of teacher quality.* Princeton, NJ: Educational Testing Service.

CHAPTER 8

STEM SUMMER INSTITUTE

A Model Program
for Stem Integration for Girls

Crystal T. Chukwurah
Stacy S. Klein-Gardner

INTRODUCTION

Rising concern about America's ability to maintain its competitive position in the global economy has renewed interest in science, technology, engineering, and mathematics (STEM) education (Chen & Weko 2009). The economy of the United States depends upon engineering and technology advancement; the growth of jobs in the STEM workforce is outpacing overall job growth by 3:1 (Lam, 2011; National Science Board, 2008). If there is such high rate in job growth, why are there so few people, specifically among women and minorities, entering the STEM field?

The answer to this question may be found at the root of the problem, K–12 education. Although children are natural engineers, with strong impulses to investigate, construct, create, and share their knowledge with others (Genalo, Bruning, & Adams, 2000), current curricula does not take advantage of their natural curiosity. Therefore, children's ability to analyze,

Girls and Women in STEM, pages 153–174
Copyright © 2014 by Information Age Publishing
All rights of reproduction in any form reserved.

develop, build, and test as engineers and scientists may be stifled in school. K–12 students tend to shy away from engineering fields simply because they have a limited understanding of what engineering is (Jeffers, Safferman, & Safferman, 2004). It does not help that many K–12 teachers have just as limited an understanding of engineering as the students do (Fadali, Robinson, & McNichols, 2000). Unless students have family members or friends who are engineers, they are often never introduced to the field (Abbitt & Carroll, 1993).

This chapter describes a 2-week long STEM Summer Institute for Girls (SSI) that focused on engaging rising 9th- and 10th-grade underrepresented girls in STEM through enrichment of their self-efficacy and knowledge of engineering. Data will be presented as to the outcomes of this institute and the degree to which the designers and presenters were effective in increasing girl's self-efficacy in STEM fields. The need for effective role models from science and engineering fields is also discussed.

BACKGROUND

Self-efficacy, girls in STEM, minorities in STEM, and service learning in STEM are essential aspects of STEM. Careful understanding of these aspects is needed for execution of programs such as the STEM Summer Institute for Girls. Further descriptions are given in the following paragraphs.

Self-Efficacy

Self-efficacy reflects personal expectations. It is an effective predictor of task-specific performance (Bong & Skaalvik, 2003; Britner & Pajares, 2006; Zimmerman, 2000). Self-efficacy is based on four primary sources of influence: mastery experience, social persuasion, physiological reaction, and vicarious experience (Bandura, 1997; Gist & Mitchell, 1992; Pajares, 2005). The following four terms are reflected throughout this chapter:

1. *Mastery experience* refers to previous task experiences. By referring back to past experiences, individuals can determine their capability to succeed.
2. *Social persuasion* refers to feedback and support from others. Positive feedback and encouragement enhance self-efficacy; this is further evident when feedback is given from influential others (e.g., parents, teachers). For example, when women receive positive feedback related to specific jobs or tasks, their self-efficacy is increased (Betz & Schifano, 2000).

3. *Physiological reaction* affects self-efficacy through symptoms of nervousness and a fear of failure; under such conditions, individuals are likely to doubt their ability to succeed.
4. *Vicarious experience* refers to learning from tasks performed by others. As research suggests, vicarious experience is a particularly powerful determinant of girls and young women's STEM self-efficacy (Seymour, 1995; Zeldin & Pajares, 2000).

Girls in STEM

Although women have nearly achieved equality with men in formerly male-dominated fields such as medicine and law, they remain underrepresented in STEM (Diekman, Brown, Johnston, & Clark, 2010). Factors that contribute to women's underrepresentation in STEM include gender differences in self-efficacy, discouragement from pursuing STEM careers, and cultural stereotypes (Ceci & Williams, 2007; Halpern, Benbow et al., 2007; Spelke, 2005). During K–12 education, STEM courses presumably do not meet the needs of female learners.

Knight, Mappen, and Knight (2011) relay that increasing women's involvement in STEM can best be achieved by having young women participate in civic engagement. Contextualizing STEM subjects with practical problems can help contribute to girls' present and future interest in the subjects (Halpern, Aronson et al., 2007). Brotman and Moore's (2008) work supports how females have a high interest in topics related to real-world issues. Clewell and Campbell (2002) assert using "real life" situations in problem-solving as an effective method in the classroom. Additionally, Carlone and Johnson (2007) recommend emphasizing the relationship between altruism and science. For minority females in particular, recruitment efforts may be more successful for disciplines such as health sciences in which there is a tangible benefit to society.

Minorities in STEM

Similarly, while engineering has been considered a noble profession, it has been dominated by White males (Gibbons, 2009). Although efforts have been made to attract and retain minorities in STEM over the past 25 years, only little progress has been made, leaving minorities an untapped resource (Burke, 2007). Diversifying the engineering profession brings additional perspectives that lead to exciting advancements in technology (Wilson, 2000).

People, specifically minorities, must be exposed to STEM at a critical point in their education, that is, K–12 education. Most children begin to discover which subject areas they are skilled in at the age of 12 (Burke, 2007). Thus, secondary education should be targeted and enhanced to attract these underrepresented groups to engineering and other STEM areas (Crawford, Wood, Fowler, & Norrell, 1994). With low numbers of minorities in the STEM workforce, minority children are less likely to have parents in STEM careers. Thus, there is more of a need to reach out to K–12 minority students, inside and outside of the classroom, possibly through STEM activities, programs, or camps.

Service Learning in STEM

One successful practice in introducing girls to STEM is incorporating STEM with service learning and within a global context. Connecting engineering and science as fields that benefit people has long been cited as a way to increase interest among women as well as underrepresented populations (Knight et al., 2011). The Engineering Projects in Community Service learning (EPICS) program, a Purdue University design program, uses a service-learning model to meet the educational needs of undergraduates and the compelling needs of the local community (Coyle, Jamieson, & Oakes 2005). Additionally, the EPICS high school model introduces high school students to engineering using service-learning design. The EPICS program is built around partnerships between student teams and nonprofit organizations in the community who often possess neither the expertise to use nor the budget to design and acquire technological solutions within their organization. Each team and its community partner work to identify and solve the partner's technology-based problems. The projects lie in four different areas: education and outreach, access and abilities, human services, and the environment. Using qualitative inquiry, EPICS concluded that service-learning draws a significantly more diverse population than traditional approaches to precollege engineering, through both gender and ethnicity.

STEM Summer Institute for Girls

The SSI focused on engaging rising 9th- and 10-grade underrepresented girls in STEM. The Institute itself is set to occur for an additional four summers at the Harpeth Hall School in Nashville, Tennessee. Unlike many other STEM summer programs, the SSI was based on service learning and engineering design. Each year, the STEM Summer Institute tackles engineering problems sponsored by the Lwala Community Alliance, a nonprofit health and development agency founded by Drs. Milton and Fred Ochieng, who are natives of Lwala, a rural village in western Kenya (Lwala Community Alliance,

2012). The Alliance includes public health outreach, water and sanitation, and education programming. The connection with Lwala is a schoolwide one at the Harpeth Hall School, forged over several years of collaboration.

At the Institute, the Lwala Community Alliance challenged the SSI participants to improve the design of the tippy-tap hand-washing station used in girls' schools in Lwala. Participants used the engineering design process, scientific inquiry, statistical analyses, CAD drawings, and prototypes to accomplish the task. Additionally, the SSI introduced the participants to role models with a majority of female staff and visiting STEM professionals Furthermore, activities were included to give the SSI a traditional camp feel: field trips, college planning, and after-lunch activities.

The SSI evaluated the program with the use of two pre-/postquestionnaires, a satisfaction survey, and program observations. With the help of the assessment tools, the effectiveness of the SSI was evaluated through answering two underlying research questions:

- *Question 1.* How does participation in the STEM Summer Institute increase or change participants' understanding of the nature of engineering?
- *Question 2.* How does participation in the STEM Summer Institute increase participants' self-efficacy?

METHODS

The methods of the SSI were contributed to various factors. A key component of the SSI was the participants and participants' demographic. Another factor was the SSI curriculum put in place with the SSI research questions in mind.

Participants

The STEM Summer Institute exclusively served rising 9th- and 10th-grade girls in Davidson County, Tennessee. Every public high school and approximately half of the middle schools in the Metropolitan Nashville Public School (MNPS) system was contacted about this program. The majority of recruiting took place through classroom teachers, many of whom had a preexisting relationship with an SSI staff member. These teachers played a critical role in encouraging their students to apply. Whenever invited, an SSI staff member went to meet with girls who were interested in the SSI at their schools. An effort was made to encourage underrepresented female students to participate in the program and to assure all applicants that financial aid was available and that money should not hinder their application. Potential applicants were assured that they did not have to be expert students in their science or mathematics classes in order to be considered for the Institute. They were told that the Institute was looking for girls who wanted to participate and problem solve, using the engineering design process. The candidates were asked to submit an application form, one teacher recommendation, and an essay explaining why they should be chosen for the program. Of a total of 20 accepted girls, 16 committed to the Institute.

Participant Demographics

Of the 16 participating girls, 8 were African American, 1 was African American/Hispanic, 1 was Hispanic, 2 were Asian, and 4 were Caucasian. Three of these students immigrated to the United States within a year of participating in the SSI. Ten families reported self-income, as illustrated in Figure 8.1. Eleven families reported maximum education achieved by the parent or parents as revealed in Figure 8.2. Two participants' parents have a degree in science, one in technology, and one in engineering.

The SSI Curriculum

The 2012 SSI ran June 18–29, 9 am–4 pm, Monday through Friday. Tuition to attend the Institute was $300 per girl. Every girl received a scholarship ranging from half tuition to nearly full. Each participant was required to pay some amount; even a nominal $10 ensured that each girl made a personal commitment to attend. Lunch and snacks were included for participants.

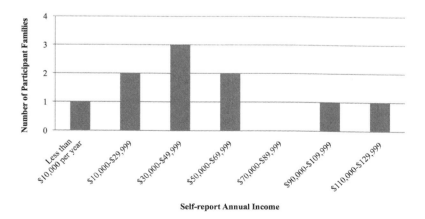

Figure 8.1 Self-reported household income of the SSI participants' families.

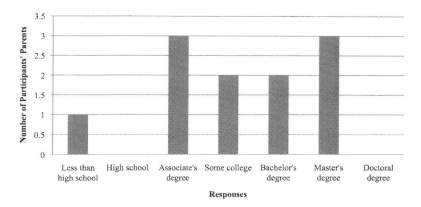

Figure 8.2 Maximum educational achievement of the SSI participants' parents.

Transportation assistance was provided as needed for participants, with 15 of 16 girls riding on Harpeth Hall bus routes created for this program. SSI staff included several Harpeth Hall upper-school science and math teachers, one Harpeth Hall middle school science teacher, two Vanderbilt University biomedical engineering graduate students and a professor, and two Vanderbilt Research Experience for Undergraduates (REU) students. The majority of the staff was female. From day one, the SSI staff oriented the girls into the world of STEM. Below is a summary of the SSI day-to-day content.

Day 1

Representatives from the Lwala Community Alliance introduced the girls to the design project: improving the tippy-tap hand-washing station. The girls learned that they would work in groups to create an original design and deliver it through a poster presentation. The best design among the groups would be chosen for implementation at a girls' school in Lwala. The girls learned about Kenyan culture and society. A lesson was given on the engineering design process, and the girls began by brainstorming for the project.

Day 2

The girls were given further information that provided an in-depth background for the project. They were taught the importance of hand washing itself and about the evident water-quality issues in Kenya. To help the girls bring the idea into perspective and to see how water is cleaned in the United States, a field trip was taken to the Harpeth Water Treatment Plant.

Day 3

The girls discussed the basics of sanitation. In pairs, they conducted an online investigation of water-borne illnesses, created miniposters on a specific illness, and delivered presentations. In addition to discussing the importance of water quality, the girls were introduced to water testing kits and shown how to use them. This day ended with teaching the girls basic statistics, including mean, median, mode, and standard deviation and how to calculate them in Excel. They discussed the basics of the normal curve and linear regression in preparation for the statistics they would use the next day.

Day 4

A field trip was taken to the Harpeth River and the Little Harpeth River, where the girls used the water test kits to catch water creatures and assess water quality based on the aquatic animals present. The girls discussed previous tippy-tap designs. New design factors were brought to their attention: budget and material limitations. They discussed how these factors might be taken into consideration along with Kenyan society and the design itself.

Day 5

The girls were split into five groups of three or four in which they would design their tippy-tap. They spent time brainstorming, individually and in teams, and documenting in the Innovation Portal, an online portfolio in which students organize their progress in the engineering design process (Project Lead the Way, 2012). The girls were introduced to the CAD software, Google SketchUp, and learned the basics of engineering drawing.

Days 6–9

The girls used the CAD software to sketch their group's tippy-tap design. The girls built prototypes, and they tested their design. If needed, the girls improved their design, documented it in Innovation Portal, and built a new prototype. After going through this cycle and finalizing a design, the girls prepared their presentation posters.

Day 10

On the final day of the SSI, the girls delivered their poster presentations. The audience included the Lwala Community Alliance representatives, external judges, SSI staff, and families of participants. A group's tippy-tap design was selected for implementation in Kenya.

Ongoing Through SSI

Through the course of the SSI, female adults involved in STEM fields were invited to speak to and eat lunch with the girls. These STEM professionals included members of industry, university professors, and STEM graduates and undergraduates.

Research Questions

Various assessment tools were used in order to answer the previously stated research questions. Question 1 was how does participation in the STEM Summer Institute increase or change participants' understanding of the nature of engineering? Question 2 was how does participation in the STEM Summer Institute increase participants' self-efficacy? Surveys and observations were used as the assessment tools.

Question 1

For the first question, the participants who gave assent and whose parents gave consent were given the assessment *Draw an Engineer Test* at the start and completion of the STEM Summer Institute (Knight & Cunningham, 2004). A discourse analysis methodology was used, with observations made throughout the 2 weeks of the Institute. Last, the survey data was aggregated; pre- and postresults were statistically compared.

Method: Draw an Engineer Test. Draw an Engineer Test (DAET) was developed to help assess students' ideas about engineering before intervention (Knight & Cunningham, 2004). Through the survey, students described their knowledge about engineering through written and drawn responses. The survey included the following questions: "In your own words, what is engineering?" "What does an engineer do?" and "Draw a picture of an engineer at work."

Method: Observations. The data collected for this study consisted of observations of the SSI participants working as engineers. Observations allowed us to explore what was happening in groups as the girls maneuvered through the engineering design process. The method was directed toward analyzing conversation and the participants' understanding of engineering itself.

Methodology: Discourse analysis. Discourse analysis usually requires data in the form of transcriptions of utterances; for example, classroom discussions and student conversations (Case & Light, 2011). Discourse analysis has been used across a range of disciplinary contexts in education, with highly productive applications in mathematics and science (Airey & Linder, 2009; Sfard, 2001). With the SSI, we observed the discourse actions of participants: practicing design to solve real-world problems, collecting and analyzing data, doing mathematical calculations, modeling, and presenting results to a range of different audiences.

Question 2

The participants were given the Pre-College Annual Self-Efficacy Survey at the start and completion of the STEM Summer Institute. The data was aggregated; pre- and postresults were statistically compared.

Method: LAESE Pre-College Annual Self-Efficacy Survey. The LAESE (Longitudinal Assessment of Engineering Self-Efficacy) Pre-College Annual Self-Efficacy Survey was a 5- to 7-point Likert assessment designed to identify longitudinal changes in the self-efficacy of students studying engineering (Assessing Women and Men in Engineering, 2008). LAESE items address the following aspects of self-efficacy with high school students: student efficacy in "barrier" situations, outcomes expected from studying engineering, student expectations about workload, student process of choosing a major, student coping strategies in difficult situations, career exploration, and influence of role models on study and career decisions (Assessing Women and Men in Engineering, 2008).

Satisfaction survey. The students completed the SSI Satisfaction Survey the final day. Consisting of 39 multiple-choice and open-ended questions, the survey focused on the camp's execution performance: the most and least meaningful student experiences and possible improvements for the camp. The survey also addressed what the girls took away from the SSI with regard to understanding of engineering and self-efficacy.

DATA ANALYSIS

Analysis of the SSI contributed by the methods of observations, Draw an Engineer Test, and LAESE Pre-College Annual Self-Efficacy Survey. These methods brought out significant findings of the SSI. Together, these findings helped with answering SSI's two research questions.

Method: Observations

Observations were noted during three activities/projects: Mini-Poster Project, Building a House on the Moon, and Design Project, as illustrated in Table 8.1. Thematic groupings were created based on the students' actions in the engineering design process: Brainstorming, Collaboration, Communication, Documentations, and Solutions, as revealed in Table 8.2, Table 8.3, and Table 8.4. Noted observations in these were given a rating from 1 to 3: 1-Rarely Present, 2-Present, and 3-Strongly present. Observations that were not present in the activity/project were not rated.

Brainstorming
Most groups began their brainstorming by identifying the main problem as a group. Most of the groups suggested more than one idea. Students were noted to give wild or obvious suggestions. At the same time, students reflected back to the main problem, leading them to thinking about

TABLE 8.1 Observed Activities Description

Group Activities	Description
Mini-Poster Project Date: 6/20 (Day 2)	Student researched and created poster on water-borne illnesses.
Practicing Design Process: Building a House on Moon Date: 6/22 (Day 4)	Students are asked to build a house on the moon.
Design Process Date: 6/25–6/29 (Days 6–10)	Students design tippy-tap.

TABLE 8.2 Noted Categorized Observations: Brainstorming

	Activities		
Noted Observations	A	B	C
Connected what they know to what they do not		2	3
Did research on brainstormed ideas			2
Brainstormed more than one possibility		3	2
Identified main problem	3		3
Looked up pictures	3		
Made obvious suggestions		3	3
Talked about living conditions		2	3
Thought about accommodations		1	3
Thought about wild ideas		3	1

Note: The Activities A, B, and C are respectively the Mini-Poster Project; Practicing Design Process: Building a House on Moon; and Design Process. Scale is as follows: 1-Rarely present, 2-Present, 3-Strongly present.

TABLE 8.3 Noted Categorized Observations: Collaboration

	Activities		
Noted Observations	A	B	C
After doing divided part, reviewed each other's work	3		
Asked others for advice		3	3
Divided up work	3		2
One person doing all of work		1	1
Worked on each step or task together			3

Note: The Activities A, B, and C are respectively the Mini-Poster Project; Practicing Design Process: Building a House on Moon; and Design Process. Scale is as follows: 1-Rarely present, 2-Present, 3-Strongly present.

TABLE 8.4   Noted Categorized Observations: Communication

Noted Observations	Activities		
	A	B	C
Asked questions to selves, each other, and teachers		3	2
Began with silent work	3		1
Drew out ideas in pictures	1		3
Off-task talk	3	3	3
Procedural talk			3
Talked about ideas in groups			3
Took turns saying ideas			
Wrote out ideas in words	3	3	2

Note: The Activities A, B, and C are respectively the Mini-Poster Project; Practicing Design Process: Building a House on Moon; and Design Process. Scale is as follows: 1-Rarely present, 2-Present, 3-Strongly present.

additional factors: living conditions and accommodations, as illustrated in Table 8.2. The students understood that brainstorming entailed generating as many ideas from the group as possible, no matter what the idea may be.

Collaboration and Communication

The students strategized the most effective way they were going to work as they designed their tippy-tap. A majority of the groups worked on each step of the design process together, while others divided up the work among one another, as revealed in Table 8.3 and Table 8.4. It was rare that a single person took on all the work for the group. Within their groups, the girls explored various modes of communicating their ideas: writing out in words, voicing aloud, and drawing pictures and diagrams. In addition to communicating their ideas, the girls asked each other questions about their proposed ideas, as illustrated in Table 8.3. This required them to partake in further group communication; evidence that the girls knew the importance of teamwork and communication in order to complete their design projects.

Method: Draw an Engineer Test

Students were asked to give a written response to the question "What is engineering?" To gain a better sense of the students' overall understanding of engineering, thematic groupings were created based on the students' written responses on the survey: Building, Brainstorming, Designing and Creating, Fixing, Improving, Operating, Solving, STEM Subjects, Technology, and Testing, as illustrated in Figure 8.3. These categories were created by one author, reviewed by the second author, and an agreement was

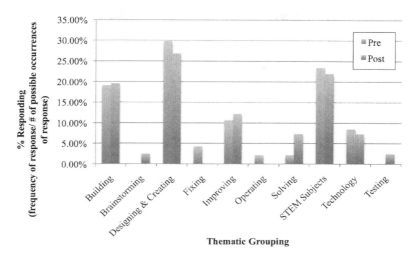

Figure 8.3   Bar graph representing responses to Question 1, "What is engineering?" split into thematic groups. The % Responding is the occurrence of image in grouping/total # of occurrence of images ($N = 11$).

reached on the categories. It is suspected that a number of participants looked up a definition for their PRE response of defining engineering, due to the fact that they were not told they could not do so, perhaps making the pre-SSI results appear stronger than they actually were.

Students were asked to respond to the question "What does an engineer do?" To gain a better sense of the students' overall understanding of engineering, thematic groupings were created based on the students' written responses on the survey: Asks, Brainstorms, Builds, Creates, Designs, Multiple Tasks, Fixes, Improves, Plans, Tests, Solves, as illustrated in Figure 8.4.

Students were asked to "Draw an engineer at work." To gain a better sense of the students' overall understanding of engineering, thematic groupings were taken from DAET_ASEE, 2004 to categorize the students' written responses on the survey: Images of Building/Fixing, Designing, Products of Engineering-Mechanical, Products of Engineering-Civil, Trains, Laboratory Work, and Unidentifiable, as illustrated in Figure 8.5.

Design

Students' drawings of engineers showed considerable evidence of engineers in the design process. Often, these pictures included a person seated at a desk holding a pen or pencil, or a person in front of a computer. Out of all the responses given, most of them fell into *Images of Design* in the pre and post, as illustrated in Figure 8.5. The increased percentage of responses of design

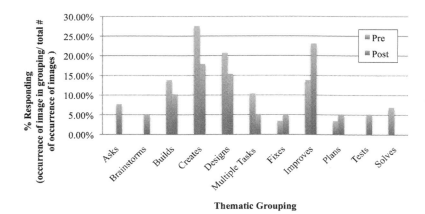

Figure 8.4 Bar graph representing responses to Question 2, "What does an engineer do?" split into thematic groups. The % Responding is the occurrence of image in grouping/total # of occurrence of images (*N* = 11).

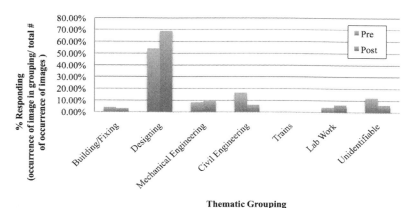

Figure 8.5 Bar graph representing responses to "Draw a picture of an engineer at work," split into thematic groups. The % Responding is the occurrence of image in grouping/total # of occurrence of images (*N* = 11).

images in the post further revealed the students' understanding that designing plays an important role in engineering, as revealed in Figure 8.5. Additionally, students realized they were acting in the design process themselves at the SSI.

Creating

In the Question 2 pre-SSI results, 28% of the students' responses attributed creating as an activity associated with engineers, as illustrated in Figure 8.4. This grouping included responses such as create, invent, make, and new. By the post, responses in the *Creates* grouping dropped to 18% in the post, as revealed in Figure 8.4. There was also an increase in Question 2's *Improves* grouping, which included responses such as innovate, make easier, better, re-design, make changes. This is further illustrated in Figure 8.4. This lined up with what the students focused on at the SSI: to improve the tippy-tap hand-washing station. These percentages showed that the students understood that engineering design is not always creating something novel but it is more often improving what already exists. Further understanding was reinforced by the responses to Question 1, wherin there was an increased percentage in the post-*Improving* grouping (responses such as improving, modify, work bet-ter) and *Solving* grouping (responses such as solving problems, brainstorm-ing), showing that the students understood that engineering is not simply making things without reason; it is purposely creating things to improve a situation or solve a problem, as illustrated in Figure 8.3.

Building and Fixing

Building and Fixing images were present in artifacts of building and fix-ing, with responses such as tools, hard hats, and safety glasses. These re-sponses are as illustrated in Figure 8.5. Post the SSI, the small percentage of building or fixing images showed that the students had an understanding of engineering beyond superficial images that suggest that engineers fix cars (car mechanics) and build houses and bridges (construction workers). This understanding was reinforced by the written responses to Question 1, wherein misconceptions such as *Operating* and *Fixing* were evident in the pre responses but not in the post, as revealed in Figure 8.3.

Method: LAESE Pre-College Annual Self-Efficacy Survey

The LAESE Survey was used to answer how participation in the SSI in-creases participants' self-efficacy. In analyzing the survey, the questionnaire items were split into 6 subscale categories, as displayed in Figure 8.6:

1. Engineering career success expectations (cs)
2. Engineering self-efficacy I (se1)
3. Engineering self-efficacy II (se2)
4,. Feeling of inclusion (fi)
5. Coping self-efficacy (cse)
6. Math outcome expectations (moe)

Cronbach's α (alpha), coefficient of reliability, for these categories is be-tween 0.73 and 0.84.

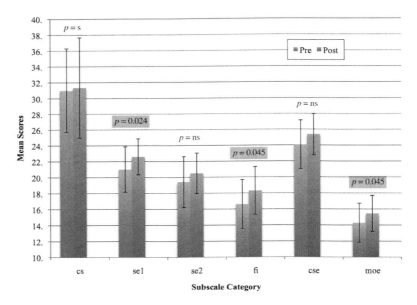

Figure 8.6 Bar graph representing responses to LAESE Pre-College Annual Self-Efficacy Survey with subscale categories. CS = engineering career success expectations. SE1 = Engineering self-efficacy I. SE2 = Engineering self-efficacy II. FI = Feelings of inclusion. CSE = Coping self-efficacy. MOE = math outcome expectations. Error bars represent the standard deviation (N = 11). P-values were considered significant at the $p < 0.05$ level and are indicated for each subscale category.

Engineering Self-Efficacy I (se1)

The students were asked five questions that addressed their beliefs about their success in STEM courses. The responses to these questions were based on a Likert scale, scaling from 0 to 6, with 6 representing Strongly Agree (Assessing Women and Men in Engineering, 2008). The Likert scores for the five items in this category were averaged to calculate the mean pre-SSI score, 5.25, and the mean post-SSI score, 5.65. When the pre and post scores were compared in the engineering self-efficacy (se1) subscale category using a paired t-test, it was found that the girls' self-efficacy improved significantly ($p < 0.05$) over the course of the SSI, as revealed in Figure 8.6. These results demonstrate that the girls had a greater belief in their success within STEM courses after participation in the SSI.

The increase in engineering self-efficacy was reinforced by the students' responses to another question on the LAESE: "How confident are you that you will complete any engineering program?" This is illustrated in Figure 8.7. Assuming the potential responses represent incremental change,

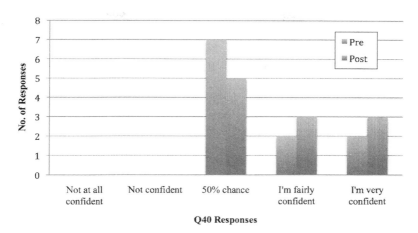

Figure 8.7 Responses to LAESE Pre-College Annual Self-Efficacy Survey Question 40: "At the present time, how confident are you that you will complete any engineering program?" N = 11. Responses indicate a shift toward more certainty after completing the SSI.

the five question options were assigned numbers values from 1 to 5: 1—Not at all confident, I am already planning not to pursue engineering; 3—There's about a 50% chance that I'll complete an engineering program; 5—I'm very confident that I will complete an engineering program. In the pre-SSI results, a majority of the students were unsure about the likelihood of completing an engineering program by giving themselves an average score of 3.5, as illustrated in Figure 8.7. Improvement in engineering self-efficacy was evident in the post-SSI survey rating of nearly a 4, in which the students were fairly confident in completing an engineering program, as revealed in Figure 8.7.

Feeling of Inclusion (fi)

The students were asked four questions that addressed how well they were able to relate to other students in the classroom and extracurricular activities. The responses to these questions were based on a Likert scale, scaling from 0 to 6, with 6 representing Strongly Agree (Assessing Women and Men in Engineering, 2008). The Likert scores for the five items in this category were averaged to calculate the mean pre-SSI score, 4.15, and the mean post-SSI score, 4.58. When the pre and post scores were compared in this subscale category using a paired t-test, it was found that the girls' self-efficacy improved significantly ($p < 0.05$) over the course of the SSI, as illustrated in Figure 8.6. The students developed a greater feeling of inclusion both inside and outside the classroom, as revealed in Figure 8.6.

Math Outcome Expectations (moe)

The students were asked three questions that addressed how they believe math will impact their future. The responses to these questions were based on a Likert scale, scaling from 0 to 6, with 6 representing Strongly Agree (Assessing Women and Men in Engineering, 2008). The Likert scores for the five items in this category were averaged to calculate the mean pre-SSI score, 4.76, and the mean post-SSI score, 5.15. When the pre and post scores were compared in this subscale category using a paired t-test, it was found that the girls' self-efficacy improved significantly ($p < 0.05$) over the course of the SSI, as revealed in Figure 8.6. There were greater expectations in the outcomes of taking math courses and doing well in math, as illustrated in Figure 8.6.

CONCLUSION

The less than 20% of woman and minorities in engineering and other STEM fields is well documented. While one cannot force persons into a given field, students ought to be exposed to these disciplines, giving them a vision of their potential futures. Recruitment of K–12 students, specifically girls, toward studies and careers in engineering is a challenging task. One of the ways the Center for STEM Education for Girls worked to meet these challenges was through its 2-week STEM Summer Institute (SSI) for students who were interested in STEM topics, but whose schools did not meet their needs fully. The program goals were to increase self-efficacy and the understanding of engineering in girls. This was done by incorporating STEM into service learning and placing it within a global context.

The girls in this institute understood that engineering design is not always creating something but is more often improving what already exists. The students were clear that there is reason behind engineering; they understood that engineering includes creating things to solve a problem. Post-SSI, the students had an understanding of engineering that is beyond such superficial ideas that suggest that engineers fix cars or build houses and bridges. It was also evident that the girls realized engineering comprises multiple disciplines and subject areas (such as math and science). By the SSI introducing the girls to real-world issues in which they can offer applicable solutions, the girls were able to make feasible connections to engineering.

The SSI was effective in increasing the girl's self-efficacy; after attending the SSI, the girls had a greater belief in their success within STEM courses. The students also had a greater feeling of inclusion both inside and outside the classroom after attending the SSI. As a result of the SSI, there were greater expectations in the outcomes of taking math courses and doing well in math. Improvement in engineering self-efficacy was evident post the SSI, in which the students were confident in completing an engineering program.

Together, the rise in self-efficacy and content knowledge serves the culture at-large. With the United States' partially STEM-dependent economy, there is an urgent need for more girls and young women to see themselves as creators, inventors, designers, and engineers (Chen, & Weko, 2009). The need for STEM outreach programs that may assist in this need is currently great, and it appears that STEM programs will continue to be developed. However, regardless of such program models, K–12 schools themselves must work to integrate engineering and technology into the core classroom curriculum so that students understand and are prepared for careers in STEM. Without full STEM integration in the classroom, students must currently rely on programs like the SSI to introduce them to STEM. If a 2-week STEM program can make an impact on girls' understanding of engineering and self-efficacy, imagine what such implementation in a year-round classroom could do.

ACKNOWLEDGEMENTS

This work was funded by the Edward E. Ford Educational Leadership Grant. We are grateful for the generous donors who have provided essential match funding for our Edward E. Ford Educational Leadership Grant for the Center for STEM Education for Girls. Major donors include the following: Lenovo, the Melkus Family Foundation, Diane and Jim Mulloy, and Nissan North America. Additional donors included Anonymous (2), the Community Foundation of Middle Tennessee, Dell, the Memorial Foundation, Regions Bank, and Virtucom. The authors wish to thank the National Science Foundation for its support of the BER-REU Site (EEC-0851930), along with Rob Linsenmeier, Penny Hirsch, Leslie Fischer, Mark Bourgeois, and Jean Alley for the organization of that program and review of this manuscript in its early stages. Any opinions, findings, and conclusions or recommendations expressed in this material are those of the authors and do not necessarily reflect the views of our donors.

REFERENCES

Abbitt, J. D., III, & Carroll, B. F. (1993). Applied aerodynamics experience for secondary science teachers and students. *Journal of Engineering Education, 82*(3), 185–188.

Airey, J., & Linder, C. (2009). A disciplinary discourse perspective on university science learning: Achieving fluency in a critical constellation of modes. *Journal of Research in Science Teaching, 46*(1), 27–49.

Assessing Women and Men in Engineering. (2008). *Pre-college annual self-efficacy survey.* Retrieved from www.aweonline.org

Bandura, A. (1997). *Self-efficacy: The exercise of control.* New York, NY: W. H. Freeman.

Betz, N. E., & Schifano, R. S. (2000). Evaluation of an intervention to increase realistic self-efficacy and interests in college women. *Journal of Vocational Behavior, 56,* 35–52.

Bong, M., & Skaalvik, E. M. (2003). Academic self-concept and self-efficacy: How different are they really? *Educational Psychological Review, 15,* 1–40.

Brotman, J. S., & Moore, F. M. (2008). Girls and science: A review of four themes in the science education literature. *Journal of Research in Science Teaching, 45*(9), 971–1002.

Britner, S. L., & Pajares, F. (2006). Sources of science self-efficacy beliefs of middle school students. *Journal of Research in Science Teaching, 43,* 485–499.

Burke, R. J. (2007). Women and minorities in STEM: A primer. In R. J. Burke & M. C. Mathis (Ed.), *Women and minorities in science, technology, engineering, and mathematics: Upping the numbers.* Cheltenham, UK: Edward Elgar.

Carlone, H. B., & Johnson, A. (2007). Understanding the science enterprises of successful women of color: Science identity as an analytic lens. *Journal of Research in Science Training, 44*(8), 1187–1218.

Case, J. M., & Light, G. (2011). Emerging methodologies in engineering education. *Journal of Engineering Education, 100*(1), 186–210.

Ceci, S. J., & Williams, W. M. (Eds.). (2007*). Why aren't more women in science? Top researchers debate the evidence.* Washington, DC: American Psychological Association.

Chen X., & Weko T. (2009). *Students who study science, technology, engineering, and mathematics (STEM) in postsecondary education.* Washington, DC: U.S. Department of Education, National Center for Education Statistics.

Clewell, B. C., & Campbell, P. C. (2002). Taking stock: Where we've been, where we are, where we're going. *Journal of Women and Minorities in Science and Engineering, 8,* 255–284.

Coyle, E. J., Jamieson, L. H., & Oakes, W. C. (2005). EPICS: Engineering projects in community service. *International Journal of Engineering Education, 21*(1), 139–150.

Crawford, R. H., Wood, K. L., Fowler, M. L., & Norrell, J. L. (1994). An engineering design curriculum for the elementary grades. *Journal of Engineering Education, 83*(2), 172–181.

Diekman, A. B., Brown, E. R., Johnston, A. M., & Clark, E. K. (2010). Seeking congruity between roles and goals: A new look at why women opt out of STEM careers. *Psychological Science, 21,* 1051–1057.

Fadali, M. S., Robinson, M., & McNichols, K. (2000). Teaching engineering to K–12 students using role playing games. *Proceedings of the 2000 annual conference of the American Society for Engineering Education.* Washington, DC.

Genalo, L. J., Bruning, M., & Adams, B. (2000). Creating a K–12 engineering educational outreach center. *Proceedings of the 2000 annual conference of the American Society for Engineering Education.* Washington, DC.

Gibbons, M. (2009). Engineering by the numbers. *ASEE profiles of engineering and engineering technology colleges.* Washington, DC: ASEE.

Gist, M. E., & Mitchell, T. R. (1992). Self-efficacy: A theoretical analysis of its determinants and malleability. *Academy of Management Review, 17,* 183–211.

Halpern, D. F., Benbow, C. P., Geary, D. C., Gur, R. C., Hyde, J. S., & Gernsbacher, M. A. (2007). The science of sex differences in science and mathematics. *Psychological Science in the Public Interest, 8,* 1–51.

Halpern, D. F., Aronson, J., Reimer, N., Simpkins, S., Star, J. R., & Wentzel, K. (2007). *Encouraging girls in math and science.* Report for Institute of Education Sciences Practice Guide. Washington, DC: U.S. Department of Education.

Jeffers, A. T., Safferman, A. G., & Safferman, S. I. (2004). Understanding K–12 engineering outreach programs. *Journal of Professional Issues in Engineering Education and Practice, 130*(2), 95–108.

Knight, D. B., Mappen, E. F., & Knight, S. L. (2011). A review of the literature on increasing the representation of women undergraduates in STEM disciplines through civic engagement pedagogies. *Science Education and Civic Engagement, 3*(1), 36–47.

Knight, M., & Cunningham, C. M. (2004). Draw an Engineer Test (DAET): Development of a tool to investigate students' ideas about engineers and engineering. *Proceedings of the 2000 annual conference of the American Society for Engineering Education.* Washington, DC.

Lam, E. (2011). Shifting skill demand. *The Gazette.* Retrieved July 27, 2012, from http://www.montrealgazette.com/news/todayspaper/Shifting+skill+demand/465124/story.html

Lwala Community Alliance. (2012). *Lwala community alliance: About us.* Retrieved July 28, 2012, from http://lwalacommunityalliance.org/about/

National Science Board. (2008). *Science and engineering indicators 2008* (Vol. 1, NSB 08-01; Vol. 2, NSB 08-01A). Arlington, VA: National Science Foundation.

Pajares, F. (2005). Gender differences in mathematics self-efficacy beliefs. In A. M. Gallagher & J. C. Kaufman (Eds.), *Gender differences in mathematics: An integrative psychological approach* (pp. 294–315). Cambridge, UK: Cambridge University Press.

Project Lead The Way. (2012). *About us: Innovation portal.* Retrieved July 29, 2012, from http://www.innovationportal.org/about

Seymour, E. (1995). The loss of women from science, mathematics, and engineering undergraduate majors: An explanatory account. *Science Education, 79,* 437–473.

Sfard, A. (2001). There is more to discourse than meets the ears: Looking at thinking as communicating to learn more about mathematical learning. *Educational Studies in Mathematics, 46*(1), 13–57.

Spelke, E. S. (2005). Sex differences in intrinsic aptitude for mathematics and science? A critical review. *American Psychologist, 60,* 950–958.

Wilson, S. S. (2000). Developing a plan for recruiting and retaining women and minorities in engineering technology at Western Kentucky University.

Proceedings of the 2000 annual conference of the American Society for Engineering Education. Washington, DC.

Zeldin, A. L., & Pajares, F. (2000). Against the odds: Self-efficacy beliefs of women in mathematical, scientific, and technological careers. *American Educational Research Journal, 37,* 215–246.

Zimmerman, B. J. (2000). Self-efficacy: An essential motive to learn. *Contemporary Educational Psychology, 25,* 82–91.

CHAPTER 9

ROBOTICS PROGRAMS

Inspiring Young Women in STEM

Cecilia (Ceal) D. Craig

INTRODUCTION

Robots inspire and grab the attention of young and old. Since the 1940s, when Isaac Asimov (1947) first proposed the Three Laws of Robotics, young people have dreamed about, designed and built, and competed with robots. Robotics is a frequently used outreach platform in the K–12 grades, often via exciting competitions. However, do these programs inspire young men and young women equally to enter STEM careers? Are influences different for females and males? This synthesis of educational robotics research describes programs for K–12 grades, highlighting specific differences and unique findings for females. Robotics programs can help grow spatial abilities, critical thinking skills, problem-solving abilities, and increase interest in STEM subjects and careers for young people. Studies showed that doing robotics helps girls break through stereotype barriers and provides them an environment to explore STEM. More research is needed to better understand gender nuances in the influences from these programs, specifically, longitudinal studies plus race and ethnicity factors

Girls and Women in STEM, pages 175–192
Copyright © 2014 by Information Age Publishing
All rights of reproduction in any form reserved.

in confluence with gender. However, research shows these programs have promise and are worth implementing to encourage more young women to enter the STEM fields.

ROBOTICS PROGRAMS:
INSPIRING YOUNG WOMEN IN STEM

Robotics has been inspiring young people for decades. In 1942, Isaac Asimov (1957), in *Runaround*, outlined for the first time Three Laws of Robotics. In subsequent books, Asimov's characters brought robotics to life for his readers: Dr. Susan Calvin, a roboticist; R. Daneel Olivaw, a humanoid robot; and Elijah Baley, a human detective. Dr. Calvin was a positive role model for young women who read how she created robots. Daneel and Elijah, while solving mysteries on Earth and other planets, learned about human-robot interaction when a robot could be taken for a human being, a vivid memory for me growing up.

Another early robot that inspired young people was *Robbie the Robot*, starring in the 1956 movie, *Forbidden Planet* (IMDb, 2012). Altaira Morbius, the daughter of Dr. Morbius, pleaded with Robby the Robot: "I must have a new dress, right away! ... with lots and lots of star sapphires" (IMDb, 2012, Quotes). He commits she will have it by breakfast. Robby was a character portrayed as a mechanical gizmo developed by Hollywood. A year before Sputnik was launched by the Soviet Union, the idea of Robby inspired young men and women to enter engineering and study fields enabling them to build robots (T. T. Craig, personal communication, October 29, 2012).

Over the succeeding decades, robots appeared in many venues. At Massachusetts Institute of Technology (MIT), Seymour Papert (MIT Media Lab, n.d.), who in Geneva had previously worked with Piaget, was inspired to use technologies for children's education. In 1985, LEGO began collaboration with MIT Media Lab to launch the ubiquitous LEGO bricks with Logo, a simple existing programming language that found quick use in education. This collaboration led to the MINDSTORMS robotics platform, moving programming to an onboard "programmable brick" (MIT Media Lab, n.d., How, para. 1). FIRST LEGO League (FLL), begun in the late 1990s, targeted elementary students using MINDSTORMS (FIRST, 2012d). In 1992, For Inspiration and Recognition of Science and Technology (FIRST) launched the FIRST Robotics Competition (FRC) aimed at high school students with large, complex robots (FIRST, 2012b). The Boosting Engineering Science and Technology (BEST) Robotics (BRI) organization, aiming at middle and high school students, launched its competition in 1993 (BEST Robotics, 2011). Other curriculum and competitions evolved involving underwater robotics, vehicle robotics, other mechanical platforms, as well as many robots using LEGO's platform. Robotics was embraced by education and by young people.

ROBOTICS PROGRAMS OVERVIEW

Educational robotics programs are multidisciplinary and mimic processes used by engineers and scientists for product development. These programs aspire to improve problem-solving skills, increase science and math subject-matter understanding, and show connections to real-world problems. Young people who participate in them are able to experiment and learn what it might be like to be an engineer or scientist. "Robotics fosters creativity" (Notter, 2010, p. 84). Competitions bring excitement and recognition. Barak and Zadok (2009) found that students learning robotics and competing with their robots were motivated and learned science concepts more effectively. What remains to be seen is the long-term influence on females and if it is different or the same as for males. The programs outlined below are major players but do not represent every educational robotics program and are limited to K–12 grades.

Elementary Grades

With its easy-to-use software and hardware, the LEGO MINDSTORMS[1] platform is widely used by K–12 grades and university classes as part of their curriculums and to stimulate interest in STEM. One ubiquitous elementary age competition is FIRST LEGO League (FLL), aimed at ages 9 through 14 (through 16 outside the United States). Begun in 1998 (FIRST, 2013b) as a collaboration between FIRST and LEGO, the 2012 season saw 12,500 teams with over 200,000 children participating, with 40% from some 60 countries outside the United States. Within the students participating, only 30% of those students were female (FIRST, 2012d).

In FLL, each season a new game arrives at the beginning of the school year "creat[ing] an exceptional learning environment that brings with it the excitement of building a robot that is applicable to real-world situations" (Holland, 2004, p. 127). Small teams (average of 10 members) have several months to brainstorm, design, build, teardown, and build again, trying out different ideas, easily modifying their LEGO robots (FIRST, 2012d). Student teams earn awards for a winning robot, demonstrated teamwork, and effective research, with some teams going to the championship, where thousands of students participate from all over the world.

Other programs targeting elementary age include other platforms, such as those using the PicoCricket, based on a development at MIT's Media lab and sold by Playful Invention Company (PICO) for children (PICO, 2010). The PicoCricket offers an integration of technological and artistic interests, a blend that might appeal to females, but no research was found using it. Another platform targeted at a broad age range is iRobot's Create robotic platform (iRobot Corporation, 2013). This customizable but functional out-of-the-box robot is used by several competitions and programs, some discussed in later sections.

Middle and High School Programs

Botball Program: Grades 7–12

Begun in 1997, organized by the KISS Institute for Practical Robots (KIPR), Botball is targeted at middle and high school students (KIPR, 2013). The primary season starts in January, beginning with educator workshops for team instructors and mentors. Student teams design and build autonomous robots using an iRobot Create base (iRobot Corporation, 2013) with LEGOs and other parts, running software created in C, C++, or Java, over 7 weeks, culminating in a spring regional competition (KIPR, 2012). The reusable components can be used by teachers in classrooms after competition ends (KIPR, 2013), extending the overall reach of Botball throughout the school year. In 2012, the teams were 30% female, with 29% underrepresented minority students. Participants were from middle (40%) and high school (60%) (KIPR, 2012).

FIRST Tech Challenge (FTC): Grades 7–12

Begun in 2005 initially with a VEX platform (see below), FIRST developed FTC to provide an experience that was more financially and technologically accessible than FRC (see below). The smaller FTC robots can provide a more challenging experience than LEGO robots for middle school and high school level students (Morrison, 2006), yet are easier to build than FRC robots, because simpler mechanical systems are involved in building them.

Females in FTC were only 23% of teams per the 2011 report (Brandeis University, 2011, p. 4). Recently, FIRST positioned FTC with an accessibility goal emphasizing teamwork and "an atmosphere where everyone contributes" (FIRST, 2013c, Accessibility, para. 1) with specific marketing targeting young women, emphasizing the importance of communication "to ensure everyone is heard" (FIRST, 2012a).

VEX: Middle to High School and College

VEX was the hardware platform for FTC's first seasons. Many schools made large investments in VEX kits and knowledge. While FTC has moved to a different platform, VEX has its own competitions, independent of FIRST and is used in educational curriculums (VEX Robotics Design System, 2013).

FIRST Robotics Competition (FRC): High School

FRC has grown from 28 teams in 1992 to more than 2,300 active teams, over 58,000 students, in 49 states and 12 countries in 2012 (FIRST, 2012c). The first Saturday of January, all teams learn about that year's competition, what the challenge will be, and all the many rules. In the 2013 game, robots could weigh up to 120 pounds (without battery and bumpers), had to fit within a 54-inch diameter, and no more than 84-inch high cylindrical space (FIRST, 2013a). These robots are physically among the largest in the competitions discussed in this chapter. Teams compete at regional events and potentially the championship event. The FRC teams were only 30% female in the most recent report (Brandeis University, 2011, p. 4), similar data for prior years was not found by this researcher.

Boosting Engineering, Science, and Technology: Grades 7–12

Begun in 1993, the design and build portions of this program are 6 weeks in length followed by regional competitions. Teams participate in BEST for free and "equipment and construction materials are provided at no cost to participating schools" (BRI, 2011, p. 2). In 2011, BEST had a presence in 16 states with about 18,000 students participating. BRI has grown its female participation since 2007 (31%) to 34% in 2012, a number similar but slightly higher than other robotics competitions for which I have obtained data. BEST is aimed at both middle and high school students building robots similar in size to VEX and FTC programs (BRI, 2011).

Robotics Programs Summary

Educational- and competition-based programs are available from early elementary through graduate school. FIRST offers four levels of programs (Jr. FLL was not discussed above) covering the gamut of K–12. BEST, VEX, and KIPR (Botball) offer programs for middle and high school students. All of these have the potential to inspire people to careers in STEM and scaffold STEM learning. However, specific data on female participation in these programs was not consistently available until recently for most programs, with the exception of BEST, as reported above.

DIVERSITY NUANCES IN ROBOTICS PROGRAMS

Considering the information available from robotics programs described in prior pages and research outlined below, female participation in robotics teams has been typically about one third of teams on average with minimal change in that ratio in the past several years (e.g., Brandeis University, 2011; BRI, 2011; KIPR, 2012). Another common finding is girls and young women tend not to be involved as much in design and build activities, instead they are more involved in business, website, outreach, and presentation activities for the team (e.g., Adolphson, 2002; Brandeis University, 2011; Weinberg, Pettibone, Thomas, Stephen, & Stein, 2007). However, this situation does apparently vary by program; for example, "the differences were substantially more pronounced on FRC teams, suggesting that the smaller FTC teams provided more opportunities for girls to get directly involved in the 'technical' aspects of the program" (Brandeis University, 2011, p. 8). The next sections describe research segmented by age groups (elementary, middle school, and high school) integrated with unique gender findings, followed by research about robotics and spatial abilities, race and ethnicity findings, concluding with a summary of research gaps.

Curriculum and Classroom Research on Robotics

In this section, I will first summarize recent research involving robotics programs in elementary, middle school, and finally high school. This section will show the breadth of influence robotics can have and that has been studied. Specific gender findings on robotics programs are integrated within.

Elementary Program Research

In a week-long program with 5th- and 6th-grade students centered on LEGO robotics, Gibbon (2007) investigated student problem-solving (both convergent and divergent or creative) and spatial abilities changes (more on that in a later section). "Students are led by the work rather than following a prescribed plan, and ... students have the flexibility to learn ... constructing with concrete objects" (p. 23). A positive increase in divergent problem-solving skills occurred in the treatment group using LEGO, and fifth graders appeared to benefit slightly more than sixth graders. Gibbon found no gender differences in his study of fifth and sixth graders using LEGO robots. Study teams included single-gender (boys or girls) and mixed-gender teams. He recommended continuing gendered data gathering because of the continuing low percentages of females in engineering and science programs and suggested longer-term studies of young women in college who had used LEGO in their youth to explore any relationship between that use and career decisions (pp. 88–89).

Investigating how problem-solving abilities change over time, Varnado (2005) evaluated FLL team members at multiple times within an 8-week FLL design period. The students had no formal training in problem solving to begin with; thus, Varnado concluded the changes were the result of the FLL activities. Varnado found no gender differences in problem-solving abilities considering measurements taken at four different points within the FLL design period. Moreover, the perceptions of boys and girls about their "technological problem solving styles" (Varnado, 2005, p. 61) were the same.

In Holland's (2004) mixed methods, yearlong LEGO-based technology study of gifted 5th-grade students, students explored robotics through a multistep LEGO robotics curriculum. Students were assessed via an instrument developed by Holland, "Student Attitudes Towards Technology" (p. 139) before the program began and afterwards with some participating in focus group interviews at the end. Those participating in the program had increased scores measuring their ability to use technology. Girls who participated in the programs had higher mean scores for attitudes and perceptions about robotics posttest than the boys in the program (this result was opposite pretest scores), whereas means for girls and boys in the classes without the intervention were similar (pp. 167, 202–203). One of Holland's conclusions was that the "program gave [the girls] a chance to advance and take risks" (p. 203). In focus group interviews, as one girl expressed it, "I think you should do robotics because today . . . in our world a lot of things are surrounded by technology and all the greatest discoveries are mostly in technology" (p. 182).

Notter (2010) studied girls through focus groups held on an FLL competition day. She gleaned four themes: "*It's all about the competition, It's like everyone is rootin' for you, What do you do with robotics, and I know who I am*" (Notter, 2010, p. 54, emphasis in original). The theme *what do you do with robotics* connected robotics to STEM careers; Notter suggested that younger girls had not yet connected robotics to STEM and were still picking careers in non-STEM fields, whereas the older girls were more commonly focused on STEM careers. Another finding was that the girls embraced the activity's competitive nature. However, as Notter mentioned in several places, the girls' positive attitudes might be due to the positive collaborative attitudes found in FLL teams. Some girls reported issues at their schools or environments with their FLL interest. "Though these issues seemed rather mild, it still implies that girls who don't have a strong will or mindset to follow what makes them happy might miss out on STEM related coursework due to negative connotations" (p. 55). Consistent with findings from a recent American Association of University Women report (Hill, Corbett, & St. Rose, 2010), Notter's point (2010) brings home how important programs like these can be to avoid limiting a girl's opportunities, instead expanding those opportunities and helping her visualize how she *can* do this.

Middle School Program Research

Robotics programs have been used to offer many possibilities for this age group. Students can be involved in "meaningful open-ended problem solving activities" (Adolphson, 2002, p. ix). Adolphson (2002) explored how designing and building robots influenced students' understanding of mathematics perceptions and how they "cooperatively organized their efforts and negotiated meaning as they solved complex, open-ended tasks" (p. 112). The activities helped students connect mathematics with robotics and improved their understanding of mathematics, though they did not see any connections to their math classes in school.

Robotics programs can be exciting, and students seem to enjoy them; however, it is less clear what influence these programs have on young people, specifically on young women. Weinberg et al. (2007), using a backdrop of Expectancy-Value Theory developed by Wigfield and Eccles (as cited in Wienberg et al., 2007), investigated the influence of Botball robotics on young women's self-perceptions related to STEM and if it affected career choice, considering nuances from single- and mixed-gender teams. They recruited 36 seventh-grade teams "from 13 states, representing all regions of the country" (Weinberg et al., 2007, p. 2) to participate, one third of them from single-gender teams. They "found that beliefs in traditional gender roles led to negative self-concepts of ability [with resultant] lower expectations for success in science and math" (p. 3) and ultimately the same for STEM careers. If traditional roles were rejected, then positive results occurred. By participating in Botball, more girls did not accept traditional roles and demonstrated a "significantly increased" (p. 3) positive attitude toward engineering.

Weinberg et al. (2007) also explored the influence of mentors and what roles girls took on the teams. After the program, girls in mixed-gender teams showed a higher self-concept about STEM with "good mentors" (Weinberg et al., 2007, p. 3), though girls in single-gender teams saw no difference. By helping girls learn about engineering processes and "seem[ing] to neutralize ... the impact of traditional gender roles on self-concept and performance" (p. 3), effective mentors had a positive influence in both types of teams. Also, girls more often took soft-skills roles on the team or did software development versus being involved in hardware design or build. This was consistent with other researcher's findings (e.g., Adolphson, 2002; Brandeis University, 2011) that girls' roles and interface techniques were different than the boys. The boys more consistently were involved in either hardware or software but not both. Whereas girls were comfortable in various roles, often seeming to not be involved at all and then quickly becoming involved in a problem to help resolve it (Adolphson, 2002, pp. 114–116).

Whitehead (2010) aimed to improve middle school attitudes toward STEM (specifically the latter three of these, or TEM) via LEGO robotics.

He asserted that being exposed to robotics and STEM in high school some-times left students with insufficient math efficacy to succeed in those college pathways. Mathematics teachers used the LEGO robotic kits to supplement mathematics curriculum. Whitehead's results from the quantitative study showed some increases, though not significant, were found in beliefs about TEM; however, the students' interest in answering questions through experiments showed significant positive increases. He did not publish any gender-specific results, though about one third of the participants were female (a proportion of participation similar to other robotics programs reported in this chapter). He mentioned that two participating schools had no girls on the teams; teachers thought "a popular girl had influenced oth-er girls to not participate in the study" (Whitehead, 2010, p. 67).

Vollstedt (2005) found in her three-part study (teacher training, sum-mer camp, and science classrooms) that science curriculum using LEGO educational robotics kits improved middle school student STEM knowl-edge. Students designed, programmed, and built robots that moved to mu-sic, competitively shot ping pong balls into hoops, raced a robotic car, and finally engaged in "a tug-of-war, sumo, and relay competition" (Vollstedt, 2005, p. 41). While the test results were mixed in Vollstedt's study, the quali-tative results provided positive feedback about the approach and its poten-tial to positively influence STEM attitudes in middle school students and teachers. Like Whitehead (2010), Vollstedt had about one third female and two thirds male participants across the two-year study of 12 middle schools, but no specific gender results were shared.

Some middle school studies did examine gender data. For example, Mo-jica (2010) used LEGO kits as one unit in a three-unit quasi-experimental study "to improve higher-order critical thinking skills" (Mojica, 2010, p. 11) in 8th-grade technology students. The other two study units involved telling stories by making a movie and a challenge event using marbles. Mojica ob-served an increase in critical thinking skills and the girls' skills "increased more than twice as much [as] the males" (p. 110), though the increases were not statistically significant.

From a different perspective, Bernstein (2010) used the *hummingbird* CREATE robot (BirdBrain, 2013) in a study of technological fluency growth in girls. The girls involved used both artistic and engineering styles to en-gage with the hummingbird robot (Bernstein, 2010). These home-schooled girls, ages 9 to 14, wrote "Robot Diaries" (Bernstein, 2010, p. 164), created costumes, and programmed its actions, demonstrating creativity from many perspectives. Bernstein observed, "consistent pre-post gains in certain areas (e.g., confidence in designing and building robots)" (p. 175). This easy-to-use robot base showed that simple programs can help girls embrace many facets of their personality and style while inspiring them to enjoy STEM.

High School Programs Research

Jewell (2011) found no gender differences in attitudes toward science or STEM careers in her quasi-experimental study involving an elective LEGO robotics-based high school class; however, the small number of females in the intervention program (9 out of 57) might have skewed the results one way or the other. She did find significant ethnicity and race differences. Welch (2007, 2010), in a quasi-experimental study of changes in attitudes toward science, about scientists, and using scientific principles, found students participating in FRC showed improvements compared with students who were in a science class but did not participate in FRC. She found no significant differences by gender or ethnicity.

In a longitudinal study commissioned by FIRST, Melchior, Cohen, Cutter, and Leavitt (2005) found a significant number of FRC alumnae (adults who had participated in FRC as high school students) had selected engineering and science careers compared to national averages. Female FRC alumnae selected engineering major to a lesser extent (32.8%) when compared to male alumnae (48.1%) and significantly less for computer sciences (1.7% vs. 18.2%), but significantly higher for business (22.4% vs. 6.5%). However, the national averages for engineering were 12.7% for males and 2.1% for females; thus, FRC did inspire more males and females to enter engineering (p. 36). A more recent study (Brandeis University, 2011, pp. 50–53) found somewhat similarly in a cross-program study of FTC and FRC that 72.4% (FRC)/75.6% (FTC) of females versus 87.6% (FRC)/87.9% (FTC) of males agreed or strongly agreed they "want[ed] to be a scientist or engineer" (Brandeis University, 2011, p. 50).

Like the Botball study of seventh graders (Weinberg et al., 2007), Welch (2007), in a study of high school student science attitudes after being in FRC, found girls were more involved in "scrap booking, photography, and record keeping" (Welch, 2007, p. 147) than in build activities. Hurner (2009), using a community of practice framework to explore social identity in an all-girls FRC team, noted that "the RoboGirls [were] intensely aware of their subordinate status as girls involved in a male dominant activity" (p. 292). The girls experienced this attitude in the competition from other teams and from "local, familiar interactions on campus" (p. 292). During the competition, as part of the typical three-team FRC alliances, the girls did not complain or push back when the boys on other teams told the girls what to do, though the girls complained privately later (p. 297).

Hurner (2007) also reported the amount of influence that negative feedback from a mentor can have. As one student shared with Hurner, "she felt dismissed when '[an instructor and team coach] blew me off' and discouraged" (p. 301). Webb (2009) observed a similar reaction exploring discourse while observing a mixed-gender FRC team. Girls were not much involved in the design or building of the robot, feeling they were "allowed to participate rather than entitled" (p. 152). A cross-program (FRC and FTC) report commissioned by FIRST (Brandeis University, 2011) had similar findings, concluding "an effort [is needed] to ensure that girls participate equally in the 'technical' aspects . . . designing, programming, building and operating the robots" (Brandeis University, 2011, p. 85), though girls on FTC teams experienced less of this issue. Nonetheless, as reported earlier by Brandeis University (2011) and Melchior et al. (2005), Griffith (2005) found that girls' interest in engineering and computers as a career did increase after participating in the FRC program (pp. 101–102).

Summing Up Robotics Educational Program Research

Robotics programs can positively influence young people's interest in STEM subjects and careers. Three key points arose in the synthesis (only some of the research reviewed is detailed above). Teacher training (Vollstedt, 2005) is a key success factor for how well a robotics program goes and for the direction of its influence, positive or negative (Jim, 2010). Without teacher training, young people see robots as "just . . . another 'foreign' object" (Jim, 2010, p. 100). The level of comfort a teacher has might support more frequent playful inquiry and be important for creative problem-solving skills development (Sullivan, 2011) as well as whether girls participate in the program (Whitehead, 2010). Webb (2009) shared how mentors provided another success element for FRC programs, though implementing FRC in a science classroom would be difficult, as an extracurricular activity, mentors can supplement teacher learning. Bottom line, the success of these technology-rich programs is dependent on knowledgeable and motivated adults.

The second point concerns the value of these kinds of intervention programs. Ward, Miller, Sienkiewicz, and Antonucci (2012) asserted that "intervention . . . by the early middle-school level [is] imperative" (p. 96), drawing that conclusion from a study of National Educational Longitudinal Study (NELS) data. They also suggested afterschool programs were a key intervention component. Ward et al. found that both girls and boys equally demonstrated increased learning in subject-matter skills after a program using robot-driven astronomical instruments. Thus, programs like those described above could be a cornerstone influence for stimulating young women's interest in a STEM career.

The last point is what was found about gender. Some did not study it at all. Some found nuances worthy of further research: Griffith (2005) showed increases in girls' interest in engineering, Whitehead's (2010) recommendation for research about peer pressure influences, Holland (2004) and Notter's (2010) findings about girls and risk taking opportunities in robotics, Weinberg et al. (2007) noted increases in positive attitudes toward engineering after Botball, and Mojica (2010) finding that girls increased their critical thinking skills after participating in robotics. Some found no significant differences in results by gender (Gibbon, 2007; Varnado, 2005; Welch, 2007), though most suggested further gender-filtered research or reported nuances not showing up in data (e.g., statements about girls being more involved in nondesign or build aspects of robotics, found in Brandeis University, 2011; Webb, 2009; Welch, 2007).

Spatial Ability Differences

Spatial ability is a predictor for STEM careers (Newcombe, 2007). Coxon's (2011) experimental study investigated spatial ability changes in elementary and middle school-age gifted students after a concentrated version of FLL robotics. Male students in the intervention program showed increased spatial abilities post- versus pretest, whereas females showed no significant change. Coxon's insights (Ch. 5) on the possible causes for this gender difference is recommended reading on this subject as well as Newcombe (2007). Spatial ability has several ingredients, and robotics programs may influence only one or two of those, most notably transformations. In Coxon's (2011) description of gender differences, he noted the "abstract reasoning subtest may have less gender bias" (p. 84). However, males in the experimental group "made significant gains" (p. 84) compared with those in the control group, whereas the females in both groups showed similar gains. Thus, he posited, "the treatment [FLL robotics] may be less effective for females" (p. 84) at raising spatial abilities.

Coxon's (2011) finding on the gender nuances of robotics influence on spatial ability development is consistent with other research. Newcombe (2007) stated that while intervention programs have been shown to be successful at improving spatial ability for both males and females, achieving "convergence [may be] hard to get" (p. 75). She asserted that problem-solving, analytical, and leadership skills may be as important as spatial abilities in reaching high achievement levels in science and engineering. Moreover, spatial-focused training results in larger deltas than gender-based deltas. Gur and Gur (2007) concluded from their meta-analysis that women and men use their brains differently to perform the same spatial task (p. 194). Thus, the type of intervention and how it influences males and females could be different (Coxon, 2011; Newcombe, 2007). Designing an intervention program ultimately aimed at improving women's participation in engineering, physics, and computer science needs to consider these nuances.

Race and Ethnicity Findings

Latina/o Students

Ortiz (2010) evaluated the use of LEGO robotics to enhance student learning of mathematical concepts of "ratios and proportions in an extracurricular program" (p. iii) in a mixed-methods, limited duration study of fifth graders from a "public urban elementary school located in a low socioeconomic status (SES) community" (p. 51), "who were representative . . . of Latino students" (p. 192). Ortiz found that students who participated in the program had higher understanding of these principles and retained the learning for a longer time when tested 10 weeks later (p. 192, 201). Another study (Sullivan, 2011) involving Latina/o students explored the use of "playfulness and bricolage" (p. 63) within a focal group of three students solving a robotics problem involving light and energy. The dialogues showed how these elements of creative problem solving were used by 6th-grade Latina/o science students.

African American Students

Ward et al. (2012) targeted a middle school robotic telescope program at underrepresented and female students to inspire them about STEM and to improve their subject-matter knowledge of science concepts. Learning after completing the program was the same when analyzed by gender, race, and ethnicity. However, girls showed a markedly smaller interest in STEM careers compared with boys, regardless of race or ethnicity.

Jewell (2011) explored the influence of a LEGO robotics curriculum on science attitudes of high school students. While she found no gender differences, she did find significantly lower scores for African American students after experiencing the program (insufficient Hispanic students participated to make conclusions). She speculated that the program may not speak to the minority student in the same way it does to majority students (p. 90). It was not clear if these conclusions varied by gender.

Research Gaps

Most studies have investigated relatively short-term influences of robotics programs. They have tested only after a competition, not years later or after the students are in college. Only a few studies have investigated or explored the longer-term influence on young women's perceptions of STEM or career decisions (e.g., Melchior et al., 2005).

In keeping with the National Academy of Engineering's (2008) concept of *Changing the Conversation,* one aspect of robotics that might more strongly positively influence young women is seeing robots as more "sociable" (Lu & Mead, 2012, p. 1). Bernstein (2010) found this in her mixed-method study in which girls made creative robots using the hummingbird CREATE robot with construction paper and other typical arts and crafts items, showing both artistic and engineering skills. "The gender gap . . . lies not in capability, but rather in social constructs for girls and boys, and what they early on expect to do later in life, and possibly how they perceive their adult responsibilities will affect their careers" (Bernstein, 2010, p. 98). More research is needed in this area across different platforms and age levels. This potentially has a connection to the finding across multiple studies (e.g., Brandeis University, 2011; Welch, 2007) that females were less likely to be involved in design and build of robots and more involved in presentations, marketing, and creating other visual collateral.

Two distinctions to note from two studies (Hurner, 2009; Notter, 2010): One involved preteens/early teen girls (Notter, 2010) in a LEGO program, and one involved high-school girls in an FRC program (Hurner, 2009). A wealth of difference occurs cognitively and emotionally during that time. Moreover, today FLL and FRC are implemented very differently. A longitudinal study with alumnae from both programs might better study long-term influences.

Underrepresented minority data, in particular by gender, for robotics programs is another area needing more research. Mosley and Kline (2006) from Pace University in New York developed a LEGO-based introductory problem-solving class that incorporates service learning to engage students from all majors, though it was not specifically targeted at underrepresented students. The college students take a class learning to use LEGO themselves and then take the project on the road to middle schools in the community, helping those schools develop LEGO clubs and get involved with the FLL program. The Baltimore City Community College (BCCC) implemented a plan building on Pace's class concept; "ninety percent of BCCC's student body is African-American" (Mosley, Liu, Hargrove, & Doswell, 2010, p. 1). This longer-term preengineering program concept begins with 11th-grade underrepresented students and works with them into BCCC and beyond. As noted, several researchers have recommended further research on gender, race, and ethnicity gaps (e.g., Jewell, 2011). For example, Coxon (2011), in his FLL study of gifted students, attempted to include race and ethnicity differences but was unable to obtain sufficient participants to gain statistical worth and recommended future studies. Thus, outcomes from the BCCC program as well as other research will inform this research gap, it is hoped, sometime in the near future.

SUMMARY

Educational robotics programs can inspire young people to pursue STEM careers. The panache or "gee-whiz" excitement of robots has been doing this for decades. Robotics intervention and curricular programs have been shown to build scientific inquiry and engineering problem-solving skills in young people from elementary age through high school. Young women benefit from participating in these programs with increased interest and skill in STEM. The long-term influence of these programs is not as well studied. What roles the girls and young women take in these programs and why is also an area for further research. In addition, the confluence of race or ethnicity and gender presents another challenge that has only minimally been studied. Nonetheless, on balance, robotics programs provide important intervention tools for education and the community as a way to influence young people, and young women in particular, to pursue STEM careers.

NOTE

1. Unless otherwise noted, when LEGO robotics or LEGO kits are mentioned, this means LEGO MINDSTORMS robotics kits.

REFERENCES

Adolphson, K. V. (2002). *Mathematical embodiment through robotics activities.* (Doctoral dissertation). Retrieved from ProQuest Dissertations and Theses database. (UMI No. 3053169)

Asimov, I. (1957). *The Naked Sun* [eBook]. New York, NY: Bantam Book/Random House Digital.

Barak, M., & Zadok, Y. (2009). Robotics projects and learning concepts in science, technology and problem solving. *International Journal of Technology & Design Education, 19*(3), 289–307. doi:10.1007/s10798-007-9043-3

Bernstein, D. L. (2010). *Developing technological fluency through creative robotics.* (Doctoral dissertation). Retrieved from ProQuest Dissertations and Theses database. (UMI No. 3435373)

BEST Robotics (BRI). (2011). *2010–2011 annual report.* Retrieved from http://www.bestinc.org/documents/2010-2011 BRI Annual Report.pdf

BirdBrain Technologies. (2013). *Inspire! Create! Educate!* Retrieved from http://www.birdbraintechnologies.com/

Brandeis University, Center for Youth and Communities. (2011). *Cross-program evaluation of the FIRST Tech Challenge and the FIRST Robotics Competition: Final report.* Manchester, NH: FIRST.

Coxon, S. V. (2011). *The malleability of spatial ability under treatment of a FIRST LEGO League-based robotics unit* (Doctoral dissertation). Retrieved from ProQuest Dissertations and Theses database. (UMI No. 3492309)

For Inspiration and Recognition of Science and Technology (FIRST). (2012a). *The FIRST tech challenge: Inspiring women.* Retrieved from http://www.usfirst.org/

For Inspiration and Recognition of Science and Technology (FIRST). (2012b). *Making it loud: 2011 annual report.* Retrieved from http://www.usfirst.org/sites/default/files/uploadedFiles/Who/Annual_Report-Financials/2011_Annual-Report.pdf

For Inspiration and Recognition of Science and Technology (FIRST). (2012c). *FRC: 2012 season facts.* Retrieved from http://www.usfirst.org/

For Inspiration and Recognition of Science and Technology (FIRST). (2012d). *FLL: At a glance.* Retrieved from http://www.usfirst.org/roboticsprograms/marketing-tools/fll/promotional-fliers-brochures-annual-report-and-presentations

For Inspiration and Recognition of Science and Technology (FIRST). (2013a). *FIRST robotics competition: Administrative manual. Game manual.* Retrieved from http://frc-manual.usfirst.org/

For Inspiration and Recognition of Science and Technology (FIRST). (2013b). *FIRST history.* Retrieved from http://www.usfirst.org/aboutus/first-history#ftc_history

For Inspiration and Recognition of Science and Technology (FIRST). (2013c, May). *FTC promotional flyers, brochures, annual report, presentations, and scholarships.* Retrieved from http://www.usfirst.org/roboticsprograms/marketing-tools/ftc/ftc-promotional-fliers-brochures-annual-report-presentations-and-scholarships

Gibbon, L. W. (2007). *Effects of LEGO Mindstorms on convergent and divergent problem-solving and spatial abilities in fifth and sixth grade students* (Doctoral dissertation). Retrieved from ProQuest Dissertations and Theses database. (UMI No. 3268731)

Griffith, D. S., Jr. (2005). *FIRST robotics as a model for experiential problem-based learning: A comparison of student attitudes and interests in science, mathematics, engineering, and technology* (Doctoral dissertation). Retrieved from ProQuest Dissertations and Theses database. (UMI No. 3170164)

Gur, R. C., & Gur, R. E. (2007). Neural substrates for sex differences in cognition. In S. J. Ceci & W. M. Williams (Eds.), *Why aren't more women in science: Top researchers debate the evidence* (pp. 189–198). Washington, DC: Sage.

Hill, C., Corbett, C., & St. Rose, A. (2010). *Why so few? Women in science, technology, engineering, and mathematics.* Washington, DC: American Association of University Women. Retrieved from http://www.aauw.org/learn/research/whysofew.cfm

Holland, S. M. (2004). *Attitudes toward technology and development of technological literacy of gifted and talented elementary school students* (Doctoral dissertation). Retrieved from ProQuest Dissertations and Theses database. (UMI No. 3160780)

Hurner, S. M. (2009). *Robotics as science (re)form: Exploring power, learning and gender(ed) identity formation in a "community of practice"* (Doctoral dissertation). Retrieved from ProQuest Dissertations and Theses database. (UMI No. 3369846)

IMDb. (2012). *Forbidden Planet.* (1956). Retrieved from http://www.imdb.com/title/tt0049223/?ref_=ttqt_qt_tt

iRobot Corporation. (2013). *SPARK: Starter programs for the advancement of robotics knowledge.* Retrieved from http://spark.irobot.com/

Jewell, S. L. (2011). *The effects of the NXT robotics curriculum on high school students attitudes in science based on grade, gender, and ethnicity* (Doctoral dissertation). Retrieved from ProQuest Dissertations and Theses database. (UMI No. 3456063)

Jim, C. K. W. (2010). *Teaching with LEGO Mindstorms robots: Effects on learning environment and attitudes toward science* (Master's thesis). Retrieved from ProQuest Dissertations and Theses database. (UMI No. 1489918)

KISS Institute for Practical Robotics (KIPR). (2012). *2012 national Botball impact.* Retrieved from http://www.kipr.org/2012-botball-national-impact

KISS Institute for Practical Robotics (KIPR). (2013). *Botball: A standards-based educational robotics program.* Retrieved from http://www.botball.org/

Lu, D. V., & Mead, R. (2012, March). *Introducing students grades 6–12 to expressive robotics* (Video session). Presented at the ACM/IEEE international conference on Human-Robot Interaction, Boston, MA. Retrieved from www.acm.org

Massachusetts Institute of Technology (MIT) Media Lab. (n.d.). *LEGO's Mindstorms.* Retrieved from http://media.mit.edu/sponsorship/getting-value/collaborations/mindstorms

Melchior, A., Cohen, F., Cutter, T., & Leavitt, T. (2005). *More than robots: An evaluation of the FIRST robotics competition participant and institutional impacts.* Retrieved from http://www.usfirst.org/

Mojica, K. D. (2010). *Ordered effects of technology education units on higher-order critical thinking skills of middle school students* (Doctoral dissertation). Retrieved from ProQuest Dissertations and Theses database. (UMI No. 3468158).

Morrison, A. (2006). Robotics competition expands—FIRST Vex Challenge inspires creativity, ingenuity and innovation. *Tech Directions, 66*(2), 10–12.

Mosley, P., & Kline, R. (2006). Engaging students: A framework using LEGO robotics to teach problem solving. *Information Technology, Learning, and Performance Journal, 24*(1), 39–45.

Mosley, P., Liu, Y., Hargrove, S. K., & Doswell, J. T. (2010). A pre-engineering program using robots to attract underrepresented high school and community college students. *Journal of STEM Education: Innovations and Research, 11*(5), 44–54.

National Academy of Engineering. (2008). *Changing the conversation: Messages for improving public understanding of engineering.* Washington, DC: National Academies Press. Retrieved from http://www.nap.com/catalog/12187.html

Newcombe, N. S. (2007). Taking science seriously: Straight thinking about spatial sex differences. In S. J. Ceci & W. M. Williams (Eds.), *Why aren't more women in science: Top researchers debate the evidence* (pp. 69–77). Washington, DC: Sage.

Notter, K. B. (2010). *Is competition making a comeback? Discovering methods to keep female adolescents engaged in STEM: A phenomenological approach* (Doctoral dissertation). Retrieved from ProQuest Dissertations and Theses database. (UMI No. 3412882)

Ortiz, A. M. (2010). *Fifth grade students' understanding of ratio and proportion in an engineering robotics program* (Doctoral dissertation). Retrieved from ProQuest Dissertations and Theses database. (UMI No. 3422310)

Playful Invention Company (PICO). (2010). *About PICO.* Retrieved from http://www.picocricket.com/aboutpico.html

Sullivan, F. R. (2011). Serious and playful inquiry: Epistemological aspects of collaborative creativity. *Journal of Educational Technology & Society, 14*(1), 55–65.

Varnado, T. E. (2005). *The effects of a technological problem-solving activity on FIRST(TM) LEGO(TM) League participants' problem solving style and performance* (Doctoral dissertation). Retrieved from ProQuest Dissertations and Theses database. (UMI No. 3164186)

VEX Robotics Design System. (2013). Retrieved from http://www.vexrobotics.com/vex/

Vollstedt, A.-M. (2005). *Using robotics to increase student knowledge and interest in science, technology, engineering, and math* (Master's thesis). Retrieved from ProQuest Dissertations and Theses database. (UMI No. 1429847)

Ward, R., Miller, J. L., Sienkiewicz, R., & Antonucci, P. (2012). ITEAMS: Increasing the self-identification for girls and underserved youth in pursuing STEM careers. *Journal of Systemics, Cybernetics & Informatics, 10*(1), 95–99.

Webb, H. (2009). *Factors affecting construction of science discourse in the context of an extracurricular science and technology project* (Doctoral dissertation), Georgia State University. Retrieved from Dissertations and Theses: Full Text (Publication No. AAT 3401618).

Weinberg, J. B., Pettibone, J. C., Thomas, S. L., Stephen, M. L., & Stein, C. (2007). *The impact of robot projects on girls' attitudes towards science and engineering* [unpublished manuscript]. Provided by Steve Goodgame, KISS Institute for Practical Robotics, Executive Director.

Welch, A. (2007). *The effect of the FIRST robotics competition on high school students' attitudes toward science* (Doctoral dissertation). Retrieved from Dissertations & Theses. (Publication No. AAT 3283939)

Welch, A. G. (2010). Using the TOSRA to assess high school students' attitudes toward science after competing in the first robotics competition: An exploratory study. *Eurasia Journal of Mathematics, Science & Technology Education, 6*(3), 187–197.

Whitehead, S. H. (2010). *Relationship of robotic implementation on changes in middle school students' beliefs and interest toward science, technology, engineering and mathematics* (Doctoral dissertation). Retrieved from ProQuest Dissertations and Theses database. (UMI No. 3433457)

CHAPTER 10

LOOKING THROUGH A MIRROR WITH A THIRD EYE

Improving Mathematics Teaching in Culturally Diverse Classrooms

Sylvia Taube
Barbara Polnick

My students understand more because I understand more.
—Middle School Teacher

There was no life in my classroom before TQG.
—High School Teacher

This is the first time I ever liked math . . . I never want to miss class!
—Middle School Student

Girls and Women in STEM, pages 193–216
Copyright © 2014 by Information Age Publishing
All rights of reproduction in any form reserved.

INTRODUCTION

Motivating teachers and students to pursue the study of mathematics can be challenging. This challenge becomes even more difficult when working with teachers who must engage and motivate students from diverse populations. As schools across the United States become more diverse in language, culture, and race, mathematics teachers are being challenged to critically analyze their current teaching to increase the number of students who have access to STEM learning opportunities in an equitable manner to equip the diverse groups representative of the nation's population. Professional development research in mathematics education has not completely addressed how teachers are gaining competency in effectively teaching STEM-related content to students from diverse backgrounds even though there is some agreement on what those teaching competencies are. In a recent study in a large urban school with a high diverse population, researchers found that middle school teachers whose students had high academic gains in mathematics were more likely to implement teaching practices that (a) developed students' conceptual understanding of mathematics, (b) made connections between mathematics and other disciplines, and (c) used textbooks as a resource rather than as the primary instructional tool (McDonald, Polnick, & Robles-Pina, 2013). Additionally, in a keynote address at the 2012 annual National Association of Professional Development Schools conference, distinguished researcher and educator Linda Darling-Hammond summarized common findings from several studies which included that effective teachers (a) understand subject matter deeply and flexibly, (b) connect what is learned to student's prior knowledge and experience, (c) use instructional strategies that help students to draw conclusions, and (d) apply and practice new skills learned. The characteristics and behaviors described above also embrace many elements of what is described as culturally responsive teaching (Ladson-Billings, 2009).

In this chapter, we describe how an extended professional development model that utilized teacher self-reflections and peer feedback, mathematics modeling and the integration of technology in instruction, and the implementation of culturally relevant instructional strategies helped secondary mathematics teachers improve their teaching in their diverse classrooms. The Mathematics Professional Development Program (MPDP) was supported through a Teacher Quality Grant (TQG), a state-funded grant the goal of which was to improve mathematics content, pedagogy, and technology use by secondary teachers; thus, you will see comments by teachers regarding TQG when referencing MPDP. Nineteen female teachers attended three summer institutes and follow-up sessions during the inclusive dates, July 2009–March 2012.

In this chapter, we share the journey of 19 women who, as secondary mathematics teachers, represent a population of teachers who have overcome the documented gender issues in early mathematics learning and pursued mathematics as an area of concentration in their academic study. They participated in the process of improving their mathematics teaching in diverse classrooms and the process is described through the eyes of four archetypes. It is significant to note, in these stories, the ways in which culturally responsive and inclusive teaching strategies enhance their practice while their own identities as women are not considered a subset of the larger paradigm. Their understanding of new methodologies for secondary mathematics instruction are informed by their desire to be inclusive and reach diverse learners, while at no time seeing themselves as "other" to learning mathematics.

BEFORE...

Winona taught in a large junior high school in a rural setting for 10 years. Her classes were very diverse, with about half of the students being Hispanic or African American. Over half of the student body on her campus was identified as "economically disadvantaged." Winona was White and lived in a middle-class neighborhood. Winona taught from her Saxon textbook series in most of her 7th- and 8th-grade classes. She occasionally used a calculator to demonstrate some pre-algebra skills. In addition, there were class sets of calculators for the students to use.

Brittany taught mathematics in a small rural high school (approximately 500 students). About 25% of her students were either African American or Hispanic, with over 60% coming from homes identified as being "economically disadvantaged." In addition, over half of the students on her campus were identified as being "at risk." She was one of three math teachers in her school, so her classes were fairly small, but she had several preparations. She was involved in mentoring new teachers by observing their classrooms, planning lessons together, and coteaching some classrooms. On her campus, there was one Spanish teacher who acted as a translator for those students who were not fluent English speakers. She was less traditional than most teachers in the program. She attended professional development sessions such as Mathematics for English Language Learners (MELL), where she learned how to implement strategies for second language learners. She was not afraid of using technology, but there was a limited amount of technology in her school. Brittany was White and lived in a middle-class neighborhood.

Virginia was a White mathematics teacher at a large rural high school (1,738). She had mostly seniors in her classes, including AP Calculus. Most of these students were White and college bound. Her teaching style then could be considered traditional, with minimal use of collaborative learning, differentiation, or performance-based assessments. Graphing calculators were the primary tools for solving problems, and they were used daily. No other technology was used on a frequent basis.

Theresa was a White teacher who lived near and taught in a suburban affluent international junior high where over 70% of the students were White and less than 12% were identified as "at risk." Most of her students were taking Pre-AP classes, receiving high school credit during their 7th- and 8th-grade years. In these classes, her students used TI-84+ calculators to solve math problems. At her school, she also prepared students to take the state assessment exam, some for the second time. Therefore, during a 3-week period in the spring, some of her classes were taught by others while she was pulled out to teach students who needed extra help to pass the state assessment. During these pull-out classes, she engaged students through good questioning, student explanation of answers, peer tutoring, and intense feedback on their errors. No technology was used during these classes.

As noted in the scenarios above, before participating in the MPDP model, teachers used traditional techniques (teacher directed, curriculum driven, whole group instruction) and did not incorporate many strategies for meeting the needs of all learners. Typically, they taught lessons using the textbook and the same direct instruction to all the students with very little differentiation or culturally diverse strategies. Lessons were presented by the teacher following the same instructional routine of review, demonstration, practice, and assignment for additional practice and reinforcement. Minimal use of manipulatives/models or technology, as well as little group work, was integrated into their instruction. When models or technology were used, they were mostly in the hands of the teacher, not the students. Students, upon observation, were typically passive learners. In many cases, the teachers lacked the confidence in themselves to make needed changes, specifically in higher-level mathematics courses. These teachers reflected who Hull (2007) described as typical of the many who teach mathematics in American schools today.

The above 4 teachers are archetypes of the 19 women who completed a mathematics professional development program described in this chapter. They all had an intense desire to learn more about how to teach mathematics to all students, especially those from culturally diverse backgrounds. All were hoping to help their students meet the challenges of a newly legislated 4x4 curriculum requirement, which required students to complete an additional mathematics course in high school. Previously, students had to complete only 3 years of math and science on their graduation plans, and many did not take any advanced mathematics courses. The change to a 4 x 4 model meant that all students had to take two additional math and science courses in order to graduate. This challenged the schools and the teachers to offer more upper-level mathematics courses, for which many teachers did not feel prepared to teach. In short, the teachers coming into the program were lacking content knowledge, experiences in integrating technology, and pedagogy for teaching higher-level courses to diverse student populations.

Teaching in Culturally Diverse Classrooms

Winona, Brittany, Virginia, and Theresa taught in classrooms where students represented diverse cultures. This diversity played out in terms of cultural, linguistic, racial, and socioeconomic backgrounds, with high levels of especially English language learners (ELLs). As diversity in student populations across the United States continues to increase (Korn & Bursztyn, 2002), mathematics teachers are challenged to analyze their own teaching in order to develop a personal and professional critical consciousness about racial, cultural, and ethnic diversity. The program designers viewed learning to self-analyze and reflect on classroom teaching as a first step for teachers to become sensitive to the different learning needs of their students. The *one-shot for all* method would not serve the teachers well when trying to get all students to master the more advanced mathematics curriculum.

Professional development in mathematics teaching needs to examine how teachers are addressing or gaining competencies in using culturally relevant pedagogy. While more research is needed in this area as U.S. schools are becoming more diverse in language, culture, and race, most agree that understanding culturally relevant pedagogy contributes not only to our understanding of the achievement gap that still persists among subpopulation groups in mathematics classes but also in finding viable solutions to equity in accessibility in mathematics-related careers. For example, by implementing meaningful practices, teachers validate the importance of using students' experiences in their teaching (Calderon-Kaplan & Billings, 2008; Ladson-Billings, 2009). Culturally relevant pedagogy bridges the home-school cultural divide in order to promote student achievement (Darling-Hammond & Bransford, 2005). Current teaching evaluation protocols, however, have not been refined to incorporate cultural relevant teaching, especially in secondary mathematics classrooms. One of the challenges of the MPDP model described here was to help teachers see the need for such strategies and how they can be beneficial in teaching students math content (Ramirez & Celedon-Pattichis, 2012).

MATHEMATICS PROFESSIONAL DEVELOPMENT PROGRAM DESCRIPTION

The mathematics professional development program in this study offered secondary mathematics teachers the opportunity to increase their mathematics content knowledge; pedagogical content knowledge (PCK), including strategies for integrating technology into instruction; and heighten teachers' critical thinking through self-reflection and peer feedback. The model used in the program was designed to meet the needs of secondary math teachers faced with the challenges of preparing their diverse student populations to graduate under more rigorous standards. These teachers were faced with meeting a state curriculum mandate known as the 4 x 4 Curriculum Model, which was required for all students in order to graduate. Specifically, students who used to only take Algebra I and Geometry were now required to take Algebra II. This meant that teachers in Algebra II would now be challenged to work with a more diverse group of students; therefore, the teachers who enrolled in this program felt that they needed more professional development content and pedagogy. The MPDP model, therefore, included concentration in Algebra II content, pedagogy, and assessments for meeting diverse learners and integrating a variety of technology to facilitate learning the content and prepare students for advanced coursework. Figure 10.1 illustrates an outline of the timeline of the MPDP model, which spanned from Summer 2009 through Spring 2012.

Mathematics Content

An example of how the program goals and summer institute topics aligned over the second and third summer sessions are reflected in Figure 10.2.

The major strategies used for teaching the Algebra I and II content incorporated the following into the summer institutes: (a) multiple representations, (b) mathematical modeling, (c) collaborative learning, (d) activity-based, (e) integration of technology, (f) problem-solving tasks, (g) teacher self-reflection, (h) small group and whole group discussions on effective strategies, (i) use of manipulatives, and (j) building relationships (instructor-participant and participant-participant). By using these 10 different strategies, instructors were better able to help these teachers develop

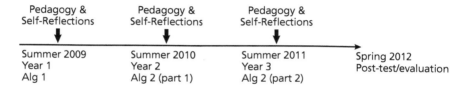

Figure 10.1 Professional development program timeline. This figure illustrates how content, pedagogy, and assessments were delivered over the 3-year period.

Program Goals	Topics (2010–2011)	Topics (2011–2012)
Increase math content knowledge of teachers	**Summer I:** Sequences Linear, Exponential function Transformation of functions Inverse functions Logarithm Real World Problems Matrices	**Summer II:** Quadratic and Sq. root functions Power functions and polynomials Rational functions Conics
Increase Pedagogical Content Knowledge and technology used by teachers	**Follow-Up Sessions (Fall–Spring)** Questioning Assessments Technology use and resources End-of-year course issues	**Follow-Up Sessions (Fall–Spring)** Curriculum adjustments Mathematical knowledge for teaching (MKT) Algebra 2
Heighten teachers' critical thinking and self-reflection of teaching (Professional Development)	**Artifacts Collected by Teachers:** 7 videotaped math lessons Reflect on taped lessons Share reflections with peers	**Artifacts Collected by Teachers:** 3 videotaped math lessons Reflect on taped lessons Share reflections with peers

Figure 10.2 Mathematics content aligned with program goals. This figure illustrates topics taught over the 3-year period.

a deep understanding of the advanced mathematics content as well as to model alternative ways to teach.

Pedagogical Content Knowledge

Participants increased their pedagogical knowledge through experiencing effective teaching, reading about effective practices, discussions around classroom challenges, and practice with teacher observation and feedback. Through modeling and practice, teachers learned to ask essential questions and integrate the state curriculum standards into their daily lessons. One strategy that the instructors modeled was the process of mathematical modeling. Mathematical modeling involves the use of challenging and meaningful problem-solving situations that allow for multiple approaches and solutions (English, 2005). Munakata (2006) found that "many students have been conditioned to think of mathematics as a cut-and-dried subject where the quest is always for the one correct answer" (p. 30). This belief can be counterproductive to students who do not approach problems in a traditional mode. Through mathematical modeling, teachers do what

Kohn (2004) describes as "teaching by doing." The mathematical modeling model used in this program contained four stages.

Stage 1: Observing, Interpreting, Formulating

This stage includes (a) describing the context in math terms, (b) identifying important variables under context, (c) identifying additional conditions, and (d) demonstrating the problems embedded in context.

Stage 2: Obtaining a Math Model

In this stage, teachers (a) describe math relationships among variables, (b) interpret relations among variables, (c) describe math model for a situation, (d) use variety of representations model, and (e) use appropriate technology to aid interpretation.

Stage 3: Mathematical Analysis of Model

This stage includes (a) use appropriate representation of model, (b) perform required math skills accurately, (c) use appropriate math language, and (d) describe the role of the various parameters.

Stage 4: Apply Model in Context

In this stage, teachers (a) identify and apply correct data to test model, (b) show evidence of reasonable and plausibility of the model, (c) interpret and communicate results of the model, (d) use available technology correctly, and (e) show evidence of testing and refining model.

For example, Algebra II content was taught through multiple strategies as outlined above. In so doing, conversations regarding how to teach students were integrated into each content session. Experts provided instruction on how to effectively use rubrics to evaluate student understanding, including hands-on experience with feedback in each session. By using rubrics and other authentic assessment measures, teachers learned how to more effectively measure student achievement and provide feedback to meet individual needs of the students. By learning how to assess their own problem-solving skills, they learned more effective ways to incorporate rubrics in the classroom.

While one goal of the MPDP model was to support teachers in gaining deeper mathematics content and pedagogy in the secondary schools, a second goal was to help teachers gain skills in meeting the needs of diverse learners, especially the ELLs. Several strategies were implemented to address this goal. Teachers were presented with a variety of language support tools, including technology. The use of informal and formative assessments was also modeled by the instructors to encourage participants to take risks and implement alternative evaluation strategies. For example, participants learned to effectively use formative data to improve instruction by seeing the presenters adjust course content, timelines, and strategies based on this data. Informal assessments were also utilized to demonstrate the need for using a variety of assessment strategies in their classrooms, including technology. In the MPDP courses, for example, participants' understanding was assessed using online apps such as Moodle, Google Docs, Quizlet, and so on.

Teacher Self-Reflections

A critical component to the model was teacher self-reflection. Through the effective use of self-reflection, teachers became aware of the challenges to their own learning, thus helping them to "stand in the shoes" of their students. This self-reflective process included reviewing and critiquing seven videotaped mathematics lessons. Moreover, each teacher shared his/her reflection with the group of participants and received feedback on ways to improve their lesson content and teaching strategies. One assumption of this MPDP model was that, by allowing sufficient time, space, and direction for engaging in self-directed professional development, teachers would gain critical thinking skills that would empower them to continue improving their practice in collaboration with peers long after the MPDP ended. These 19 female teachers were able to improve their teaching over the course of the 3-year program in such a way that both they and their students experienced changes in attitude (i.e., beliefs about their own teaching and learning) as well as their own deeper knowledge about mathematics.

Studies have found that when teachers reflect on their own practice, explicitly describing classroom events, they can more clearly define the direction for their own improvement (Artzt & Armour-Thomas, 2002; Climent & Carillo, 2001; Gay & Kirkland, 2003; Gosselin, 2007). Climent and Carrillo (2001), for example, found that an important step in improving mathematics teaching was to make available opportunities for reflection on one's own knowledge and beliefs. Schielack and Chancellor (1994) further argued for the importance of self-reflections in professional development programs. In addition, past studies further indicate that, by using teachers' videotapes of their actual teaching, teachers are more effectively able to improve their own teaching (Gay & Kirkland, 2003; Penny & Coe, 2004). In their research, Gay and Kirkland (2003) found that reviewing videotaped lessons within the context of guided practice, authentic examples, and realistic situations was most effective. Overall, the limited research in this area indicates that self-reflection and lesson feedback are beneficial in helping teachers integrate the science and art of teaching, especially important when improving teaching and learning in culturally diverse classrooms. As we consider issues of gender and STEM fields, it is important to observe that the construct of gender as a limiting factor in their own or their students' mathematics education is not attended to overtly. The significance of this lies in the experience of these women as insiders to mathematics and seeking strategies for bringing diverse populations into their world while not indicating that gender issues (Koch, 2003), if they existed for these women, had at all impacted their mathematics educations.

THE EFFECTIVENESS OF THE MATHEMATICS PROFESSIONAL DEVELOPMENT PROGRAM

Both formative and summative evaluation measures were used to determine the effectiveness of this program in meeting the goals as established in the Teacher Quality Grant, the funding agency. Teachers were assessed on their mathematics content knowledge with open-ended problem-based questions, developed by the project instructors. Understanding of mathematics content was also assessed during the classroom observations by instructors and the program evaluator. Evaluation of the program also included measuring the impact of self-reflection as a type of professional development at three levels: the impact on the conceptions of teaching of the participants, the resultant impact on teaching practices, and the consequential effect on student learning. The following were used as measures of the effectiveness of the self-reflection component: paper-pencil questionnaire, an online survey, and written reflections of teachers on their videotaped lessons were analyzed. The instruments were administered and data collected at different times throughout the 3-year period. The assessment of technology use was measured through classroom observations and participant presentations at local and state math conferences, where they were required to share their skills using technology. In addition, participants taught minilessons, which also required the integration of technology into instruction.

Participants videotaped seven lessons using a content structure, which required them to reflect on the lesson by describing the objectives and activities used in the lesson, as well as examples of student engagement and student understanding. In addition, the reflection asked participants to discuss how they would improve the lesson. These reflections were shared in presentations to the class in which peer feedback was given to assist in how to improve the lessons. They then received feedback from their peers. Initially, no structured guidelines were given to the teachers for writing the self-reflections. They were told to reflect on only their strengths, weaknesses, and plan for improving their pedagogy. On the last videotaped lesson, however, a rubric was given to the teachers, and a format for writing the critique was recommended, as well. The rubric can be found in Appendix B.

Following each of the three summer MPDP sessions, teachers were asked to implement the strategies and content they learned. Teachers completed self-assessments regarding (a) the program content they learned (i.e., To what extent did you learn in-depth and rigorous content?); (b) the degree to which they felt effective in using the professional development content (i.e., How effective are you in using technology in your math teaching today?); (c) the degree to which they developed critical thinking (i.e., To what extent have you developed critical thinking and improved your teaching from viewing your videos?); and (d) what they learned about improving their own teaching (i.e., What have you learned about your teaching after watching and critiquing your videotaped lessons?). Results from these questionnaires were used to improve the summer sessions for the next year.

Five months after the participating in the 3-year program, teachers were asked to complete an online survey (included in Appendix A), consisting of four questions soliciting their perceptions about the usefulness of the teaching reflection and peer feedback process in improving their teaching. This data was used to measure the extended impact the MPDP had on teacher implementation of what they had learned. It was believed that the additional time for reflection would provide valuable information regarding the long-term impact of the program on classroom implementation.

In this chapter, we share the evaluation findings in three parts. Part I includes the results from the pre-/posttests and the paper-pencil questionnaire (Appendix B) administered at the end of the MPDP. Data were analyzed and summarized using descriptive statistics. Two items on the questionnaire specifically referred to the video reflections. Part II contains the results of the videotaped lesson self-reflections; Part III describes the results from an online survey (Appendix B), which asked teachers their perceptions of the value and benefits of the self-reflection and videotaping process in terms of impact on their classroom teaching 3 months after they had completed the program;

Part I: Increased Content Knowledge

The teacher participants were administered a pretest consisting of open-ended problems, and the same instrument was administered four times during the culmination of each summer institute. As shown in Table 10.1, only 15 teachers had taken the initial pretest and stayed with the program for 3 years. Among these participants, there is evidence that they had gained content knowledge significantly from pre- to posttest.

TABLE 10.1   Content Knowledge Gain Based on Pretest and Four Posttest Scores

Measures Being Compared	N	Mean Difference	SD of the Difference	T-Statistics	p-value
Pretest & Posttest 1	23	13	11.35	5.42	8.31169E-06*
Pretest & Posttest 2	16	18	11.378	6.17	6.67795E-06*
Pretest & Posttest 3	15	20	10.5	7.39	1.12111E-06*
Posttest 2 & Posttest 3	22	6	6.5	3.97	.000325827*
Posttest 3 & Posttest 4	24	4	6.49	2.95	.003453243*
Pretest & Posttest 4	15	23	9.76	9.16	7.87129E-08*

* Significance level, p < .01

Supporting Evidence of Knowledge Gain From Other Measures

Data from the evaluation questionnaire support gains in content knowledge in which 75% of teachers indicated that they had learned "very much" in-depth and rigorous content during the program. The other 25% said they have learned "much" content. A follow-up question asked teachers to list 3 mathematics topics they had learned the most. Some 50% of them listed topics related to functions (linear, quadratic, transformations), 29% identified conics, 66% listed matrices, and 33% felt they learned log/exponential equations the most. Additionally, about a third of the teachers said they had understood ellipses and conics better by using the *Geogebra* software. Meanwhile, 95% of the participants said all the topics presented were clearly understood, while the rest of them found logarithm, sequential/parametric mode, matrices, and rational equations as somewhat challenging and not clearly understood. Additional support for content knowledge gain by participants was observed in the last classroom observations in Spring 2012. Using the classroom observation instrument showed that teachers made fewer or minor mathematics content errors in their teaching and were able to respond readily to students' questions about the content they were learning.

Part II: Self-Reflection Through Videotaping

Overall, each participant submitted a reflection for each of the seven videotaped lessons. An analysis of teachers' written reflections was conducted using both quantitative data (rubric scoring) as well as qualitative methods (content analysis). The platform for getting feedback on videotaped lessons occurred during monthly sessions with their peers and instructors over a 2-year period. Data were triangulated with paper-and-pencil questionnaires and a follow-up online survey at the end of the program. More than 150 videotape reflections were analyzed for common themes.

Comparing Initial and Last Reflection on Videotaped Lessons

The first videotaped lesson reflection was submitted 2 years after the first summer institute (July 2009). Analysis of 18 teachers' reflections revealed the following:

- Teachers' reflections on their first videotaped lesson were short and lacked depth (ranging from one short paragraph to half a page), indicating less effort and insufficient time spent;
- Teachers' reflections were centered mostly on their behavior (I said "OK, so" several times; I talked too fast; I looked at my notes a lot);
- Of the things they did well in their teaching, they mentioned monitoring students, technology use, praising students, good questioning, and student involvement;
- One teacher realized she was "doing all the work" and that she needed to engage students, while other teachers found they needed to have students demonstrate/explain more;
- Teachers thought they needed to provide real-world examples, use proper vocabulary and higher-order questions; and
- Some teachers saw the need to practice using their technology before coming to class.

Teachers' last written self-evaluation of their videotaped lesson showed more substantive write-ups with richer descriptions of instructional events. Overall, teachers did very well on the analysis of their teaching related to student learning, but fell short of outlining a clear plan for improving their pedagogy or content knowledge. Close to 88% of the teachers felt they had learned "much" or "very much" about their teaching from reviewing the videotapes. Watching themselves teach seven times made them feel they had gotten better at their craft. For example, one teacher wrote, "My teaching gets better overtime; I am now student-centered." They also reflected on *lessons learned* about themselves, their teaching, and their students' learning, as well.

When teachers were asked on paper-pencil evaluation questionnaires what they had learned about their teaching after going through the process of self-assessment, they reported the following in terms of increased use:

- Student-centered
- Student involvement and discussing
- Questioning techniques, formative assessment
- Use of technology-investigative questioning with use of tech works
- Sequencing of concepts, increased student involvement

- Public speaking, fewer errors
- Wait time for students to discuss and discover
- Use of proper terms
- Efficiency with time and premade files ready to display
- Lesson flow due to better preparation
- More guided practice

The responses listed above centered on teachers' teaching strategies and what teachers thought they needed to change. This self-analysis process definitely became a mirror for the teachers in which they were able to view themselves and change what they felt needed improving. They became in charge of their own improvement in teaching. When comparing the scenarios of the teacher archetypes before the professional development, you can see definite improvements in those areas that reflected teaching effectiveness, as outlined by Darling-Hammond (2012), including (a) understanding subject matter deeply and flexibly (i.e., sequencing concepts, increased vocabulary), (b) connecting what is learned to student's prior knowledge and experience (i.e., increased questioning, student-centeredness), (c) using instructional strategies that help students to draw conclusions (i.e., wait time for students to discover answers), and (d) applying and practicing new skills learned, as reflected in the changes described in example comments.

Part III: Results From the Online Survey

The purpose of the online survey was to capture teacher perceptions of the impact the MPDP had on their teaching 1 year later. Four questions were asked. The first question on the online survey gathered demographic data information about the diversity of their current classrooms by asking teachers to describe the extent to which their classes were culturally and/or linguistically diverse. Twelve (86%) out of nineteen teachers indicated that their classrooms ranged from "some" to "very much" diversity, with 26% of the respondents saying their classrooms had "very much" diversity and only two teachers (14%) indicated "little" diversity in their classrooms. Teachers reported they were still challenged with meeting the needs of a diverse group.

The second question asked teachers to report to what extent the videotaped component of the model had a positive impact on their mathematics teaching. A total of 13 out of 14 respondents indicated "some" or "much" on this question. When requested to elaborate further on their responses, teachers wrote the following:

- It is always useful to observe oneself from a distance;
- Filming my instruction helped me see how my classroom ran rather than just feeling it;
- I think it was very valuable to not only hear how I sound to the students but actually to see my interactions with the kids;
- Viewing instruction on the videotapes helped me improve time management, focus on main ideas, improve communication with students;
- It helps me to discover how the students were receiving materials I was presenting; I was busy presenting and did not have time to notice many of the students' reactions;
- I have increased my wait time for student responses;
- It was helpful to see what I was doing and was not doing in terms of good teaching strategies; and
- I was able to notice things in my lesson that I needed to work on.

The above comments reflect changes in teaching strategies, content, communication, and classroom management when the self-reflective process was integrated into the MPDP model. Teachers clearly felt that viewing their own lessons (and their students' behaviors) was beneficial to improving their teaching because they targeted specific areas to improve.

The third question was a complement to the second question in that it asked teachers whether they thought their self-reflections on the videos had a positive impact on their mathematics teaching. Eight teachers replied "much," five responded "some," and one teacher said "little." Their elaborations on their responses on the third question included the following:

- It was beneficial to find positives and negatives.
- It was helpful to reflect on what was taught and how I could have improved the lesson.
- Writing down my evaluation helped me clarify my strengths and weaknesses and gave me goals to improve upon.
- I liked being able to reflect and come up with strategies that could better help me in my teaching.
- I could see different ways to teach a subject.
- I was able to see what corrections are needed.

Setting a structure for reflecting on their own lessons helped teachers see strengths and weaknesses in their own teaching, which then helped them direct their improvement goals. Many times teachers are asked to set goals with little or no personal awareness of where they need to improve. In this model, teachers expressed a need to focus on what they could see, not feel.

The fourth and last question on the survey asked teachers to indicate the extent to which the peer feedback component of the TQG program had a positive impact on their mathematics teaching now. On a 4-point scale, 64% of the respondents chose "much" or "very much." Four teachers (29%) indicated "some" impact.

Teachers' elaborations on their responses to the last question included the following:

- Sharing with colleagues has always been a huge part of growing as a teacher.
- Getting feedback from other teachers always improves my teaching.
- It always helps to get the opinions of other teachers who share the same goals and expectations as I do; this was very helpful.
- Having my peers review my work was very rewarding; much better than having an administrator review my lesson.
- It was very helpful having someone else, a quality teacher, to bounce ideas off and to reinforce the good things that were happening on the video.
- They were able to give me suggestions on how to solve whatever I wanted to improve on.
- Listening to others in our groups talking about shared or unique problems.
- Discussing how problems were solved helped bolster my spirit and appreciate my working situation.
- I think my self-reflection was more helpful than the peer reflections.

An important source for improvement that is often missing in other professional development opportunities is peer feedback. In this study, teachers responded positively to receiving critiques from their peers, enjoying both the focused communication and the extra set of eyes of their peers. Bouncing ideas off of each other and hearing issues other teachers face seemed to be more rewarding than the usual feedback from occasional administrative reviews. This collegiality and openness to colleagues' stories and suggestions indicate the lack of defensiveness on the part of these women as they seek to improve their mathematics teaching practice. Clearly, mathematics has been a vehicle for personal empowerment, allowing these women to examine their practices in a nonthreatening, risk-free context.

From the teachers' comments on the follow-up survey open-ended questions, it was evident that the MPDP model had an impact on teachers in several ways: change toward student-centered teaching, increase in strategies for culturally diverse students, a deeper level of mathematical understanding, an increased use of technology, and a transformation in confidence and attitude toward professional development. Additional data focusing on student impact was collected from the teachers' self-reported data. The quotes and comments are highlighted in the next section.

Clearly, these female secondary mathematics teachers were serious about improving their teaching, and their flexibility and engagement in the process opened doors for growth. The following archetype scenarios reflect the numerous indicators of how these teachers changed during the 3-year intensive professional development model. Comments reflect increased understanding of higher-level mathematics content, increased content level performance in their students, greater confidence to take risks and try new strategies, improvement in how they and their students used technology to learn, and improvement in the way they assessed student learning in their diverse classrooms.

AFTER...

Winona, from a large rural junior high, reported that she can now take their students' understanding to a higher level with a more logical approach. She felt confident and more willing to try new activities. She described herself as transformed and motivated to become a better teacher as she observed more students' success and understanding.

Brittany, from a small high school, expressed that she had grown in her technology skills and now felt confident their uses. She reported that she strongly believed that technology had improved her students' attitudes toward mathematics. As she made her math classroom learner-centered, she became more of a guide to her students. She said, "My students are more driven to learn and explore mathematics using technology."

Theresa, from an affluent junior high, reported that she improved her teaching by learning how to provide students clearer explanations, because she had a clear understanding of the content. She noted that she now realizes that she had a lot to learn and that it was important to continue learning and studying ways to best teach math concepts.

Virginia, from a large rural high school, described her teaching style as changed, with a better understanding of her students. She was more able to assess students to determine what they needed to learn. In addition, she became aware of the importance of vocabulary building in her classroom. She wrote that she had grown so much and gained more confidence.

SUMMARY AND RECOMMENDATIONS

In this chapter, we have described an extended professional development for secondary mathematics teachers teaching culturally, economically, and linguistically diverse students. The population studied included women who had not faced early mathematics learning challenges but who pursued mathematics as a field of study and were successful. Their openness to new pedagogical strategies that would render their instruction more inclusive never considered "gender" as a limiting factor in the teaching and learning of mathematics.

The teacher education model had a three-pronged approach: increased content knowledge, improved teaching practices through use of current technology, and heightened critical thinking through more ownership in their own professional growth. A critical feature of creating teacher ownership in professional development was the self-reflection of several videotaped mathematics lessons by the teachers, with follow-up feedback (critique) from their peers during sharing periods.

By systematically incorporating self-reflection in their teaching and by sharing and receiving feedback from a supportive group of peers and professional development facilitators, secondary female mathematics teachers were able to more successfully incorporate culturally related teaching into their classrooms, thus preparing the path for successful learning among diverse learners. Those teachers who were most receptive to feedback from peers and lesson critiques appeared to benefit the most. The female secondary teachers in this study found video reviews and critical analysis of the lessons they had taught very helpful to their professional growth. They were interested in seeing how they were interacting with their students and how they could improve communication with them. More importantly, the teachers were focused on how their students were "receiving the materials" as well as students' reactions to their teaching. Interestingly enough, these responses to their taped lessons are indicators of culturally related teaching.

Increasingly, teacher evaluation processes include the effective use of self-reflection on one's teaching and beliefs about how students learn. The evaluation of teachers in professional development programs needs to expand to include a variety of measures, including the use of self-reflection (Artzt & Armour-Thomas, 2002), videotaped lessons (Penny & Coe, 2004), and peer review/critique (Esquivel, Lashier, & Smith, 1978; Topping, 1998) as well as value-added measures wherein student growth (content and attitudinal) is used as an indicator of teaching success (Darling-Hammond, Amrein-Beardsley, Haertel, & Rothstein, 2012; McDonald et al., 2013).

One recommendation we have regarding the use of self-reflections as a professional development tool or strategy is that teachers need support in learning how to effectively self-reflect, especially in the early stages of the professional development. When reviewing and analyzing teachers' early written reflections, we found that without guided steps, initial written reflections were "superficial" and centered mostly on the teacher's physical behavior and attributes. The later self-reflections were more focused on students, with details regarding their strategies and management; however, they still lacked clear plans for future improvement. We recommend improving the process of self-reflection by including increased measures of cultural relevance with an analysis of student learning, motivation, and other critical components associated with equity and culture. Our findings support and extend earlier research on the use of extended professional development of teachers (Hill & Ball, 2004), which concluded that greater performance gains are linked with the length of time allotted for the professional development mathematics institutes and the use of a rigorous curriculum involving critical thinking and self-reflection.

More importantly, professional development for mathematics teachers needs to include lesson plan analysis using critical indicators for CRT, such as those identified by Aguirre (2012), as well as modeling practices that accommodate language and culture with high-level content. Current research by Aguirre and del Rosario-Zavala (2013), for example, has focused on developing a protocol for lesson plan analysis using dimensions of CRT. This type of classroom teaching observation protocol that values student participation, rich mathematics content, and mathematical reasoning of students could be beneficial to school leaders who support culturally related mathematics teaching at all levels.

ACKNOWLEDGMENTS

The following people were directly involved in either designing, procuring, evaluating, managing, training, and/or participating in the Professional Development Program Grant: Dr. Max Coleman, Project Director; Dr. Patrice Poage, Project instructor; the Texas Higher Education Coordinating Board; and Secondary Mathematics Teacher Participants. The authors' views do not necessarily represent the views of the project director and grant funder.

REFERENCES

Aguirre, J. M. (2012). Developing culturally responsive mathematics teaching. *Fall 2012 TODOS newsletter TODOS- Mathematics For All*. Retrieved from http://www.todos-math.org/assets/documents/noticias/noticiasv8n2fall2012.pdf

Aguirre, J. M., & del Rosario-Zavala, M. (2013). Making culturally responsive mathematics teaching explicit: A lesson analysis tool. *Pedagogies: An International Journal*, 1–28.

Artzt, A. E., & Armour-Thomas, E. (2002). *Becoming a reflective mathematics teacher*. Mahwah, NJ: Lawrence Erlbaum.

Calderon-Kaplan, K., & Billings, E. S. (2008). Developing socio-political active teachers: A model for teacher professional development. *Forum on Public Policy,* (1), 1–28. Retrieved from http://forumonpublicpolicy.com/archivespring08/cadiero.pdf

Climent, N., & Carrillo, J. (2001). Developing and researching professional knowledge with primary teachers. In J. Novotná (Ed.), *CERME 2. European research in mathematics education II, Part 1* (pp. 269–280). Prague, Czech Republic: Charles University, Faculty of Education.

Darling-Hammond, L. (2012, March). *Teacher education and teaching quality: What will it take to build a true profession?* Paper presented at the National Professional Development Schools Conference, Las Vegas, NV.

Darling-Hammond, L., Amrein-Beardsley, A., Haertel, E., & Rothstein, J. (2012). Evaluating teacher evaluation. *Kappan, 93*(6), 8–15.

Darling-Hammond, L., & Bransford, J. (2005). *Preparing teachers for a changing world: What teachers should learn and be able to do.* San Francisco, CA: Jossey-Bass.

English, L. (2005). Problem posing and solving with mathematical modeling. *Teaching Children Mathematics, 12*(3), 156–163.

Esquivel, J. M., Lashier, W. S., & Smith, W. S. (1978). Effect of feedback on questioning of preservice teachers in SCIS microteaching. *Science Teacher Education, 62*(2), 209–214.

Gay, G., & Kirkland, K. (2003). Developing cultural critical consciousness and self-reflection in preservice teacher education. *Theory into Practice, 42*(3), 181–187. doi:10.1207/s15430421tip4203_3

Gosselin, C. (2007). Philosophy and role of teacher reflections on constructing gender. *Educational Foundations, 21*(3).

Hill, H. C., & Ball, D. L. (2004). Learning mathematics for teaching: Results from California mathematics professional development institutes. *Journal for Research in Mathematics Education, 35*(5), 330–351.

Hull, T. (2007). Manager to instructional leader: Developing teachers as leaders. *NCSM Journal of Mathematic Education Leadership, 9*(2), 7–12.

Koch, J. (2003). Gender issues in the classroom. In W. Reynolds & G. Miller (Eds.), *Handbook of psychology, volume 7: Educational psychology.* Hoboken, NJ: John Wiley & Sons.

Kohn, A. (2004). Challenging students... and how to have more of them. *Phi Delta Kappan, 86* (3), 184–194.

Korn, C., & Bursztyn, A. (Eds). (2002). *Rethinking multicultural education.* Westport, CT: Bergin and Garvey.

Ladson-Billing, G. (2009). *The dreamkeepers: Successful teachers of African American children,* Hoboken, NJ: Wiley & Sons.

McDonald, B., Polnick, B., & Robles-Pina, R. A. (2013). Impact of instructional practices on students' mathematics achievement in urban middle schools. *Delta Kappa Gamma Bulletin, 79*(2), 52–65. Retrieved from www.dkg.org

Munakata, M. (2006). A little competition goes a long way: Holding a mathematical modeling contest in your classroom. *Mathematics Teacher, 100*(1), 30–39.

Penny, A. R., & Coe, R. (2004). Effectiveness of consultation on student ratings feedback: A meta-analysis. *Review of Educational Research, 74*(2), 215–253.

Ramirez, N. G., & Celedon-Pattichis, S. (Eds.). (2012). *Beyond good teaching: Advancing mathematics education for ELLs.* Reston, VA: National Council of Teachers of Mathematics.

Schielack, J., & Chancellor, D. (1994). Stop, look, listen: Building reflection into continuing professional development. In D. B. Aichele (Ed.), *Professional development for teachers of mathematics* (pp. 304–307), Reston, VA: National Council of Teachers of Mathematics.

Topping, K. (1998). Peer assessment between students in colleges and universities. *Review of Educational Research, 68*(3), 249–276.

APPENDIX A
Online Survey of Videotaping
and Self-Reflective Process for the Professional
Development Mathematics Program

Purpose: This survey is being conducted as a follow-up to the professional development you received through the Total Quality Grant at ***** under *******. Your responses will be held strictly confidential. Data from the survey will be reported in the aggregate (whole group), with no individual identifiers attached to your responses.

We appreciate your taking the time to give us this feedback!

Directions: Please indicate your response by clicking on the answer choice that most correctly identifies your experiences and feelings.

Q1. Background Information: Please indicate the extent to which the classes you teach are culturally diverse (race, ethnicity, linguistic, etc.)

    Little   Some   Much   Very Much

Q2. To what extent did the videotaping component of the TQG professional development have a positive impact on your mathematics teaching?

    Little   Some   Much   Very Much

Q2b. Comments are appreciated.

Q3. To what extent did the self-reflection component of the TQG professional development have a positive impact on your mathematics teaching?

    Little   Some   Much   Very Much

Q3b. Comments are appreciated.

Q4. To what extent did the peer feedback component of the TQG professional development have a positive impact on your mathematics teaching?

    Little   Some   Much   Very Much

Q4b. Comments are appreciated.

APPENDIX B
Teacher Quality Grant (2009–2012)
Award period: May 1, 2009–April 30, 2012
Survey of Participants

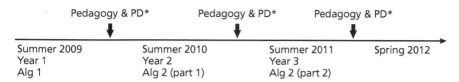

	Pedagogy & PD*	Pedagogy & PD*	Pedagogy & PD*	
Summer 2009	Summer 2010	Summer 2011	Spring 2012	
Year 1	Year 2	Year 3		
Alg 1	Alg 2 (part 1)	Alg 2 (part 2)		

* Professional Development (PD) is defined as teachers' self-evaluation of their own teaching by reviewing their 7 videotaped lessons.

Dear Teacher Participants,

The diagram above shows the timeline of the TQG program that you have participated in. Please use this to help you recall and reflect on the program objectives, implementation, and how you have benefitted from this 3-year program.

1. **Content**

    1A. To what extent did you learn an in-depth and rigorous content (math)? Circle one.

    Little   Some   Much   Very much

    1B. As evidence, give three examples of math topics that you have learned the most.
    a.
    b.
    c.

    1C. What math topic/s do you feel were not clearly understood and how could the instructors do a better job next time?

2. **Processes**

    2A. To what extent did the project staff (director, instructors, invited presenters) support the program objectives? Circle one.

    Little   Some   Much   Very much

    2B. Give three examples indicating the project staff did their best to implement the project goals.
    a.
    b.
    c.

3. **Use of Technology to Support Instruction**

   3A. How effective are you in using technology in your math teaching today? Circle one.

   Novice   Good   Very good   Highly effective

   3B. Provide your favorite example that you have actually used with success.

   3C. How effective are you in using technology for assessing student learning? Circle one.

   Novice   Good   Very good   Highly effective

   3D. your favorite example that you have actually used with success.

4. **Professional Development**

   4A. To what extent did you develop critical thinking and self-reflection from viewing your videos? Circle one.

   Little   Some   Much   Very much

   4B. What have you learned about your teaching after watching and critiquing your videotaped lessons?

5. **Program Implementation**

   5A. List the top three benefits of having a 3-year-long professional development over the traditional 1-year program.

   a.
   b.
   c.

   5B. Give three suggestions for improving the 3-year program.

CHAPTER 11

THE FORWARD PROGRAM

Catherine Mavriplis
Rachelle S. Heller
Paul Sabila
Charlene Sorensen

INTRODUCTION

A significant fraction (43%) of the scientists and engineers in research and development in the United States are in academia (National Science Board, 2006; National Science Foundation, 2005). In addition, American female scientific and engineering researchers tend to be more often in academic and nonprofit settings (National Academy Press, 2001; National Science Board, 2006). From 1973 to 2003, doctoral women employed in U.S. science and engineering academia increased from 9% to 30% or 754,600 (National Science Board, 2006; National Science Foundation, 2005). By 2003, the engineering, academic workforce was 15.5% female, with women making up 4.6% of the engineering faculty at the rank of full professor, 8.9% at the associate rank, and 22.8% at the assistant rank for a total of 2,300 women engineering professors (National Science Board, 2006). While academic professors conduct research as a significant component of their efforts at top-tier research-intensive universities (Thomson, 2000), the balance of intended effort between research, teaching, and service can be as high as 100%-0%-0%, respectively, but is typically considered to be 40%-40%-20%, respectively. At less-research-intensive institutions,

Girls and Women in STEM, pages 217–235
217

such as liberal arts colleges and primarily undergraduate institutions, the balance tends to be closer to 5%-80%-15%, respectively, however many institutions of higher education in the United States are pushing for more research by their faculty members. A total of 41% of academic science and engineering doctorate holders in academia reported research as their primary activity, and 69% reported research as their primary or secondary activity in 2001. Indeed, 68.4% of engineering academic doctorate holders report receiving federal support in 2002 (National Science Board, 2006; National Science Foundation, 2005). In this case, women fare better than men, wherein 68.4% of the women versus 63.4% of the men were funded (National Science Board, 2006). When broadened to all science and engineering fields however, only 35.8% of the women are supported versus 45% of the men (National Science Board, 2006).

Why are such large percentages of U.S. women not choosing to work in engineering research as professors? Certainly they are faced, at the end of their doctoral research studies, with the difficult choice of pursuing positions in academia, working in private industry or government, or selecting a totally different career or life path. Many female doctoral students report that they have no intention of pursuing an academic career based on what they have seen at their own institutions (Thomson, 2000). Two issues arise that may deter them from pursuing academia: small or nonexistent numbers of women in their academic field and/or the treatment or challenges they've observed regarding the few academic women they do see at their institutions. Then, for all the efforts to attract, train, and fund women in science and engineering to pursue careers in research, much of that is *lost* at this important junction of doctoral degree to professorship. For example, there were 7,073 engineering doctoral degrees awarded to women in the period 1994–2002 in the United States (Rosser, 2004); however, only 1,200 of those with less than 10 years within graduating with their doctorate were engineering professors at U.S. institutions in 2003 (National Science Board, 2006). This represents a yield of about 17%. This may, of course, be due to several reasons, including the possibility that fewer women are being hired as tenure-track professors. Indeed, Nelson and Rogers (2003) have shown that the pool of doctoral scientists and engineers is underutilized in academic hiring. Furthermore, many drop out or are marginalized in the career stage before tenure is achieved (or not achieved), typically 7 years after the first tenure-track professorship appointment.

GENESIS OF THE FOCUS ON REACHING WOMEN FOR ACADEMICS, RESEARCH, AND DEVELOPMENT (FORWARD) PROGRAMS

The origin of the FORWARD program dates back to an engineering course that the first author of this chapter, Mavriplis, taught at George

Washington University (GW) in which a deaf Gallaudet University (GU) female student was enrolled, since GU did not offer engineering curricula. Through the mentoring of this student, the author discovered how difficult it was for deaf scientists or engineers to communicate due to lack of technology and American Sign Language (ASL) vocabulary. One of our professors reached out to the GU faculty for help in addressing this difficulty. At the same time, the GW faculty of Engineering and Applied Science were sorely lacking in support for women students, and the second chapter author approached Mavriplis to start a mentoring program. Consequently, chapter authors Mavriplis and Heller, along with chemistry professor Sorensen and physics professor Snyder, both from GU, created the FORWARD program and applied and received a substantial grant from the NSF Program for Women and Girls in 1997 to encourage more women and underrepresented minorities to bridge the undergraduate to graduate juncture. This first FORWARD program involved not only the two collaborating universities (GW and GU), but also four cooperating institutions, including two women's colleges, Smith and Hood; Hampton University, a historically Black university; and the National Technical Institute for the Deaf (NTID), with a faculty representative at each of those institutions, thereby covering four more STEM communities and discipline fields.

FORWARD TO GRADUATE SCHOOL

Our first FORWARD project had five different components: FORWARD to Graduate school workshops, a graduate student research competition, an interdisciplinary STEM course called *A Walk on the Moon*, student support at the four cooperating institutions, and a deaf STEM education ASL tool development project. The most successful of these was the FORWARD to Graduate School workshops, a set of engaging and effective one-and-a-half-day workshops. In 1998, it was quite unheard of to bring a group of women together for a workshop that addressed the challenges faced by women and underrepresented minorities (including individuals who were deaf or hard of hearing). The purpose of these workshops was to provide attendees with the information and skills needed to apply for graduate study in STEM fields. Mentoring success from this first workshop fell into two categories: mentoring of individual students and the creation of a system or process for future mentoring. Our greatest success from this workshop was a deaf young woman from GU, who did not initially consider herself a scientist but who worked with us on her Graduate Record Exam scores and then successfully entered and completed a graduate program at a hearing at Research 1 (R1) University (pseudonym).

We offered the FORWARD to Graduate School workshop four times with similar success, impacting more than 90 students.

Success Stories

Even after 3 years after the completion of their participation in this program, students provided us feedback on their success. Below is an unsolicited email comment from one of the students, Janet (a pseudonym), who expressed her excitement regarding completion of her dissertation and her job opportunities in medicine.

> I am doing great. As you can see by the email forward, am almost finished! this is so exhilarating for me. I have been interviewing in Pittsburgh for jobs. I head to NC for an interview in May. The regenerative medicine company grows bladders in the lab and implants them into patients . . . really exciting work. I interviewed with a small start-up company in San Diego but I have yet to hear from them. I will let you know where I end up. (personal communication, 2001)

In addition, this same student expressed a desire to continue the mentoring process, as illustrated in the following comment.

> Can you please forward my abstract to Vivian Pinn at NIH (as we discussed in March)? When I visit DC again next month, I would like to try to coordinate a meeting with her. I think it would be really nice to chat with her and learn more about her. She really sounds like an interesting person. (Janet, personal communication, May, 2001)

FORWARD TO PROFESSORSHIP

In 2001, based on our success with the workshops, we designed the FORWARD to Professorship Workshops to try, once again, to bridge a critical juncture: the doctoral and postdoctoral student's step to professorship. Awarded an NSF ADVANCE Leadership grant with a shoestring budget, we mounted the workshop free of charge to the participants, including travel and subsistence. Based on our work with undergraduates, we designed and offered a multiday workshop with information, skills, and activities (i.e., grant writing, negotiation, teaching strategies, work-life balance) to support women and underrepresented minorities as they moved from graduate school to academic positions in STEM fields. In the follow-up to the workshop, we maintained a telephone bridge for ongoing mentoring. Our most memorable "success" from these workshops was an ongoing discussion with Jane (a pseudonym) who was set to abandon her doctoral program. With the help of the mentoring from the program, she completed her PhD and is now a successful professor. Another email comment sent after a workshop was written by this participant.

> Thank you so much for taking time from your busy schedule to organize such a great program. It was very helpful to learn so much about how to enter academia and be a successful professor. Thank you so much for providing us with a clear view of the tenure process. It was my pleasure to meet you and have the opportunity to be in this program again. Also, I would like to share a great news with you. I was just being offered a temporary "visiting assistant professor" position from our department (ME) at Virginia Tech. I think it would give me a great chance to look for a permanent position while serving here at Tech. (personal communication, 2001)

Description of the Workshop

The FORWARD workshop (Mavriplis, Heller, Sorensen, & Snyder, 2005) was designed as a national workshop, bringing together participants from a wide geographical area (across the United States), a wide array of STEM disciplines, and a range of career levels, from doctoral student, to postdoctoral level, non–tenure track professors and research scientists, tenure-track assistant professors, tenure-track or tenured associate professors, and some nonacademic scientists and engineers. The organizers strive to achieve a 50%-50% balance between scientists and engineers both for participants and speakers. They also strive to include as many members of underrepresented groups such as ethnic minorities as possible. The national workshop is held at Gallaudet University, the United States' only university for the deaf and hard of hearing and includes at least a handful of such participants every year. Every formal and informal session of the workshop is facilitated by American Sign Language (ASL) interpreters and the non-deaf participants are urged to learn a bit about deaf culture and challenges for deaf scientists and engineers. The workshop is open to men and women. Approximately 5% of the participants are male and are often spouses of women participants. A great majority of the participants are from research universities or R1 institutions, as defined by the Carnegie classification (Carnegie Foundation, 2012).

The workshop is designed to address the critical aspects of a modern-day tenure-track STEM faculty position. The three traditional legs of a faculty member's responsibilities, namely research, teaching, and service, are discussed. Acknowledging that these are the three main areas of accomplishment upon which a faculty member's performance is evaluated, we also discuss the many challenges of interacting with other academics and setting up an academic career for oneself: sessions on writing research statements, teaching statements and cover letters, negotiation, interaction with administrators, and work-life balance round out the 2.5 day experience. The work-life balance panel presents specific data from dual-career-couple research, examples of women who have found creative solutions to their work-family balance challenges, and information on career breaks. One of the main aims of the workshop is to create a community of women in STEM fields, so much of the first day's events are aimed at creating a collegial and supportive atmosphere. The strategy is to showcase a variety of models/paths so that all can find the strength and resources to build their own paths to a successful and rewarding STEM career or other life choice.

The workshop is evaluated every year, and feedback is used for improvements. In the final-day evaluation forms, participants rated the overall workshop experience highly: 4.9/5 (where 1 is poor, 2 fair, 3 average, 4 good, and 5 excellent). The organization, the selection of speakers, and the activities in relation to meeting the participants' needs and expectations were also highly rated. Detailed comments on the evaluation forms reflect the high approval rating and sense of empowerment that many participants felt. For example, one participant wrote, "Probably the most inspiring and confidence building thing I've ever done as far as science goes."

Fully 100% of the evaluation from respondents said they would recommend this workshop to their friends and colleagues. And many did! The following quote is typical of unsolicited emails received after the workshop. Dana (a pseudonym) said,

> I must say that the experience has reinforced my decision to enter academia and I feel more knowledgeable about how to proceed. I'm already sharing what I've learned with my colleagues here at [XXX] and the information is being well received. I'll be sure to keep you posted on my PhD completion. (personal communication, 2001)

The workshop at MIT has a compressed format: a 1.5-day workshop runs Friday evening and all day Saturday and almost entirely skips the session on teaching (at MIT's request). Furthermore, the participants are all from the same institution (MIT) and are more predominantly doctoral students, with a significant fraction at the postdoctoral level. The MIT workshop includes only women participants. MIT is also a premier research-intensive institution.

Moving Beyond FORWARD to Professorship.

After these national FORWARD workshops had been presented numerous times, the challenge became how to disseminate the workshop information and impact and move the workshops beyond the current chapter authors. As is often said, you cannot be in two places at once. Therefore, in 2009, the FORWARD organization moved to create a training program for trainer/observers, called Pay It FORWARD. The intent is to create a cadre of trainers who are able to provide a structured mentoring workshop targeted at specific regions (e.g., the U.S. Southwest, U.S. Midwest, U.S. Northeast, etc.), specific disciplines (e.g., those involving field studies, computer and mathematical sciences, planetary sciences, etc.) or societal groups (i.e., African American, Pacific Islanders, and Latina women), thereby increasing the impact of the program with these specializations. In order to inform our training program, we also assembled a group of Experts in Leadership Development (termed ELDers) for a one-day workshop to synthesize best practices for women's leadership development programs. They were Telle Whitney from the Anita Borg Institute, Eve Riskin from University of Washington ADVANCE program, Ted Hodapp from the American Physical Society, Katie Flint from the National Postdoctoral Association, Jeanne Narum and Judy Dilts from Project Kaleidoscope, Michele Montgomery from the American Astronomical Society Committee on the Status of Women, and Anke Lipinsky from the European Union's Encouragement to Advance—Training Seminars for Women Scientists. Some of these ELDers act as mentors to our trainees. The reach of the entire series of workshops is demonstrated in the Figure 11.1.

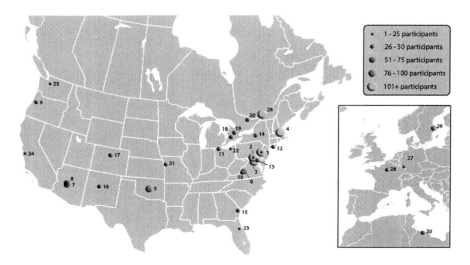

Figure 11.1 Geographical impact of national and local workshops.

EVALUATION

The First Survey

A web-based survey consisting of 18 questions was administered by email to participants of the five earliest offerings of the workshop: the national workshop in Washington, DC, at Gallaudet University in May 2003, 2004, and 2005, and the MIT workshop in October 2005 and 2006. The survey collected standard demographic data (e.g., gender and minority status) as well as data and written comments about the participants' career development, experiences and achievements since their attendance at the workshop, elements of the workshop that influenced their careers, perceptions of their competence to perform key activities for a research and/or academic career, perceptions of their likelihood to achieve significant milestones, and experiences in and outlook for balancing personal and career goals. The survey was sanctioned by the George Washington University's Institutional Review Board, indicating that those being asked to respond to the survey could be assured of anonymity and the adherence to federal research compliance regulations regarding the protection of human subjects. A request to complete the online survey was sent by email to 173 past workshop participants, using the email addresses they had given us at the time of their workshop participation. Some effort was made to find new email addresses (using Google) for the 20 participants for whom the messages were undeliverable. At least 12 participants remained unreachable. A reminder was sent after three weeks and the survey was closed out 10 days later.

Survey Results

There were 81 responses obtained, for a response rate of 46.8%. The breakdown by workshop attendance is given in Figure 11.2. We note that there are fewer respondents from the first workshop, as expected, since it is harder to reach these people because they may have moved on and are hard to find.

General Characteristics

Although we had some male participants at the workshops (approximately 5%), 100% of the respondents were female; 26% of the respondents identified themselves as being part of a minority group in the United States. Only one identified herself as deaf or hard of hearing, therefore no conclusions may be made about this group. Respondents were predominantly doctoral students (53%) at the time of the workshop: this makes sense since this group is easiest to locate if they have not moved on too many times

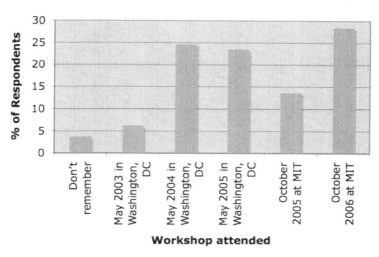

Figure 11.2 Workshop attendance by year and location.

from the last known address. For the other respondents, 28% were postdoctoral researchers at the time of the workshop, 13.5% assistant professors, 1% ($n = 1$) associate professors, 1% ($n = 1$) research scientists, and the rest identified as "other." At the time of the survey however, only 25% remained students, 31% were postdoctoral researchers, 21% were assistant professors, 5% associate professors, 1% ($n = 1$) full professor, 5% research scientists, 4% in industry or government, and 5% indicated "other." A comparison between the employment status at the time of the workshop and at the time of the survey is given in Figure 11.3.

Employment and Success Indicators

The respondents seemed very confident about their abilities to secure employment of their choice. Of those who had not already achieved these types of employment typical of or possible in a research or academic career, at least half and often much more than half indicated that they were likely or more than likely (i.e., ≥ 4 range 4–7 on a scale of 1–7, with 1 being "not likely at all" and 7 being "very likely") to achieve these. These are given in Table 11.1. Note however that they were less confident in obtaining employment in industry or government. It is not clear if these respondents wished to do so or not.

The respondents also seemed quite confident about their level of competence in performing key activities to secure a position and launch a

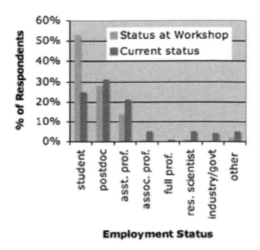

Figure 11.3 Employment status of survey respondents at the time of FORWARD workshop and then at time of survey.

TABLE 11.1 Respondents' Confidence in Their Ability to Obtain Employment

Respondents	Percentage Confident, Likely, or More Than Likely to Achieve	Number of Respondents for These Questions
Obtain a postdoctoral or research position	83	6
Obtain a tenure-track position at a research university	89	37
Obtain a tenure-track position at a liberal arts college	62	21
Obtain a non-tenure-track position at a university or college	50	14
Obtain a position in industry	33	18
Obtain a position in government	20	15

successful career in research or academia. Overwhelmingly, a large majority indicated that they felt competent or very competent (i.e., ≥4 range 4–7 on a scale of 1–7, with 1 being "not at all competent" and 7 being "very competent") in the areas listed in Table 11.2.

The respondents were confident perhaps because they had already achieved a lot and had been well-trained. Table 11.3 summarizes some of the major research milestones they had achieved and, of those who had not achieved them, how confident they were in achieving them (using the same definition as above). An astonishing 88% of those who had not attained tenure yet felt confident that they would. It is exciting to also see that 77% of those considering administrative roles were confident that they would attain them.

In terms of professional development, the respondents seemed to be engaging in a variety of activities to broaden their networks and lines of research and improve their skills. For each of the following activities, a substantial majority of the respondents reported having done these: attended professional development sessions provided by the employer as well as outside the place of employment, attended professional meetings, read professional articles in their field, worked with peers and/or mentors inside as well as outside their department and even outside their research field (86%), which may indicate the growing interdisciplinarity of research. The written comments in their evaluation of the workshop on their professional development are all positive. Again, they underscored confidence and proactive behavior, for example Participant One wrote,

> I pursued two significant programs after Forward—one inside my organization (Leadership training) and one outside (Executive Management training). I think the Forward program helped me realize the importance of this

TABLE 11.2 Respondents' Confidence in Their Competence to Perform Key Activities for a Successful Research or Academic Career

Respondents	Percentage Confident, Competent, or More Than Competent to Achieve	Number of Respondents for These Questions
Negotiate a salary	85	59
Negotiate a start-up package	84	50
Write a grant proposal	90	62
Write a teaching statement	89	65
Write a research statement	94	71
Teach	95	64

TABLE 11.3 Respondents' Achievements Related to Research and Moving Toward Tenure and Confidence in Their Competence to Achieve These if Not Yet Achieved.

Respondents	Percentage who had achieved (n = number of respondents to this part of the question)	Percentage of those who had not achieved who feel confident they are likely or more than likely to achieve (n = number of respondents to this part of the questions)
Completed dissertation	73% (n = 73)	100% (n = 17)
Presented research findings at a conference	99% (n = 79)	100% (n = 1)
Prepared an article for publication	95% (n = 80)	100% (n = 4)
Has had article accepted for publication	87% (n = 79)	100% (n = 10)
Has obtained funding for research	50% (n = 68)	94% (n = 34)
Has obtained tenure	7% (n = 56)	88% (n = 52)
Has taken on administrative role	10% (n = 50)	77% (n = 44)
Has participated in grant review process as a reviewer or panelist	31% (n = 58)	82% (n = 39)

sort of professional development—these have significantly positively contributed to my career advancement. (personal communication, November, 2006)

Negotiation

Of those who had secured university or college positions (n = 30), 77% indicated that they did negotiate the terms of their positions. Specifically, 74% negotiated salary, 56% negotiated space, 65% negotiated start-up funds, 43% negotiated research student fellowships, 35% negotiated their teaching load, 35% negotiated time flexibility, and 22% negotiated other terms of their own choosing and creativity! When asked if "there was something [from the workshop] particularly useful to [their] career[s]," negotiation was the most-often-cited topic. Many of the respondents reported using the advice gained at the workshop to negotiate their first tenure-track positions, not only for salary, as in this example from Teresa (a pseudonym):

I have now achieved tenure myself and am about to be promoted again within months. I think this program was a critical component of this success. The negotiation session was really key. There was a GWU law professor as I recall and this was instrumental to me negotiating the salary for my first position, but also to accommodate work/life balance issues. (personal communication, November, 2006)

The following example by Beverly (a pseudonym) also supports these beliefs.

I wish I had taken more advice on negotiating my contract but I must admit that at the time I was so focused on negotiating the start date that I ended up not negotiating on the salary and start-up. The issue was that I was pregnant at the time and wanted to start after the birth of my child. Even with that negotiation I was only able to delay 2.5 months after his birth rather than the 10 months I was hoping for. Nevertheless, I was given a light course load my first semester in its place. (personal communication, 2006).

Tenure Criteria

Those who had secured tenure-track or tenured academic professor positions were asked if they were informed about the criteria for tenure. A total of 79% of the respondents to this question ($n = 19$) said they were informed, 74% said the criteria were made clear to them, and almost all (95%) of them had discussed the criteria with an administrator or committee. A handful of these respondents wrote in comments, many of them still expressing uneasiness with the ambiguity of the tenure process.

Work-Life Balance

When asked about their personal development, the respondents were also optimistic. While 52% of the respondents said they had already achieved a well-rounded lifestyle, 86% of those who had felt they were likely or more than likely to (using the same definition as above). A total of 62% of the respondents felt they were able to deal with stress effectively, and of those who did not feel that way yet, 83% felt they were likely or more than likely to. Overall though, the respondents felt stressed: 88% of the respondents felt a moderate to high level of stress (rated ≥ 4 (or in the range 4–7 on a scale of 1–7, with 1 being "not at all stressed" and 7 being "very stressed"). And 51% of respondents ($n = 77$) said they had already achieved a career/family balance. A total of 74% of those who had not yet achieved that balance felt confident they were likely or more than likely to (using the same definition as above); 35% of respondents ($n = 46$) said they had taken time off for childrearing, and 57% of respondents ($n = 30$) said they were likely or more than likely (using the same definitions as above) to do so.

About 68% of the respondents were part of a dual-career couple, 51% of these had partners in a similar career path, and 67% of these had encountered employment or geographic location problems. These people were asked for written comments about how their employment or geographic problems had been resolved. The tone was understandably far less positive on this topic. Overwhelmingly, the responses indicated huge struggles to stay together, unhappiness, and stress. However, the respondents realized the sacrifices they may have had to make or had already made and seemed to accept them. Furthermore, some recounted the ins and outs of their perseverance and connected it back to the examples they heard at the workshop. For example, Wanda (a pseudonym) reported,

> Initially we had offers that were not even in the same city or state (closest was 5–7 hour drive away and the job for my spouse was mediocre). We had to choose a large, urban area where there were multiple potential options. When we first chose, my spouse did not have a job offer. When an offer did come, it was hours away from my place of employment. Then another offer came a bit closer and my spouse took the offer. Two years later I was offered a position (completely independently!) at the same place as my spouse. Now we have a good situation but there was a lot of STRESS involved. The story that the University of Cincinnati math professor told at Forward though gave me hope one has to work through some difficulties before solutions arise. My closest colleague and friend had a similar 2–3 year period of "angst" where she and her husband were in the same town, etc. but just hadn't achieved anything close to stability with two good jobs." (personal communication, 2006)

Networking

While 38% of the respondents were in contact with people they met through the workshop, 91% said the workshop did not broaden their network much (rated ≤ 4, or in the range 1–4 on a scale of 1–7, with 1 being "not at all" and 7 being "very much"). For the MIT respondents, wherein the participants were perhaps better able to continue their relationships while being on the same campus and for whom less time has elapsed, 53% were still in contact with people they had met through the workshop. Furthermore, MIT has continued some interim activities throughout the year. The written comments in several of the sections of the survey seemed to be in contradiction to the numerical result of the respondents feeling their network was not broadened. A consistent theme in the comments is the appreciation for and impact of the "stories" and "experiences" offered up by our speakers in many different areas of the workshop. For example Maria (a pseudonym) reported,

I remember being quite taken by real life personal stories of several speakers at the workshop. Determination and passion for work allowed these women to succeed in their professions. I have to say the workshop was more than I expected it to be—I left it being confident and inspired and for ME this was very important. (personal communication, 2006)

Perhaps the respondents are taking the "networking" term more literally as a long-lasting relationship. Many expressed regret at their inability to keep up contacts with fellow participants and suggested that we organize a second workshop: several of the respondents even volunteered in the survey to help organize it. Others seemed to have understood the benefits of such networking and were since then practicing more networking skills to advance themselves.

Overall

Overall, the respondents were positive about their career progress: 90% indicated that they thought their careers were progressing moderately to very well (rated ≥ 4, or in the range 4–7 on a scale of 1–7, with 1 being "not at all well" and 7 being "very well"). Regarding the workshop itself, the response has been overwhelmingly positive, best summed up by one of the respondents, Sarah (a pseudonym).

The FORWARD to Professorship workshop was extremely beneficial for me. I learned skills for negotiating the job I wanted as well as had a forum to discuss specific issues facing women in academia. Hearing the experiences of women at different stages of their career was helpful. While I chose a position at a small liberal arts college for work/life reasons, I was also offered a position at a "R1" research institution. I strongly feel my experience at the workshop helped me both in the application and the interview process to obtain job offers at these diverse institutions. I felt more prepared for the process than many of my fellow graduate students. I have recommended such workshops to my fellow graduate students. (personal communication, 2006)

Since as many as 4 years have passed between the workshop experience to this survey, it is difficult to indicate a direct link between the workshop and the current status of the participants. That said, as noted in the research literature, this group of women are, by and large, more focused than their peers on their careers, less daunted by the concepts of negotiation and employment. Results from surveys of participants before the start of a workshop indicate that fewer felt likely or very likely to obtain a position of employment than the participants surveyed in the years after their workshop. Their personal expectations for delivering papers at conferences, publishing, and obtaining grants were high before the start of the workshop and were even higher afterward. For those considering academic careers, their outlooks for achieving tenure and taking on administrative roles were very positive.

The most outstanding aspect of change, whether directly or indirectly, related to the workshop is in relation to negotiation. More than two thirds of the most recent (2007) participants had no negotiation experience before the workshop and in these postworkshop reports, that same fraction indicated they had negotiated a salary, package, space, or other aspect of their academic life. More importantly, preworkshop, over three fourths indicated that they had little or no confidence in doing so. This fact is reflected in many of the respondents' comments. For example, Anna (a pseudonym) stated, "The workshop on negotiating over your contract for your first faculty job was extremely informative, and something I would not have thought about otherwise" (personal communication, 2007).

The high percentage of women who had, or were considering having, children reflected another confidence among the former participants. Research studies have found that women who have children early in their academic careers are less likely to achieve tenure than men with children. In addition, many academic women have sacrificed the number of children they would have liked to have for their career. This group, however, seemed confident in their abilities to juggle the demands of an academic career with family responsibilities.

The Second Survey

The second survey began in the fall of 2012. A total of 368 participants from all previous national and trainer workshops were surveyed, and 165 responses were gathered as of February 1, 2013. Respondents were exclusively pre-tenured faculty or entering academics when they were workshop participants. Today, nearly 75% are in a career position. Our web survey also shows a clear career progression from graduate student to postdoctoral position, postdoctoral to tenure track and tenure track to tenured. This trend reflects the fact that the responders have advanced in their own careers from students and post-docs to career academics.

While the complete analysis is yet to be finalized, the current analysis of this data shows that participants referred to materials and information provided by their workshop. They pointed to actively relying on the peer network (nearly 30% indicated they agree or strongly agree on their reliance on the peer network), more than 35% reported actively relying on the negotiation information, which included strategies and skills on start-up packages (more than 60%), salaries (6% indicated they had asked for salary increases after the workshop), staff support, and managing student assistants. They also reported that their confidence was increased in interactions with other faculty and search committees, the latter reported as agree or strongly agree by nearly 50% of respondents. The respondents also indicated significant successes, such as publishing 42 papers since the workshop.

In responding to questions about the quality of life and personal development, the participants pointed to materials on career plan (nearly 40% indicated that they agree or strongly agree that this was a value of the workshop) and balancing service commitments (over 35% indicated that they agree or strongly agree that this was an important and useful take-away from the workshop) as a workshop value. Additionally, material on teaching strategies and grant resources were noted as valuable. Grant writing and abstract writing remained a highly valued activity and one that continued to have impact on their personal academic career development.

The survey inquired about the participants' involvement with mentoring beyond the peer network established in the workshops. More than 65% of the respondents reported serving as a mentor, and nearly 50% of respondents pointed to the workshops as helping them see the need to have a mentor. Nearly 75% of the participants were not in institutions where there is a mentoring program within their department or college. Many have established an informal mentoring relationship, perhaps because of the lack of a structured mentoring program. While confidence in approaches to their career remained a major outcome for the majority of responders, and negotiation was a valued lesson from our workshops, at least one new topic has emerged as important: participants dealing with new work-life changes. Two participants reported leaving academia (one for industry, one for science editing). Dual-career-couple issues were noted by more than 30% of responders, especially among participants of the early workshops, as an important issue.

CONCLUSIONS

The FORWARD program has, since 1996, been designing, implementing, and extending the impact of mentoring workshops and other activities to empower women and other underrepresented groups such as the deaf and hard of hearing to successfully tackle the junctions of the *leaky pipeline* (Holton, 1995) in science, technology, engineering, and mathematics (STEM) fields. Over a 15-year period of workshop activities, the FORWARD program has reached over 1,300 doctoral women and more than 250 other women and men in STEM fields with skills-building and personal mentorship activities. The national workshops have a sustained national draw and attendance in Washington, DC. A version of the FOR-WARD workshop for doctoral candidates has also been instituted at MIT in Boston. FORWARD's emerging regional workshop series has geographical reach as far afield as Guam and Pacific Islander women, to women of color in the U.S. Midwest, Latina women in the U.S. Southwest, and to women in the Northeast.

Overall, the survey respondents from workshop evaluations seemed to be a very confident and successful group of female scientists and engineers. They achieved many of the traditional markers of early success for research and/or academic careers in these fields. They reported being confident in their abilities to balance demanding career work with family and personal responsibilities and lifestyle. While it is possible that this is a self-selecting group, those who were trained at some of the best institutions in the world, sought out the workshop, and have actively pursued other opportunities to advance themselves certainly expressed a different tone coming through the workshop survey than those we have seen in other publications describing the post-PhD experience. While it is possible that the training and the climate are improving for doctoral students and, in particular, for women, we believe that programs like the FORWARD to Professorship workshop can aid tremendously in motivating and advancing these women in STEM research and academic careers through fellowship (collegiality and networking), information delivery (transparency), exposition of many different examples of how to navigate the career path, and empowerment.

ACKNOWLEDGEMENTS

This work and the participant support for the workshop are supported by the National Science Foundation's ADVANCE program under awards #0123582, 0123454, 0540801, 0540800, 0540016, with the exception of the workshops held at MIT, which were funded by MIT's Office of Graduate Students. We appreciate the encouragement, support, and cooperation we have received from MIT, in particular from Dean Blanche Stanton, Dean Isaac Colbert, and student assistants Shani Daly and Virginia Rich. We are indebted to our speakers, a list of whom is available on the workshop website: http://www.student.seas.gwu.edu/~forward/speakers.php. The workshop logistics were arranged by Dr. Yell Inverso, an audiology doctoral student at Gallaudet University, and evaluation help was supplied by Patricia Freitag. Any opinions, findings, and conclusions or recommendations expressed in this publication are those of the author and do not necessarily reflect the views of the NSF.

REFERENCES

Carnegie Foundation. (2012). *Carnegie classifications FAQs.* Retrieved from http://classifications.carnegiefoundation.org/resources/faqs.php

Holton, G. (1995). *Who succeeds in science: The gender dimension.* New Brunswick, NJ: Rutgers University Press.

Mavriplis, C., Heller, R. S., Sorensen, C. C., & Snyder, H. D. (2005). *The FORWARD to professorship workshop* (ASEE Paper 2005-1352).

National Academy Press. (2001). From scarcity to visibility: Gender differences in the careers of doctoral scientists and engineers. Washington, DC: National Academy Press.

National Science Board. (2006). *Science and engineering indicators 2006* (NSB 06-01). Arlington, VA: National Science Foundation.

National Science Foundation. (2005). *Division of science resources statistics, federal scientists and engineers:1998–2002* (NSF 05-304). Arlington, VA: National Science Foundation.

Nelson, D. J., & Rogers, D. C. (2003). *A national analysis of diversity in science and engineering faculties at research universities.* Retrieved from http://users.nber.org/~sewp/events/2005.01.14/Bios+Links/Krieger-rec4-Nelson+Rogers_Report.pdf

Rosser, S. (2004). *The science glass ceiling: Academic women scientists and the struggle to succeed.* New York, NY: Routledge.

Thomson, E. A. (2000, March 29). Study points to career/family concerns among women engineering faculty. *MITnews.* Retrieved from http://web.mit.edu/newsoffice/2000/women-0329.html

ABOUT THE EDITORS

Janice Koch, PhD, is Professor Emerita of Science Education at Hofstra University on Long Island, New York where she directed IDEAS- the Institute for the Development of Education in the Advanced Sciences. She is the Past Chair of the SIG: RWE (1997-1999) and Past President (2007-2008) of the Association for Science Teacher Education (ASTE). In 2004 and 2005 Long Island Business News named her one of Long Island's Top 50 Women. Dr. Koch taught courses addressing gender issues in the classroom and is the author of the chapter of the same name for Educational Psychology, Volume 7 of the Comprehensive Handbook of Psychology (2002). She is the author of TEACH 2nd edition (2014), an introduction to education textbook and Science Stories: Science Methods for Elementary and Middle School Teachers (2013), now in 5th edition. Janice has written extensively on what it "looks like" to engage pre-service and in-service teachers in making explicit their own gendered expectations for the males and females in their classrooms and addressing the "hidden" curriculum.

Barbara Polnick, EdD, is an associate professor in the Educational Leadership and Counseling Department at Sam Houston State University, Huntsville, Texas. Her expertise lies in writing and evaluating grants, leading school improvement initiatives, and conducting research on gender and social justice issues, women in leadership, teacher leadership in mathematics, early childhood and mathematics learning, and teaching in online environments. Dr. Polnick's scholarship contributions include 51 national presentations, 22 peer-reviewed articles, six book chapters, as well as 14 research monographs and technical reports. She is currently serving as co-editor of

Girls and Women in STEM, pages 237–238
Copyright © 2014 by Information Age Publishing

the Advancement of Women in Leadership online journal and Association for Supervision and Curriculum Development P.A.L. Research Online Journal. A recent recipient of the Excellence in Service Award for her college and nominee for her university, Dr. Polnick holds leadership roles in several local and national organizations and is currently the Chair for the AERA SIG Research on Women and Education. She has over 26 years of experience in public education as a teacher, regional consultant, instructional supervisor, assistant principal, and district curriculum director.

Beverly J. Irby, EdD, is Professor and Chair of Educational Administration, Department of Educational Administration and Human Resource Development at Texas A&M University, College Station, Texas. She earned her doctorate from the University of Mississippi in 1983. She has earned the reputation of an excellent professor and her mentored students have garnered numerous research awards. Dr. Irby's research focus is that of social responsibility for instructional leadership; theory development/validation; women's leadership; gender equity; early childhood, bilingual/ESL, gifted, and science education; online learning; reflective practice portfolios; international leadership; principal and teacher evaluation/professional development; program evaluation; and various research techniques including bricolage. A national/international speaker, she and her research group have developed studies and garnered over $35,000,000 in grant funding. She developed the Hispanic Bilingual Gifted Screening Instrument and the Synergistic Leadership Theory. Dr. Irby, who holds the Texas State University System Regents Professor since 2009, has several awards and honors among which are Bilingual Research Journal Senior Reviewer 2012, AERA Educational Researcher Reviewer 2010, AERA Research on Women and Education Information Age Publishing Legacy Award 2012, Editor of Mentoring and Tutoring Journal, Board of Reviewers for ELCC, and AERA Willystine Goodsell Award 2005.

ABOUT THE CONTRIBUTORS

Catherine Martin-Dunlop, PhD, has been involved in science education for 35 years—she narrated the killer whale and beluga whale shows at the Vancouver Public Aquarium in Canada during her first position. After a 10-year career in informal environmental education with the provincial and national park system as a park interpreter, she began teaching general science, biology, mathematics, and environmental science in elementary, middle, and high school classrooms in British Columbia, Canada; Hong Kong; and in California. Always believing in lifelong learning, Catherine returned to the university after being in the classroom for 8 years and obtained a master's from the University of Southern California and a PhD from Curtin University of Technology, both degrees in science education. Between 1999 and 2010, Catherine worked at California State University, Long Beach, where she taught courses for both preservice elementary and secondary science teachers, a Nature of Science course for graduate students, and supervised student teachers. In 2011, she became associate professor at Morgan State University, a historically Black college and university (HBCU) in Baltimore, Maryland. She is currently developing a STEM research program focusing on aspects of the urban learning environment that serve to promote or depress student outcomes in science, characteristics of student/teacher interactions in urban science classrooms, and environmental literacy and assessment.

Whitney Johnson, PhD, earned her bachelor's degree in mathematics at the University of Delaware, her master's degree in mathematics at Michigan State University, and her doctorate in teacher education, curriculum and

Girls and Women in STEM, pages 239–247
Copyright © 2014 by Information Age Publishing
All rights of reproduction in any form reserved.

educational policy at Michigan State University. She spent 10 years preparing secondary undergraduate preservice mathematics teachers. She has spent the last 2 years teaching doctoral-level courses in mathematics curriculum, introductory research, and the history and philosophy of mathematics as assistant professor at Morgan State University. Her current research interests include African American doctoral students' perspectives on Black education and the schooling experiences of Black students in mathematics from the time of segregation to the present. She co-directed a 3-year study of African American math teachers in the Washington, DC, and Maryland areas on how they create a sense of purpose for their students to study Algebra I. Her recent publication, entitled *Teaching with Speeches: A Black Teacher Who Uses the Mathematics Classroom to Prepare Students for Life*, appears in volume 115, issue 2 of *Teachers College Record*. Her long-range goal is to begin a nonprofit organization that provides out-of-school learning experiences for K–12 students and works with teachers and schools to improve the in-school learning experiences for students in Baltimore City.

Ezella McPherson, PhD, earned her bachelor's degree from the University of Michigan-Ann Arbor. She earned her Masters of Education and Doctorate of Philosophy in Educational Policy Studies from the University of Illinois at Urbana-Champaign. Dr. McPherson's research focuses on equity in K–20 schools. Her past scholarship focused on school tracking, school desegregation, and health in African American communities. Her dissertation, Undergraduate African American Women's Narratives on Persistence in Science Majors at a Predominantly White Institution (PWI), centered on the persistence of African American women in science majors. It examined why some African American women remained or departed from science majors. Her current research focuses on college student success, including underrepresented populations in STEM fields. For the last decade, she spent time serving P–20 populations as a tutor, mentor, academic advisor, supervisor, instructor, career counselor, and/or leadership program coordinator. She is committed to the retention, persistence, and graduation of college and graduate students. Currently, she serves as an administrator at Wayne State University, an urban public research university in Detroit, Michigan.

Carolyn Parker, PhD, is a STEM education faculty member in the Division of Teaching and Learning of Johns Hopkins University. Her research interests include equity issues in STEM education, teacher professional development, and the equitable distribution of teachers. Her work appears in the *Journal of Research in Science Teaching, Written Communication*, and Association for Teacher Education Yearbook IX. Dr. Parker is a co-principal investigator for JHU's National Science Foundation STEM Achievement in

Baltimore Elementary Schools (SABES) grant. The SABES grant is a $7.4 million award that leverages the skills and resources of the schools, community, and businesses in three high-minority, low-resource Baltimore city neighborhoods. The goal is to integrate science into a child's world as opposed to bringing a student into the world of scientists. From 2003 to 2007, Dr. Parker was co-principal investigator for a $1,577,169 National Science Foundation Supported Instructional Materials Design Grant, entitled Engineering Inquiry-Based Learning Modules for Technology Education, which focused on increasing the participation of women and minorities in STEM careers through innovative curriculum development. Dr. Parker earned her bachelor's degree in biology from Binghamton University (formally, SUNY-Binghamton). She began her career as a science educator as a Peace Corps volunteer in Guatemala. Upon her return to the United States, she earned an MA in science teaching and then taught high school science in New York State and Miami, Florida.

Louise Ann (Lou Ann) Lyon, PhD, received her doctorate in learning sciences with a graduate certificate in feminist studies from the University of Washington. Prior to pursuing her graduate degree, she worked as a software engineer, developing user interface software for video products, first for Grass Valley Group (at the time, a division of Tektronix) and then for the small startup company Telestream. Her software engineering work came on the heels of her MS degree in computer science from California State University, Chico. More recently, Dr. Lyon spent 5 years teaching computer science and developing a non-majors curriculum at the Institute of Technology at the University of Washington, Tacoma. Dr. Lyon's research focuses on pathways to success for women in STEM fields. She is particularly interested in qualitative and quantitative approaches to women's entry into computer science and sociocultural influences on underrepresented minorities.

Roxanne Hughes, PhD, is the Director of the Center for Integrating Research and Learning at the National High Magnetic Field Laboratory, an NSF funded multisite facility that includes Florida State University, University of Florida, and Los Alamos National Laboratory. Dr. Hughes runs the educational and public outreach programs at the lab, which includes K–12, undergraduate, graduate, postdoctoral, and general public. Her research interests focus on policies and programs that improve underrepresented minorities' persistence in STEM fields at all educational levels. Dr. Hughes examines the concept of STEM identity as it relates to persistence in STEM.

Nicole Wallace, MS, is a middle and high school science teacher at an all-girl, independent school in Cape Town, South Africa. She is passionate about innovative methods of teaching science, which engage students beyond the curriculum and classroom, with the hope of encouraging them to continue in STEM courses at university. In 2010, she won an award from the Microsoft Partners in Learning for producing an innovative unit on HIV/Aids. She recently completed her master's degree at the University of Cape Town, where she explored the relationship between alternative assessments and attitudes toward science. Her current academic interests are the long-term effects of these assessments on the choices of girls for tertiary studies and careers.

Annemarie Hattingh, PhD, worked at the Centre for Science, Mathematics and Technology Education at Pretoria University and in 2010, joined the University of Cape Town (South Africa). In 2008, she won an award that acknowledged her work as project leader of a 10-year African-Norwegian collaboration called "Productive Learning Cultures," which supported women in their doctoral studies. She is a co-author of a book on teacher education entitled *The Brave New World of Education: Creating a New Professionalism.* Her latest research explores dispositions and patterns of innovation of exceptional science teachers working in difficult, underresourced environments.

Merle Froschl has more than 35 years of experience in education and publishing, developing innovative programs and materials that foster equality of opportunity for students regardless of gender, race/ethnicity, disability, or level of family income. Since the 1970s, she has developed outstanding curricular and teacher training models in the field of educational equity and is a nationally known speaker on issues of gender equity and equality of opportunity in education.

Currently, Ms. Froschl is co-director of Educational Equity at FHI 360, where she provides leadership to projects that promote girls' interest and persistence in STEM, including Great Science for Girls, After-School Math PLUS, and After-School Science PLUS. Publications include Great Science for Girls: Gender-Equitable STEM & Afterschool Programs, *SB&F,* May/June 2006; Building Diversity Through Science and Science Through Diversity, *Connect,* Vol. 19, Issue 4, March/April 2006; and *Science, Gender, and Afterschool: A Research-Action Agenda,* New York: Educational Equity Concepts and the Academy for Educational Development, 2003. Recent publications include *Supporting Boys' Learning: Strategies for Teacher Practice, Pre-K-Grade 3,* Teachers College Press, 2010 and "Improving Boys' Achievement in Early Childhood and Primary Education" in *Lessons in Educational Equality,* Oxford University Press, 2012. Merle Froschl holds a BS in journalism from Syracuse University and is a graduate of the Institute for Not-for-Profit Management, Columbia University.

Barbara Sprung is the Co-Director of Educational Equity at FHI 360 and has four decades of experience in bias-free education, as a teacher and as an innovator of programs and materials to promote equality of opportunity for children regardless of gender, race/ethnicity, disability, or family income. Recent STEM projects she has co-directed include After-School Science PLUS, Great Science for Girls, Science: It's a Girl Thing! and After-School Math PLUS. Sprung has written extensively about equity in education. She is a co-author of *Playtime is Science* (EEC, 1997), *Quit it! A Teacher's Guide for Use with Students in Grades K–3* (EEC, 1998), the *Anti-Teasing Bullying and Teasing Book for Preschool Classrooms* (Gryphon House, 2005) *Supporting Boys' Learning: Strategies for Teacher Practice, Pre-K-Grade 3* (Teachers College Press, Columbia University, 2010) "Improving Boys' Achievement in Early Childhood and Primary Education," in *Lessons in Educational Equality* (Oxford University Press, 2012), and "How a Preschool Teacher Became Free to Be" in *When We Were Free To Be* (University of North Carolina Press, 2012). Barbara Sprung holds a BA degree from Sarah Lawrence College, an MS in child development from the Bank Street College of Education, and is a graduate of the Institute for Not-for-Profit Management, Columbia University. She was the recipient of the 2011 Bank Street College Alumni Award.

Crystal Chukwurah is currently a student at Duke University's Pratt School of Engineering where she is a biomedical engineering major. She actively participates in research groups and conducts research under the VaNTH Bioengineering Education Research Summer Research Experience for Undergraduates (BER REU) at Vanderbilt University. Within the REU, Ms. Chukwurah works with the Director of the Center for STEM Education for Girls, Dr. Stacy S. Klein-Gardner, at the Harpeth Hall School in Nashville, Tennessee. Here, Ms. Chukwurah designs and implements assessment tools for both the 2012 STEM Summer Institute for Girls and the 2012 STEM Think Tank and Conference. Ms. Chukwurah dedicates her time to derive efficient results that contribute to identifying best practices from successful K–12, university, and corporate STEM programs for females. Ms. Chukwurah is currently a 2013 National Nanotechnology Infrastructure Network (NNIN) research intern at Howard University. Her work is focused on growing a new material known as graphene on multiple substrates and developing graphene devices. Ms. Chukwurah's career goals are to advance biomedical engineering research and medical care. Also, she plans to pursue her educational and research interests by earning her MD/PhD to pursue a career in health care management and conduct research.

Stacy Klein-Gardner, PhD, is the Director of the Center for STEM Education for Girls at the Harpeth Hall School in Nashville, Tennessee. Here, she leads professional development opportunities in STEM for K–12 teachers and works to identify and disseminate best practices from successful K–12, university, and corporate STEM programs for females. This Center also leads a program for rising high school girls, which integrates community service and engineering design in a global context. She continues to serve as Adjunct Professor of the Practice of Biomedical Engineering, Teaching & Learning, and Radiological Sciences at Vanderbilt University. She served as the Associate Dean for Outreach in the Vanderbilt School of Engineering from 2007 to 2010. Dr. Klein-Gardner currently serves as the chair of the American Society for Engineering Education's K–12 division. An engineer by training and in her way of thinking, she received a BSE in biomedical and electrical engineering from Duke University in 1991. She then earned her MS from Drexel University in 1993 and her PhD in biomedical engineering from Vanderbilt University in 1996. Dr. Klein-Gardner's career focuses on K–12 science, technology, engineering, and mathematics (STEM) education, particularly as it relates to increasing interest in and participation by females.

Cecilia D. Craig, PhD, is an engineer by education, technical director by experience, and now a researcher and STEM robotics education advocate. Craig earned a BSME (mechanical engineering) from The Ohio State University, an MSE (mechanical engineering) from California State University at Fullerton, and held management roles in manufacturing and program management for large and small companies, working in high tech for 30 years. In 2000, Craig took a sabbatical from high tech to teach high school math for a year. Staying in education, in 2002, a sixth-grade student in her first Johns Hopkins University's Center for Talented Youth (CTY) science and engineering class asked if she would include robotics in the curriculum. Using wall-hugging mouse robots for students to make that summer and thereafter, students loved robots in the CTY class she taught for several years. Her passion for robotics and STEM education was born. She and her engineering husband mentored a high school robotics team for 7 years and continue to bring robotics education and competitions to young people as part of the Western Region Robotics Forum since 2004. While working again in high tech, she earned a PhD in education at Walden University. She is now retired from high tech and in the middle of a dissertation study exploring the long-term influence of participating in a FIRST Robotics Competition on young women's career decisions. She plans to graduate in 2014 and continue sharing robotics with young people, hoping to inspire them to become engineers.

Sylvia Taube, PhD, is associate professor in the Curriculum and Instruction Department at Sam Houston State University, Huntsville, Texas. She was a secondary mathematics teacher in the public school for 10 years prior to earning a Doctor of Philosophy degree in educational theory and practice from the State University of New York, Albany. In addition to teaching mathematics methods courses at Sam Houston State University, Dr. Taube has been successful in writing and implementing seven Teacher Quality Grant Programs for the professional development of secondary mathematics in Texas. She has also been a program evaluator for several external grants awarded to Sam Houston State University by the Texas Higher Education Coordinating Board. Dr. Taube is currently a program reviewer for the National Council for Accreditation of Teacher Education (NCATE) and National Council of Teachers of Mathematics (NCTM) Specialized Program Area (secondary mathematics). Dr. Taube has published articles and book chapters in the following areas: mathematics for english language learners, professional development of teachers, project-based learning, and implementing a professional development schools model for teacher preparation.

Catherine Mavriplis, PhD, has worked under NSF funding to advance women in STEM since 1996, notably through the FORWARD program and the ADVANCE program, reaching up to 1,300 science and engineering doctoral women by 2013. Dr. Mavriplis has been appointed the prestigious NSERC Chair for Women in Science and Engineering (Ontario Region). Professor Mavriplis graduated from McGill University's Honours Mechanical Engineering program and continued her studies at the Massachusetts Institute of Technology in aeronautics and applied mathematics, where she earned the SM and PhD degrees. After a postdoctoral appointment at Princeton University in the Program for Applied and Computational Mathematics, she began her tenure-track career at George Washington University, where she earned tenure. She spent 2 years as a program manager in applied and computational mathematics at the National Science Foundation. As a research fellow in the Cooperative Institute for Mesoscale Meteorological Studies at the University of Oklahoma, she worked with NOAA National Severe Storms Laboratory scientists to advance modeling techniques for Numerical Weather Prediction. She recently joined the University of Ottawa in the Department of Mechanical Engineering, where she continues to pursue her interests in numerical methods and fluid dynamics.

Rachelle S. Heller, PhD, is associate provost at the Mount Vernon Campus of George Washington University. She is the co-recipient and co-principal investigator of National Science Foundation sponsored grants. The first, in 1989, was "Bringing Young Minority Women to the Threshold of Science." This 4-year grant was designed as an intervention program to raise the interest of young minority women in studies and careers in science and engineering. "Did It Work" was a significant follow-up study to assess the impact of the original intervention program. The most recently completed grants are FORWARD in STEM and CRIM. The former is an intervention program for women undergraduates and early master's students as a bridge program to offer opportunities for graduate study and research. The most recent and the current grants are NSF ADVANCE Leadership awards. The Advance is designed to promote competencies within pre-tenured women faculty to help advance their career toward tenure, and held successful workshops in May 2003, 2004, and 2005. FORWARD to Professorship was recently awarded from NSF under the Advance program for workshops in 2007 and 2008. Pay It FORWARD is a collaborative grant to disseminate the workshop model and findings by training others to conduct smaller, more regionally, culturally, or discipline-focused workshops.

Paul Sabila, PhD, is associate professor of chemistry in the Department of Science, Technology, and Mathematics at Gallaudet University (GU). GU is the leading liberal arts university dedicated to the education of deaf and hard-of-hearing individuals (D/HoH) and is located in Washington, DC. He completed a postdoctoral fellowship in the Department of Medicinal Chemistry, School of Pharmacy, at the University of Connecticut (2008). He has also worked with several institutions intending to take GU students for summer internships. Dr. Sabila has been a co-recipient of several NSF grants, including FORWARD (NSF 0930112), MRI Instrumentation Grant (NSF 1040094), Nanotechnology (NSF 1205608), and Overcoming Barriers to STEM Undergraduates (NSF 1259237). He has also formed research collaborations with faculty from several institutions, including George Washington University (GWU), Howard University, the University of the District of Columbia, Cornell University, and Harvard University. Under FORWARD, Dr. Sabila has worked as Gallaudet PI and was instrumental in organizing, coordinating, and hosting two national conferences at Gallaudet University. He has also given several presentations at the NSF Advance workshops at Arlington, Virginia, Research on Women and Education and Forward workshops.

Charlene Sorensen, PhD, holds a bachelor's degree from St. Andrew's Presbyterian College, with majors in chemistry and comparative religious studies (1989). She received her PhD from the University of Tennessee in Knoxville (1998) and a master's in pastoral ministry (2012). Her STEM concentration was in the area of physical chemistry. The focus of her dissertation was statistical thermodynamics of grafted and free polymer chains in various solvent types. From 1993 until 1996, she was assistant professor at Pikeville College, a small private college in the Appalachian Mountains. In 1996, she moved to Washington, DC, to teach at Gallaudet University. While teaching undergraduate chemistry courses, Dr. Sorensen has served as a mentor to many students, including those in preprofessional programs. She began going to elementary schools to give "chemistry magic shows" in an attempt to combat the misconception that chemistry is an elite subject that only highly intelligent and sophisticated people can enjoy. She especially noticed that women were avoiding the sciences. As a result, she began meeting with a group of about nine girls and encouraged them, over the course of 3 years to investigate science.

Made in the USA
Lexington, KY
25 August 2016